THE A-Z OF STUFF

For Michael & Jean

Very best wishes,

David

THE A-Z OF STUFF

DAVID FLETCHER

Copyright © 2016 David Fletcher

The moral right of the author has been asserted.

Apart from any fair dealing for the purposes of research or private study, or criticism or review, as permitted under the Copyright, Designs and Patents Act 1988, this publication may only be reproduced, stored or transmitted, in any form or by any means, with the prior permission in writing of the publishers, or in the case of reprographic reproduction in accordance with the terms of licences issued by the Copyright Licensing Agency. Enquiries concerning reproduction outside those terms should be sent to the publishers.

Matador
9 Priory Business Park,
Wistow Road, Kibworth Beauchamp,
Leicestershire. LE8 0RX
Tel: 0116 279 2299
Email: books@troubador.co.uk
Web: www.troubador.co.uk/matador
Twitter: @matadorbooks

ISBN 9781 785899 768

British Library Cataloguing in Publication Data.
A catalogue record for this book is available from the British Library.

Printed and bound in the UK by TJ International, Padstow, Cornwall
Typeset in 11pt Aldine by Troubador Publishing Ltd, Leicester, UK

Matador is an imprint of Troubador Publishing Ltd

In memory of sanity

Contents

Anarchic Ideas	1
BBC	15
Cultures	32
Democracy	50
European Union	69
Financial Services	91
Government	98
Human Rights	121
Islam	130
Jury System	131
Kids	140
London	153
Men	163
NHS	177
Officialdom	186
Population	202
Quaggas	217
Religion	230
Sex	244
Taxation	257
United Kingdom	265
Vatican	271
Women	289
X-rated	298
Young People	318
Zealots	334

Introduction

Life is tough, not least because one has to digest just so much 'stuff'. In fact, there is such a colossal amount of stuff that much of the really important stuff can get neglected while we were all so busy dealing with some of the basic stuff like reading and maths (and then some of the less basic stuff like coping with acne and writing some half-credible CVs).

So here it is: a brief compendium of all the important stuff that may have been neglected along the way, designed to equip all those who read it with virtually everything they need to know about the world around us. It has been compiled without any interference from the political correctness brigade and, of course, without any scrutiny of its accuracy or its merit. This, in itself, is another thing one must learn about the world: that it doesn't come in a precise, calibrated form and that it is far from being full of the worthy and the good.

Oh, another thing. To render this useful tome suitably attractive to the widest audience possible it has been thought necessary to dispense with a more sensible ordering of its component topics in favour of an 'A-Z' theme. This apparently is what 'the market' now requires, presumably because the market is so full of numbnuts who simply can't deal with other than the most infantile approach to any topic you care to mention. In fact, I really do wonder whether this work has any real chance at all and it might have been better to pen another work entitled The A-Z of Pointless Selfies. All I would need to have done then is write some stupid captions…

Anyway, I seem to have got off the point. And the point, I emphasise, is to use this book to equip oneself with all the essential important stuff one will ever need, and so make one's life just a little less tough.

Bon voyage.
David Fletcher
Spring 2016

Anarchic ideas

Right. Well, let's start with an admission, and it's that this first dose of stuff would be better titled 'Heretical ideas'. Because, you see, it's all about the need to challenge orthodoxy in all its manifestations, and that this challenge is best conducted by formulating heretical – or rebellious or unconventional or simply unorthodox – ideas, ideas that might just upset the established position on any number of issues. However, due to the constraints imposed by that idiotic alphabet format referred to in the introduction, I've had to go with 'Anarchic ideas'. And I will have to ask you to accept this on the basis that anarchy can be taken to mean 'a lack of obedience to an authority' and therefore 'anarchic ideas' could just about be interpreted as 'insubordinate thinking' – which is exactly what I intend to discuss. So, with all that bloomin' nonsense sorted out, it's time to get on, and to kick off with, 'What's wrong with orthodoxies?'

The short answer: virtually everything. The longer answer: they cause beliefs and concepts to ossify, they stifle original thinking and development and they are often hijacked by religious, political and scientific establishments for their own benefit and to the detriment of us all. And, if that's not bad enough, they're just not the sort of thing to get the blood coursing through one's veins... whereas a bit of anarchic thinking can turn one's cheeks positively scarlet and may even bring on palpitations.

That's not to say that Galileo Galilei turned puce when he suggested that the Earth revolved around the sun – in the face of the Christian orthodoxy of the time – or that Charles Darwin had to lie down for a minute when, by proposing that species evolved gradually, he was implying that the Earth had not been created perfectly (as was still the orthodoxy of the day). But it is to say that one could well understand it if their bodies did experience a physical reaction to their mental achievements, because their achievements were remarkable both in an intellectual sense and in a sodding great impact sense. I mean, it may not have happened immediately, but their 'anarchic ideas' did end up sweeping away some pretty entrenched orthodoxies – and then dumping them in a dustbin. And thank God they did. Otherwise the Dark Ages would still be alive and well and I'd be writing this piece with a goose quill – or, indeed, I wouldn't be writing it at all.

Yes, three cheers for all the world's heretics, and three cheers for the fact that they're not all historical figures. So we had people like Oscar Wilde, Martin Luther King, Jr. and John Lennon stirring up things quite recently, and we've still got people like Richard Dawkins, Stephen Hawking and Kenny Orkenninot doing it now. (And if you haven't heard, Kenny Orkenninot is the guy who recently demolished that ridiculous L'Oréal Paris orthodoxy with his radical idea, now proven beyond doubt, that not all women are actually worth it after all…)

Anyway, we owe a debt of gratitude to these chaps, not least because in confronting old, entrenched ideas they faced harsh criticism, ridicule – or even a rather unenviable situation on a pile of wood with a stake up its middle. And whilst the incineration threat is now a little less, 'original thinkers' still face all sorts of problems, and maybe ridicule more than anything else, a fact I will now demonstrate by setting out three heretical (or anarchic) thoughts of my very own, starting with the proposition that education in Britain was possibly or even probably better in the 1960s than it is now.

1. Yes, I think there is a strong case to be made for regarding the British educational system in the 1960s as superior to that of the present day. And I think the evidence for this is largely empirical and can be found in a simple comparison of the outcomes of the two very different systems. So, in my opinion, in the 1960s it was not unusual to find school-leavers who could write legibly, who knew where to shove their apostrophes, who could calculate the change required in a shop purchase in their heads and who, when talking to adults, could put a whole sentence together without the use of a single grunt. They would probably be relatively courteous as well and not find too much trouble in grasping the concept of good timekeeping at work – or, indeed, the concept of work itself. Fast-forward fifty years, and it is now not unusual to

find school-leavers – some of them emerging from universities – whose mastery of texting has both slaughtered their skills with a pen and obliterated any relationships they might have been developing with pronouns, inverted commas, capital letters and structured, well-thought-out, comprehensible prose. As for their innate numeracy… well, it doesn't seem innate any more. And as for their 'work skills'… well, not all of them appear to realise that being paid requires something in return, and that this something should preferably start at the agreed time. Furthermore, quite a few of them find it difficult to understand that one's relations with one's work colleagues might not necessarily be enhanced by one's trolling these work colleagues. In short, no matter how much education is being force-fed to pupils (yes, pupils, not students), and in whatever way it is being force-fed, the results are not what they used to be. Which does make one wonder why.

Well, let's just remind ourselves of what used to go on. How, in those cold, gloomy classrooms of the sixties, class sizes were often over thirty, there were no classroom assistants but just a single class teacher, and he or she would require his or her charges to sit upright at a desk, facing a well-used blackboard at the front of the room. Discipline was somewhere between strict and totally uncompromising, with that rare beast, the disruptive child, dealt with by a rap over the knuckles or a ruler on the palm of the hand – while the overwhelming majority of non-disruptive children got on with their times tables or practised their writing and *how* to write. Or maybe they were acquiring another fact about British history that would eventually add to their sense of identity and their pride in their country.

Sounds really grim, doesn't it? But there was worse to come. Many would now have to cope with a social mobility that had been thrust upon them as a direct result of an antiquated grammar school system, one that was based on an individual's academic ability and not on his or her parents' ability to pay. Others would have to enter adult life with only an appropriate tertiary education, courtesy of a technical college or a polytechnic, and would have to miss out on the opportunity to take a degree course in event management at Huddersfield University. *Quelle horreur!*

Well, I'm almost certain of one thing at this stage, and this is that many of you will have begun to appreciate just how much ridicule any anarchic thinking can engender. But bear with me. Because, whilst my opinion might not be shared by a single teacher or a single educationalist, these are the very people who maintain the orthodox view that teaching in Britain has never been better and that to return to the teaching of the sixties would be a disaster. And I'm sorry, but it takes a disinterested (some might say ignorant) outsider like myself to point out that they are probably completely wrong.

As further evidence in support of my case I will not dwell on the all too apparent failings of the present educational system in output terms, nor will

I argue that the overuse of technology in classrooms has reduced the role of a teacher to that of a guide – wandering among children who may or may not learn on their own with the aid of some Internet-connected device. And as for discipline… well, I will refrain from suggesting that managing classroom behaviour now requires not only an awareness of every piece of equal opportunities legislation in respect of disability, sex, religion and belief, sexual orientation, pregnancy and maternity and gender reassignment, but also the sort of skills taught to hostage negotiators and, possibly more pertinently, to the bodyguard fraternity. But what I will do is state the simple fact that educational outcomes do not depend on how much money is spent, or how many whiteboards and iPads are brought into play, but simply on inspirational teachers working in a controlled and an 'under-their-control' environment, the sort of environment that used to give them an opportunity to *teach* rather than to provide just occupational therapy.

So you might now just have a little more sympathy for my radical views. Or you might not. However, I remain convinced that in the world of education something has gone terribly wrong since the 1960s and that the orthodoxy that promotes the superiority of current educational practices needs challenging like never before. Hell, I now hear that they don't even have sticky buns in the tuck shop any more. And if that doesn't need a dose of anarchic thinking I don't know what does.

Although, there again, I do. Because I am just

reminded that my next heretical thought concerns 'social media'.

2. Yes, my contention is that, contrary to the current orthodoxy that social media is brilliant, the fact is that it actually sucks, and that the world would be a much better place if it no longer existed.

I must say, this one is a doddle, because to start with the only positives one can assemble to support the maintenance of social media are that it provides some sort of connectivity, bringing people with common interests together, and it also provides a platform to 'share one's life with the rest of the world'.

Well, pardon me while I retch – and prepare yourself for a list of just some of the negatives that accompany the unprecedented use of this captivating but ultimately addictive cyberspace drug...

- To start with, it represents a serious threat to the privacy and safety of all its many disciples. If they don't have their identities stolen or their future work prospects buggered up by that photo of their wearing that inappropriate underwear – in Waitrose – then they may well end up losing their self-esteem, their savings, their virginity or even their life. And, long before losing any of this stuff, they will have lost their self-responsibility and a good chunk of their common sense.
- Then there is the ability of social media to undermine normal, healthy social interaction. I mean, we've all seen it, haven't we? Young addicts spending excessive amounts of time on social media and in

doing so retreating from real face-to-face dealings with both their friends and their family, to the extent that their actual speech becomes fractured and fraught. And they lose eye contact as well. This would be fine if we were attempting to breed a nation of hygiene-indifferent zombies, but it's not such great news if we want the next generation to be a bunch of normal, functioning adults who can respond in real time to the spoken word – with some other spoken words of their own.

- Worse still, possibly, is the facility that social media provides to bastards of all sorts to be bastards. Yes, social media brings out the very worst in so many people. And it does this because no matter how puny, acne-ridden, brainless, smelly and downright ugly they are, it doesn't stop them bullying, trolling, acting offensively or actually intimidating fellow social media users. In fact, somebody needs to invent an embedded app which, when it detected any sort of social media abuse, would administer some immediate retribution to the originator of this abuse – by turning his or her screen into a mirror (while reminding the gargoyle reflected there of just how much he or she smells and how few friends he or she has – if any at all).
- And, talking of grotesque, it is now time to address what from a business perspective might be the most grotesque aspect of social media of them all. And this is its ability to reduce the productivity level of any enterprise down to that of the public sector. Yes, infinite amounts of time are wasted by

office workers every day in updating their Facebook pages, doing whatever one does on Twitter – and generally trying to project to others something remotely interesting in their a–million-miles-from-anything-remotely-interesting lives. It's rather sad, really. But not for the owners of these enterprises or for their customers, who have to pay for the resulting low productivity. For them… well, it's enough to make them want to troll…

- OK, time for a more 'philosophical' disadvantage of social media, and this concerns the use to which it is often put. I mean, quite simply it rarely if ever is used for what might be called a 'great purpose' – even though it has the capacity to be used in this way. No. Almost invariably it is used for the trivial or for the plain daft. And what I mean is that, rather than starting a firestorm on the way we are trashing this world, social media users are more often intent on exposing their selfies, their embarrassing grasp of some aspect of personal grooming, their half-baked views on world politics or their sheer, jaw-drop-inducing stupidity. In fact, if social media has taught us nothing else, it has taught us just how many knuckle-dragging morons we are sharing our world with. With their primary school English (at best) and with their twisted, ignorant, sometimes comical opinions on all manner of subjects, they have made us all aware that the majority of *Homo sapiens* lives up to only the first half of its name. Try *Homo hare-brained* instead…

Well, I've probably overstated my case, haven't I? I mean, my case against the orthodoxy of social media being an absolute boon. But one last thing, and this is how social media might be screwing up not only the physical well-being of its users – in terms of its impact on their blood pressure, their genes, their immune responses and their hormone levels – but also their mental well-being. Because, if you think about it, these social media junkies generally only post photos of themselves looking perfect or looking happy after receiving some good news. Images of themselves coping with diarrhoea or the aftermath of their running over the pet cat are in a distinct minority. And this selective sampling of their lives will inevitably lead to a skewed representation of their lives, and quite probably a skewed self-image. In other words they will begin to see their online presence as an accurate reflection of themselves, and they will then find it increasingly difficult to deal with who they really are and the real, *not* perfect situations that make up the majority of their lives. Result: brain problems well into their old age, and yet another reason to support my heretical views on the overwhelming drawbacks of social media.

In fact, I suspect that the ridicule level on this particular target of my heresy is lower than that on my assault on education. I also suspect that it will be at only a moderately high level on my final target – which is the orthodoxy of evolution…

3. Now I should say straight away that I am in complete agreement with Mr Darwin on all matters

to do with evolution, and that my anarchic views on this subject concern just one species, and are more a reinforcement of his general principles than any form of attack. This probably makes very little sense – so let me explain.

You see, there were these people who, as well as saluting each other with an outstretched arm, also sought to 'improve their race' by improving its genetic composition. This initiative was actually an exercise in eugenics, and eugenics is all about 'interventions', in this case, interventions that were designed to upgrade the genetic composition of humans. Well, all very nice. Or should I say all very unpleasant? But the point is that we in this modern age are making 'interventions' ourselves – in the form of *medical* interventions – in order to save people's lives and to give us all a chance to live to old age. And who could argue that this is not the noblest of things to do? And I do mean that. After all, it is indisputable that one of our very best features as human beings is our humanity to our fellow man, and our commendable desire to help all those we can.

However, there is a problem. Because interventions, no matter how well intentioned they might be, do have an impact, as they do in eugenics. Especially as the interventions may well be made in respect of some of the 'weakest' of our brethren (and I'm not ruling myself out there). But, as awful and as cold-blooded as it sounds, such interventions, although they will inevitably help the individual, will do so only at the expense of the species.

This is uncomfortable stuff, but one cannot get away from the fact that if one makes constant interventions to protect the weakest members of any species – and thereby allow them to survive – then the whole population of that species begins to degrade. Its members become slower, less agile, less physically strong than their ancestors, and indeed less able in every aspect of their make-up. And it is no different for us. Which is why I believe we are 'de-evolving'.

Yes, in our modern human-rights-for-all, best-available-medicine-for-all societies, we have been busy practising 'reverse eugenics', and in doing so we have, for our own species, put Darwin's survival of the fittest into reverse. Although, as I indicated above, this reversal of our development is more a confirmation of his theory, in that by fiddling with natural selection we have made those who are most in need of medical support and those who are closest to its provision the fittest. Which is very good news for them, but a bit of a bummer for mankind in general.

You see, if the long-term impact on the genetic composition of our very own species is destined to be... adverse, and if one accepts that our greatest quality is our intelligence, then this adverse effect will manifest itself in a diminution in this intelligence. In other words we will become dimmer and dimmer... until we can't even make use of social media any more. And then we'll become extinct, a victim of our humanity to our fellow man.

OK. Maybe my prediction of the ridicule level on this particular anarchic thought was a little off beam, and you are now laughing your socks off. But just look around you. I'm not saying that the stupid are outbreeding the intelligent – necessarily – but just look at people you see on the street and then listen to those other people on the street who give us the benefit of their views in some vox pop on the telly. Don't you suspect something? Don't you have a deep-seated suspicion that they've all got quite noticeably more brainless over the years? And then one only has to consider whole groups of our species. And I have in mind here all those Piers Morgan Twitter followers, all those HS2 supporters, all those Jeremy Kyle clods (and all the people he has in his audience), all those people who enjoy Saturday night telly and all those people who think that studs and rings embedded in their genitals improve their genitals' appearance. The list is infinite, and increasingly depressing. But the good news is that I have finally got to the end of this first dose of stuff.

Yes, having mauled the continued evolution of *Homo sapiens* with the claws of my original and heretical thinking I will now conclude this chapter, but not before making one final anarchic point. This is that anarchy itself is not necessarily a bad thing. Indeed, if it weren't for the growing stupidity of mankind, it would be the very best way to organise any society. However, I suspect that you might not agree with that statement, even if you now accept that anarchic ideas are vital in our battle with firmly established orthodoxies. And if you don't accept that, then I'm still pretty certain that you will at least have grasped the association between brave new thoughts and ridicule… which I suppose, if nothing else, is a step in the right direction.

> The orthodox is hard to budge
> It takes a shove and not a nudge
> The sort of shove, I think you'll find
> That needs a sharp, rebellious mind
>
> Yes, heresy and 'Not that way'
> Are what's still needed till this day
> To see the back of postulates
> That are beyond their use-by dates
>
> The trouble is, I have to say
> That those who use their minds this way
> Are often in for lots of flack
> And some, a mean, sustained attack
>
> But what I've found is true for me
> Is more to do with jollity
> Yes, even though I'm not a fool
> I seem to court just ridicule…

BBC

The BBC is great, isn't it? Or, there again, was it? Did it once wear a crown of greatness, but has that crown now slipped from its head?

Well, let us consider the evidence and, first, the claim that it did have a crown of greatness in the past. This shouldn't take too long because it is quite clear that for many years after its inception the BBC was a true pioneer in broadcasting and it had few if any rivals anywhere else in the world, and certainly none here in Britain. When its management philosophy was still very much 'Please hold on to the seat of your pants', and when its budget was a fraction of what it is now, its performance across the board was outstanding, even if sometimes a little stilted and a little Heath Robinsonesque. And one only needs to look at the comedy output from decades ago – which now constitutes much of the content of channels such as Gold and Dave – to realise just how imaginative and productive the BBC could be at its very best. Yes, there was a crown of greatness there in the past, and it was so firmly seated on the corporation's head that it is difficult to imagine that it would ever slip by as much as an inch. But, of course, that was when the BBC still stood for the British Broadcasting

Corporation and hadn't acquired its three alternative titles. And if you are unaware of what these are I will tell you. And then I will go on to explain how they have come about and how they illustrate that the crown may not have just slipped, but it may now have fallen off completely. So what I'm saying is that the BBC now stands not just for the British Broadcasting Corporation but also for the 'Bloated Bureaucracy Corporation', the 'Blatantly Biased Corporation' and the 'Broadcast Banality Corporation'. And I will now deal with each of these three less than complimentary monikers in turn, and first, that Bloated Bureaucracy Corporation moniker.

1. The Bloated Bureaucracy Corporation.

Unfortunately, the BBC has not been able to withstand the disease that ultimately afflicts all publicly funded institutions: the disease known as 'rampant bureaucracy'. Yes, where once there were a few heads of departments and a reasonable number of managers and assistant managers (all working with a variety of producers, technicians and administrators) there is now a huge standing army of bureaucrats. And the primary role of this army is simply to maintain itself, it having spent the last forty years or so building itself to its present size – and for no other reason than it was allowed to.

It's a familiar story. You see, the true measure of the worth of any bureaucrat, according to the bureaucrats' code, is how many other bureaucrats he has under him (or she/her). And I nearly said 'working for him/her' there, but that would be to misrepresent what bureaucracy is all about, and to suggest that an eternal round of meetings with other bureaucrats, punctuated with sending memos to other bureaucrats and reading all those memos received, could in any way be construed as some sort of work. Whereas, as we all know, this has as little to do with real work as the title 'Executive Creative Director, Future Media' has with a real job. Anyway, more of titles and fantasy in a moment. For now I will just reinforce the message that, over the years, many BBC managers, lacking an oversized bulge in their trousers, have sought to display their potency by creating 'subsidiary positions' within their own bailiwicks of responsibility, and in this way they have increased their own importance – and, of course, they have much enhanced their ability to dip into the corporation's purse – for their own financial benefit. Furthermore, by working with other managers with similar expansionary ambitions, there has been built a 'mutual gratification' system within the corporation. This system, where each manager has assisted other managers – as he has been assisted by them – has been used to justify that promotion to senior manager or controller or director or to whatever position is thought necessary to strengthen the army of bureaucrats even further, and to furnish that manager with the particular position he so desires within its ranks. It's a bit like a gathering of swingers, really, where each participant of the gathering assists his or her fellow participants in first 'swelling their libido' in order that eventually all the participants achieve the climax they require, even if it means that somebody else who doesn't want to be screwed gets screwed even more (as in the millions of poor, bound-and-gagged, defenceless licence payers).

Well, if you are possibly thinking at this stage that I am being in any way unfair here or that I am exaggerating my case, then just dwell for a moment on the following facts:

- The average pay of a BBC employee is £54,000, which must be about twice the national average.
- There are 4,500 job titles within the BBC, 2,000 of which have 'manager' in their title.
- Forty-four members of staff have the word 'strategy' in their job title.
- Somewhere around 120 senior managers in the BBC are paid more than the prime minister. (This means, incidentally, that, among other nonsenses, being Head of Drama in Wales is apparently more demanding than running the whole of the United Kingdom – drama not necessarily included.)

Anyway, something has got rather out of hand at the BBC, and to underline this statement it is worth spending just a little more time examining BBC job titles and the fantasy world they expose. In fact, until recently I thought that Alan Yentob's job at the BBC, as Creative Director, was primarily to do with creating ever more bizarre job titles. And it wasn't until he parted company with the corporation (and not before time) that I realised that his job was just to commission himself to make largely unwatched art programmes, and that the BBC needed no help whatsoever from one of its most unpopular sons to dream up the most preposterous job titles imaginable, all in the cause of expanding that rampant bureaucracy even further. So, without Alan's help, it has (within the last couple of years) come up with such masterpieces as:

- A Client Solutions Executive, who would be expected to 'work with internal stakeholders and external partners to provide sponsorship and "thematic" advertising packages'.
- A Portfolio Support Coordinator, to assist with the 'development of policy to identify and challenge demand requirements'.
- A Head of Audiences, Vision Multiplatform, who would be required to 'embed audience understanding in the creative process' and 'interrogate and find new, interesting audience insights and creative stimulus', and…
- A Decision Support Manager, who would obviously be there 'to support decision-making in the BBC workplace'.

Well, where does one start? Maybe by questioning why anybody charged with (and paid for) making decisions in an organisation should be supported in this responsibility by having a designated decision support manager – who presumably carries the can when the decision is wrong. Or how about asking whether any sort of 'Head of Audiences' was embedding audience understanding in the creative process or finding new, interesting audience insights and creative stimulus when *Yes Minister* or *Only Fools and Horses* was being produced. I can only imagine that even Jim Hacker, as the Minister for Administrative Affairs, would have found this proposition highly amusing, and Del Boy would have assumed it was one of Rodney's more ridiculous flights of fancy. Certainly no one would have taken the idea seriously, just as they shouldn't do now. Because it's all complete nonsense, and no more than a risible product of the bureaucracy that has become the BBC. It's just another brick in the wall of the overpaid, overstaffed establishment that is the current manifestation of our national broadcasting institution. And isn't that sad? And isn't it also completely reprehensible? I can only suggest that the whole management structure of the BBC is disbanded – entirely – and that they start all over again. Or they could just sack every other manager on the payroll and wait twelve months to see if anybody other than the sacked managers ever notice. Or, failing either of those solutions, it might be as well to move on to the next interpretation of the BBC – which is the 'Blatantly Biased Corporation'.

2. The Blatantly Biased Corporation.

It probably started to go wrong as soon as the BBC stopped recruiting retired wing commanders after the

War and embarked instead on a trawl of universities in order to capture a whole shoal of 'humanities-types', earnest young things who came factory-fitted with left-wing views and who would have their left-wing views nurtured indefinitely within an increasingly left-wing BBC environment that they themselves would create. This isn't bollocks. Indeed, one only has to watch – or listen to – the output of BBC News to see this blatant bias in all its glory every day. And, if you don't believe me, then consider some recent academic research that has demonstrated, with undeniable statistics, that such a bias does exist. Because what this research uncovered was that the BBC News was more likely to cover left-wing think tank reports – and to hail them as 'independent' – rather than right-wing think tank research, which would then often be 'qualified' by it being pointed out that these think tanks had a particular ideological position. That sounds like some pretty boring research to me, but it does illustrate that there is a distinct, possibly subconscious 'group think' among BBC journalists, or even a more deliberate left-of-centre bias in operation. And, frankly, I've observed it myself; a very obvious lack of balance, even on such worthy programmes as *Today*, where not only is there an ingrained antipathy to the upstart and distinctly non-pink party which is UKIP (apparent in the style of questioning employed) but even an attack on its very purpose, by giving roughly twice as much airtime to pro-EU voices as to those who are anti-EU.

Interestingly, this left-wing groupthink has led to a long list of what is 'good' and what is 'bad' in the BBC News environment. And I can report that 'good' includes, inter alia:

- The United Nations
- The European Union (although this isn't quite as 'good' as the UN)
- Soaking the rich
- Government spending (sorry, government 'investment')
- Quangos
- Islam (to the extent that it mustn't be offended)
- The NHS
- State welfare and social services
- State education.

Conversely, 'bad' includes, inter alia:

- The United States of America
- The monarchy
- Capitalism
- The defence establishment
- Banking (can't argue with that)
- The Empire
- Christians (although not strictly 'bad', but just fair game in that they won't do anything dangerous if they're offended)
- Margaret Thatcher.

I don't suppose that this bias thing should really surprise us. After all, if you're filling up your organisation with young 'arty' types – and, inevitably, quite a few ethnic characters – then you are hardly going to breed a new wing of the EDL within Broadcasting House, or even an active chapter of the Conservative Party. But even so, if the only way you can read the *Daily Mail* anywhere near the newsroom is by hiding it in a copy of *The Guardian*, then something is very wrong. No one can challenge the collective view with impunity – and by doing so, even once, you would probably compromise your future career. Indeed, this left-of-centre orthodoxy is so established in the BBC, and in its news operation in particular, that it is even apparent in the way that news is reported. And what I mean is that when BBC News is seeking to explain (let's say) another outbreak of violence in the Middle East, it often chooses to interview its own reporters rather than independent voices. Because that way it can present to the public a 'clarification of the facts', which may often be no more than an expression of its own (biased) opinion. That may sound a little harsh, but being biased certainly sees off being balanced and impartial, as anybody who has seen the BBC's reporting of the influx of migrants into Europe will be only too aware. Here the BBC has lost sight entirely of its duty as an impartial reporter and has instead become an enthusiastic cheerleader for the whole process of the mass migration of people. Migrants, it seems, have joined the first of those two lists above, and from the perspective of the BBC News establishment are now not just 'good' but possibly even 'very good'.

I don't know what can be done. Maybe they need to get some leaders in there for whom *The Guardian* and *The Independent* are not their sole reading – or their friggin' catechism. Or maybe they should make the *Daily Mail* and *The Telegraph* compulsory reading. Or maybe there should just be an acceptance that to be successful in the BBC one doesn't have to fit a particular (left-wing) template and one can express admiration, on occasions at least, for some of Mrs Thatcher's achievements. Or do we just learn to accept the status quo, and tune into Al Jazeera rather than continue to endure that smarmy Welsh autocue reader who keeps looking away from the camera? And Al Jazeera doesn't treat the results of *Strictly Come Dancing* as news, either.

At which point it must be time to turn to the Broadcast Banality Corporation, which I will do forthwith.

3. The Broadcast Banality Corporation.

OK. Some of the BBC's current output is commendable, and there are still the odd flashes of brilliance in what it produces. But there is other stuff – and a lot of other stuff – that is at best tiresome and at worst a genuine threat to the brain function of an average human being. Yes, it appears that in fighting a ratings battle with other channels the BBC has decided that it is quite OK to put the nation's mental health at risk – by filling its schedules with a series of 'popular entertainment' programmes that are quite capable of shrivelling brain cells by the second. And if you don't know the sort of programmes I'm talking about – that make up the BBC's banality offerings – then take a look below where I have made some suggestions as to how some of them might be 'improved'. Or should I be more honest and admit that they are really suggestions as to how I might just be tempted to watch any of them at all? And in any event, my proposals couldn't possibly make them any worse than they already are. So, let's see what's to do with just four of them – starting with '*Strictly*'.

- Yes, *Strictly Come Dancing* is a prime example of serving up glitz, glamour and lip gloss as something worth watching, when if people gave it just a minute's thought they would see it for what it really is: just glitz, glamour and lip gloss that isn't worth watching at all. Now I know this will not be a popular view, because so many people will have been seduced by what is essentially an amateur night on speed (where the amateurs' make-up often weighs more than their clothes). But the truth is that *Strictly Come Dancing* is a pretty dismal idea, and is more in need of a makeover than are some of its desperate contestants. So what I suggest is that the format is changed from a tinsel-type dancing competition into a tinsel-type dance marathon, the sort of dance marathon that was held in the States during the Depression and which attracted so much well-deserved scorn.

I mean, just think: a contemptible (and therefore innately interesting) format, brought up to date and embellished with a big BBC budget... with the potential to provide days of output on the telly, compared to the odd few hours for the BBC's current played-out offering. Talk about a win–win situation. The punters would be happy – observing the suffering of a troupe of underdressed, over-painted hopefuls as they succumb to injury and fatigue over seven or eight days. And the BBC would be happy with a new, stimulating programme that could fill one week a month in its increasingly threadbare schedules. I've even got a name for it: '*Carry on Dancing*', a name, I might say, that would allow Dame Barbara Windsor to push aside the rather odd Winkleman/Daly duo and thereby provide a genuine national treasure with a boost to her pension.

Better still, that panel could be done away with. There would be no subjective judging any more, but just the indisputable 'last man and woman standing' measure of who wins the ultimate prize. And they could maybe even get the panel, and possibly the W/D duo as well, to make a valedictory performance in the form of their participating in the first event. I mean, that would really set it on its way, wouldn't it? God, people would even pay to watch it, and to observe how quickly grins dissolve into looks of abject horror when the pain starts to bite.... But, even if they couldn't secure the services of these wonderful people, I'm sure there wouldn't be any shortage of contestants for this show because, as we all know, there are literally millions out there who will do anything to get on the telly – and thousands of 'celebrities' who will just do anything full stop. There again, to get the retiring crew in that first show… well, that would provide us with a display of so much real (as opposed to ersatz) emotion, it might even put some of that national brain fade into reverse, and convince millions of us to demand something better.

So, that's brilliant idea number one, after which comes a much-needed revision of the stale and frankly embarrassing format of *The Apprentice*.

- Yes, *The Apprentice* in its present form is laughable, but not actually funny. Its master of ceremonies is a hopeless clown and its would-be apprentices are essentially just plain offensive and should all be put down for the sake of humanity. So there is an overwhelming need to take some radical action, and I will now propose what this action should be.

My idea stems from the fact that the hopeless clown is a peer of the realm and sits in the Lords, and we all know how dysfunctional that institution is and how overcrowded it is. So, to thin out its numbers, why don't we replace the youthful tossers with a clutch of peers and get these older wastes-of-space to go through the usual series of preposterous challenges?

I mean, you could easily find plenty of candidates (who, of course, would have no choice in the matter) and you could make your selection from all those peers who are only peers through political patronage or because they gave a lot of money for their peerage. And, to start with, you might want to focus on all those who don't attend the Lords ever, or who are only there to abuse its expenses system. Then, when you've got your chosen gang, you set them to work on a number of stupid challenges… No, on second thoughts, you just set them to work.

Yes, I've had a really good rethink. What better challenge could there be for a peer who formerly spent his or her life in politics – or who spent his or her life saving up for a title – to be set to do an honest day's work? It would be incredibly demanding for all of them and it would see any number of them falling by the wayside within no time at all – and, in doing so, losing their peerage. Oh, yes, as I implied above, the last remaining peer in the competition is the only peer who retains his peerage and his seat in the Lords. The rest are reduced to plain old commoners and have to live out their lives like the rest of us – which, if nothing else, will be very stimulating for them.

The programme would be called either *Peer Pressure* or *Peer into the Abyss*. And its only problem would be that it would still involve Lord Sugar. But I can't think of everything. And anyway, it's now time to move on to *Dragons' Den*.

- *Dragons' Den* started off as quite a good show, but it's now just very silly and not a little unpleasant. This is because the dragons have become more and more supercilious and more and more spiteful over the years, while still maintaining the pretence that they are all good guys with the best interests of the 'victims' at heart.

    Well, the only way to redeem this programme is to introduce a good dose of honesty into it, and to do away with that pretence of there being any sympathy for the unfortunate participants. So that means keeping the present dragons but dressing them as Romans and seating them above a mini arena, into which are led the show's modern-day Christians. When these poor sods then fail to attract an investment from the dragons… well, Health and Safety might mean that we couldn't introduce a bunch of lions into the proceedings, but I think a suitable stand-in for the losers being mauled to death would be just a tweak to the present approach of abject humiliation. This could be achieved by adding to the standard round of sneering a bucket of urine – which one of the dragons would throw over the unsuccessful participants to underline just what hopeless specimens of humanity they'd turned out to be.

    So, no dramatic change of the format here, but just more honesty and more piss. And I think that should do it – and we can now move on to *The Voice*.
- Well, I've not much to say about *The Voice*

because, unlike the three programmes above that I've actually seen on a couple of occasions, I have never watched *The Voice*, ever. However, I do know that it entails judges hearing somebody's voice without seeing them (?), and that the four winning voices from the four series of this programme aired in the UK have gone on to be... well, not quite a raging success. The first winner produced an album that was described as 'a huge flop' and she was soon dropped by her label, and the other winners have produced albums that have 'not caught too many people's attention'. Which suggests to me that *The Voice* might benefit if the judges didn't just not see the contestants, but they didn't hear them either. Give them all a pair of earplugs and let the winner emerge through a combination of chance and possibly corruption. It might produce a winner who actually went on to have some success, and it might provide us with a programme that was just about watchable. Maybe.

The alternative is just to scrap it completely.

So, that's the low-down on the BBC, a crowned institution that's suffered more than just a minor wardrobe malfunction in the crown department. And I haven't even mentioned its whitewashing of past sex scandals with the attendant implausible absolution of its senior managers, its over-rewarding of its sometimes unwatchable presenters, its ineptitude with IT, its excruciatingly feeble local news programmes, its desire to paste music over any worthwhile programme, its 'We are right and you are wrong' response to any viewer/listener complaint and its rather demoralising dedication to diversity in all its forms, whether this is warranted or not.

That said, the BBC could be a lot worse. It could, for example, be FIFA.

> The BBC is big and strong
> With wavelengths short and wavelengths long
> But even so, I have to say
> I think the Beeb has lost its way
>
> To start with there are all its folk
> Whose jobs are just a dreadful joke
> And worse than this, or so I'm told
> There's quite a few paid pots of gold
>
> And then there is its state of mind
> That means it might be very kind
> To those who share its pinkish views
> But not to those of other hues
>
> And then there are its flagship shows
> The sort not meant to curl our toes
> And what I mean is all that stuff
> That's full of glitz and noise and fluff
>
> But toes *are* curled – and jaws are dropped
> At what is aired and can't be stopped
> And all because the BBC
> Is not the Beeb it used to be

Cultures

Now the first thing to note about this particular 'stuff' is that its title is '*Cultures*' and not '*Culture*'. This means that I do not intend to give you my opinion on art or on any other manifestation of human intellect. No, what I intend to do is explore cultures in the plural, as in the ideas, customs and social behaviour of various different people on this planet. And then, most importantly, I intend to examine how these various cultures are now shaping our future. Yes, it is the 'way of life' sort of culture I have in my sights here, not the sort that Mr Yentob pores over in his repeated attempts to justify his existence. What this means, of course, is that the following pearls of wisdom are not for the faint-hearted. Or, more specifically, if multiculturalism is up there for you, along with a robust rendition of *The Red Flag* and an evening of experimental theatre, then you will be well advised to ignore this section completely. However, if you are alarmed at the prospect of Jeremy Corbyn becoming this country's prime minister and are of the opinion that only a minority of your fellow humans have not yet lost the plot, then you should probably read on.

OK, I'll make a start, and I'll make this start by stating

the profusely bleedin' obvious, and this is that there are very many different cultures in the world, which must mean that there are very many different traditions, outlooks, practices, moral codes and sets of values in the world. We all know what we regard as acceptable and normal in our own culture, and equally we can see that other cultures hold very different views.

Right. So far so good, and not really contentious. But if I now suggest that some cultures are better than others then I can almost hear the hair on the back of a thousand liberal necks bristle into action, even before I've set out what I mean by 'better'. Well, let me do just that. Because I am of the firm opinion that a culture that doesn't encourage practices such as female genital mutilation, child marriage, infanticide, forced marriages and so-called honour killings is better than one that does. I also think that one that is based on law and at least a modest amount of order, even if it indulges in such arrant nonsense as *I'm a Celebrity get me out of here* and *The Apprentice*, is infinitely better than one that is cloaked in a miasma of corruption and one where 'order' only ever comes in the plural – as in the form of diktats from oppressors and thugs.

Well, I can now hear quite a few liberals sharpening their Liberty letter openers. Not ideal as daggers, I know. But they'll do, especially if buried in a heretic's neck…

Nonetheless, I am obliged to carry on, and to confirm their worst fears, which is that the very best cultures in the world – not only in terms of their rejection of barbaric practices and wholesale corruption but also in terms of their ability to nourish societies which are by and large stable, safe and fair – are those that are found in the West. And to be entirely clear about that, I mean the select assortment of cultures that are found in Western Europe, North America and the Antipodes. They are all a million miles from perfection and, like any human creation, they are more characterised by their inadequacies and their faults than by their merits. But, compared to many other cultures around the world, they are truly excellent. Compared to some they are ideal.

With their enlightened views they have encouraged, over the years, the advancement of science, the flourishing of all sorts of technologies and the flourishing of all sorts of manifestations of the Alan Yentob sort of culture. And, of course, they have encouraged the creation of largely comfortable and largely secure environments for their adherents. They have even nurtured the development of the human spirit, which now manifests itself in such diverse recreations as synchronised swimming, cheese-rolling and the epitome of uplifting pastimes: morris dancing. Such are the heights that can be attained in those societies whose cultures have 'taken the right path'.

OK. Time now to turn the spotlight on some of those less admirable cultures, cultures that have nourished the creation of societies that are far from desirable. OK, some are not too bad and their adherents lead reasonable, settled lives. But others… well, there are literally billions of people in this world who are obliged to live out their lives in what are effectively mafia states – or feudal hellholes or despotic snake pits or completely rotten narco states or states that are brazenly totalitarian in their nature. Worse still, and possibly of rather more relevance at the moment, hundreds of millions more are obliged to exist in societies whose cultures have rendered them entirely dysfunctional. And may I also say (while now dodging the thrusts of all those letter openers) that these societies are so dysfunctional that they cannot withstand the pressure of population growth, and they have either already collapsed or are in the process of doing so.

But I risk getting ahead of myself... because I did threaten, at the beginning of this essay, to explore how the world's various cultures are shaping our future. And it is now time to admit that there are two particular types of cultures that are already shaping *our* future, and my exploration will therefore focus on these two – and on their impact on our own cherished *The Apprentice*-watching culture, along with those of our immediate neighbours in Europe. Oh, and the two future-shaping cultures I have in mind are:

1. Russia's, and
2. The 'completely dysfunctionals".

I will start with Russia, and with a plea that you do not read the rest of this essay after a hard night on the town or after an overlong lunch. It will require concentration, a certain degree of stamina and a resolve to get to its end. So please organise yourself properly, and bear in mind that I probably spent longer writing this stuff than you're going to spend reading it. Oh, and as you are a member of one of the most admirable cultures on the planet, I am confident that you will heed my appeal. So, to start with Russia…, and first a bit of history, and then how history can incubate a culture…

You see, in times long past, many now more 'civilised' countries operated some sort of serf system in the development of their societies. Most European countries did. And so too did Russia. But, in the case of Russia, this serfdom habit arrived rather earlier than in other countries and it remained in place well after all the others had gone, and consequently, a serf mentality became very deeply embedded in its psyche. For centuries people had been made to think like slaves. Instilled into them was the belief that they were little more than chattels: the human property of their masters, there to do his bidding and to have no proper lives of their own. So that when serfdom was abolished in 1861 the serf mentality endured... and endured. So much so that when Stalin decided to return his people to serfdom, by driving them in their millions on to collectives and state farms, it was far easier than it might otherwise have been. It also had the effect of reinvigorating that serf mentality, which had never really disappeared. And this is why it has not disappeared even now, in the twenty-first century. Quite simply, a 'serfdom nurture' still has a huge impact on how the country – and its leaders – behave.

To explain this further, it is first necessary to recognise that a society of ex-serfs, still burdened with a serf mentality, equates to a society in which the experience of property ownership and free labour is by no means widespread. And this sort of society is not instantly going to convert itself into a society of free people or, indeed, into what might be regarded as a proper civil society. How can it, when one considers some of the characteristics instilled by serfdom, and which still persist in the minds of Russian people to this very day – such as a lack of respect for the individual (and especially for themselves), a lack of respect for private property, a disrespect for the law and, consequently, an acceptance of paternalism and an innate fear of all forms of power?

All this adds up to a bunch of citizens who might best be described as socially infantile and barely bothered by the concept of personal responsibility and personal initiative. And without personal initiative, in particular, it is very difficult to build a modern economy, where things work and people's well-being improves, and instead you just end up with a third-rate scrapheap of an economy, and even this can't be sustained. Yes, not even the Red Army could keep it all together, and all those states you'd sucked into your neighbourhood empire through the twin devices of the USSR ploy and the Warsaw Pact couldn't wait to piss off.

However, at the conclusion of this lacklustre history, Russia finally got a break. Because it seems that it had always been sitting on something that was now desperately in demand, and this, of course, was an awful lot of oil and an awful lot of gas. With this combined natural bounty (and very little else) Russia has been able to improve its situation radically in material terms, even if its people still lack initiative or many of the other qualities we now take for granted in the West. They are also undeniably still wedded to the idea of paternalism, of somebody being responsible for them from cradle to grave, and this paternalism now manifests itself as statism, whether the state in question calls itself a democratic state or a Communist state. To most Russians that's just a detail. The important thing is that the state should take care of them and that right at the top of the state should be a father figure who, like those feudal lords of the past, can punish or pardon as he wishes... and get away with just about anything he wants.

Well, congratulations for getting this far, with not even a hint of levity to assist you in your passage, and probably with no refreshments whatsoever. But take heart, because we are now not only in the present day but we are also just about to discuss that father figure at the top, one Mr Vladimir Putin, known to his friends as... errh, wait a minute, he doesn't have any friends, does he? Not any real friends, anyway... just friends who might more accurately be described as sycophants or toadies, or just terrified acolytes. But again, I am drifting off the point, and the point is that Mr Putin is regarded by most of his ex-serf citizens as a kind though strict father who has to cope with the malign influence of bad guys in the shape of corrupt officials, and who is never regarded as the source of malignancy himself. And the fact that he is not the product of a real democracy, as operated in a real, modern civil society, is inconsequential. Russians don't care. And, helped by a constant drip-feed of misinformation by the state apparatus, not enough of them care about how this acceptance of what is closer to an autocracy than a democracy is being abused by the country's elite.

Only those in that elite know how much abuse is taking place, but there are those outside who have described Russia as 'a corrupt, autocratic kleptocracy centred on Putin's leadership, in which officials, oligarchs and organised crime are bound together to create a virtual mafia state, one in which it is impossible to differentiate between the activities of the government and those of organised crime'. It probably is this bad, and it is certainly inconceivable that corruption does not exist on a grand scale, with those responsible for this corruption only in fear of the law when the law is being used against them by others who are equally corrupt.

Well, fine. But so what? Surely all this means is that Russians are being screwed by a state-sized mafia – and aren't even aware of it. And as much as Russia wants to be regarded as an efficient, effective democracy, standing up against the forces of colonialism and modern imperialism, it never will be. Because all of us outside Russia can see it for what it really is: a third-rate society born out of a history of serfdom and with no worthwhile future until eventually that serf mentality simply shrivels up and dies – if, indeed, it ever does.

However, that rather narrow conclusion fails to take account of the father figure himself, and what he might need to do to maintain his position at the top of a mafia state. Bear in mind that he is a guy lacking in both height and charisma, and it takes rather more than constant propaganda to sustain his vital cult of personality. It takes projections of (faux) virility, demonstrations of ruthlessness, successful ventures on the international stage and unrestrained duplicity, especially when one's economy is distinctly on the slide.

So, what have we observed during his tenure as head honcho? Well, there were all those photos of a short man wrestling tigers, releasing leopards, hugging polar bears and exposing himself on a horse – and there was that infamous cup of tea (one rad or two, comrade?). Then there was the most expensive Winter Olympics in history, at Sochi, the success in that open and honest competition to host the 2018 FIFA World Cup and that not so open and honest haul of athletic medals at the 2012 Summer Olympics in London. But, let's be really honest, as opposed to the honest in 'open and honest.' – and that means recognising that there is just so much mileage in showing your nipples and stealing gold medals, and that to keep it going you really have to indulge in a bit of unprovoked belligerence.

Hell, it went very well in Georgia… and then there was hardly a squeak when Crimea was taken. So why wouldn't any self-respecting delusional dictator try it on even more, even if it meant lying through his teeth about all his forces being deployed in Eastern Ukraine and then fibbing some more when his dickhead forces had managed to shoot down a civilian airliner by mistake? Hell, the peasants at home won't know what's going on because they'll be told more fibs through the state media, where illegal incursions into sovereign states will be dressed up as the protection of the motherland and a repudiation of those humiliations of the past, when somebody carelessly let the USSR fall apart. And anyway, the Malaysians probably shot down that plane – as some sort of insurance scam (a suggestion that would almost certainly be accepted without question by a majority of Russians).

Then there is the current adventure in Syria, with a bit of blowback over the Sinai Desert, and a distinct suspicion that Putin has the ability to do something really, really stupid, just to maintain his position as the Godfather of Grief and the ultimate Russian patriarch in the eyes of his 'children'. It might be as simple as one of his military jets getting too close to one of our jets in the course of a 'probing flight' towards Britain – with uncontrollable consequences. It might be a border incident with one of the Baltic states, which could trigger a response from NATO. Or, if things got really desperate for him, it might be a plain old-fashioned first strike (having previously taken care to warn the oligarchs in London that they should ship out their best vintages without delay).

Far-fetched? I don't think so. After all, the idea that a 'civilised' nation state would buy a football tournament, sabotage a Summer Olympics, facilitate the shooting down of a civil aircraft or annex a huge chunk of its neighbour's territory would all have been described as far-fetched fifteen years ago. Yet they all happened.

So the point I am striving to make is that we now live next door to a well-armed neighbour, which, through a defective culture, has now become a real threat to our very existence. If we all go up in smoke it won't be because Morocco has pressed a button. In the first place it hasn't got one. And in the second place Morocco has only a very pale facsimile of Putin, who isn't quite so dependent on image. In fact, it's not that likely that it will be another nuclear power like China or even North Korea. Like Morocco, they can manage without causing an apocalypse in Europe. No. Only Russia, with its highly flawed society – stemming from its highly flawed culture – represents the ultimate threat to our future. And it is a threat that might emerge overnight. Unlike the second major threat to our culture, a threat that is more insidious and rather more sedate in its progress, but ultimately just as fatal as the first. And this, of course, is the very scary threat posed by the number two future-shaping culture, as referred to above: the very real menace to ourselves from the 'completely dysfunctionals'.

So, just to make it clear… We've done the number one future-shaping culture (that of Russia). And we're now going to embark on the second, which – given how dedicated you must have been to get this far – may mean that you ought to take a break and then come back refreshed. I'll leave it up to you. But, in any event, please do carry on. I have, after all, been dodging the thrusts of sharpened letter openers for the last few pages. And that's before I've got to the even more sensitive part of this tale, which I will now do without further delay.

OK. Just to reiterate, my 'completely dysfunctional' societies are those societies whose cultures have rendered them incapable of providing their citizens with very much of anything and, more pertinently for us, they are also incapable of dealing with the pressures of population expansion (see my discussion of population later in this book). And, as a consequence, they are on the point of collapse or they have collapsed already.

Somalia is a prime example of a society that has already collapsed. It is a matter of debate whether Syria and Afghanistan are on the point of collapse or whether they should be bracketed with Somalia. Then there is Yemen…

Anyway, these four nations together are not the full extent of the problem. There are now a number of states in Asia and Africa and centred on the Middle East, where it looks as though it is only a matter of time before they too join the likes of Somalia on the scrapheap of national flops. Yes, there is no getting away from it, whatever those liberals might think. There are now a number of societies in this world that are completely in the shit. And there are even more of them that are in the process of toppling over and ending up in that same stinking ordure, and within only a very short time. I could name them. We could all name them. But, there again, I suspect we hardly want to encourage them (as if they needed any encouragement…).

Right. Well, even if this assertion is correct, and many will argue that it isn't, does it really matter? After all, the world has lived with dysfunctional human societies for centuries. And furthermore, why, even if things are now worse than ever for many, should it bother those of us who are fortunate enough to live in the 'desirable societies', those that are housed in Western Europe, North America and the Antipodes? Well, the answer, of course, lies in *cultures* again – and not just in the underperforming cultures, but in the cultures of the Western world as well. I will explain as follows.

The world's population is growing at an unsustainable rate (again as discussed in exquisite detail under 'Population'). Now this growth rate is by no means the same in all countries across the globe. No, the highest growth rates are found generally in the poorest of countries. This is probably because (ignoring other factors) less enlightenment in these countries leads to less development and less financial security and, hence, a desire for bigger families. I won't, of course, be the first to suggest this, but however this expansion in the number of people is coming about, it is the more dysfunctional societies that are least able to cope with the demands this creates. These societies cannot supply jobs. They cannot supply an attractive future for their youth. And some of them cannot supply even the basics to their people – in terms of food, clean water or shelter.

It is hardly a great surprise, then, that in these circumstances many of these trapped people look for a way out of their predicament – even before their society has actually collapsed. And only the dimmest of these would contemplate seeking out one of those less than attractive societies referred to at the beginning of this piece. After all, who, in his or her right mind would risk life and limb to make it to the land of the Russian mafiosi? Or to the land of some fourth-term despot in Africa, or to the land of the lockdown in China, even if they were allowed to? Even less likely is their desire to relocate their lives to another completely dysfunctional society, whether already collapsed or in the process of collapse. I cannot believe, for example, that very many destitute Bangladeshis are currently being trafficked into Afghanistan, and few Eritreans seem to be making a beeline for Gaza. No, like the hundreds of thousands of other desperate people in this world, they have in their sights one of those comfortable, generous societies, where not only will they be able to taste the fruits of economic well-being but also those famous and far from universal human rights (as discussed later in this tome). Only, of course, following the actual/imminent collapses of their own societies, it is wrong to think in terms of just hundreds of thousands. There will soon be millions of them, and what has recently been just a steady stream of these guys will inevitably turn into an absolute torrent. And this torrent will then just get bigger and bigger.

In short, there used to exist a 'cultural gradient' between 'them' and 'us', a huge incline that stretched from the depths of all those 'cul-de-sac' cultures to the heights of all those successful, 'civilised' cultures where life was sweet beyond words. And those in the cul-de-sac cultures went on enduring them largely because they had no choice or, in certain situations, because they were able to get their hands on some local resources that enabled them to make lives for themselves that were just about endurable or even rather good. But that was back in the period just after the Second World War, when the Earth's population was just one third of its present total and, very pertinently, when the Convention relating to the Status of Refugees (to which I will soon return) was drafted. Since then things have become more and more difficult, and more and more people at the bottom of that gradient have realised two things. The first is that they are at the bottom of a very large gradient, and the second is that there is nothing that can actually stop them climbing that gradient! It might be a difficult and dangerous climb but, with modern communication technology and with modern transport technology, they can do it. Oh, and there is one other vital element in their successful ascent of that gradient, and this is what has now become an integral part of all those cultures at the top of the gradient. And that, I am afraid to say, is these cultures' tight embrace of rampant liberalism…

I have just felt a stabbing pain in my back but I must struggle on, because it is vital that I make a very important point, and this point is that while all our modern Western democracies – without a single exception – have been indulging themselves in this overdose of heart-warming, make-us-feel-good-about-ourselves liberalism, they have, at the same time, forgotten that much of the rest of the world has not been doing the same. Liberalism has certainly not caught on in places like Russia and China – nor, indeed, in about a full three quarters of all the world's countries. We are in a distinct and now vulnerable minority. And our vulnerability arises from the fact that, by pampering ourselves with liberalism, we have quite simply emasculated our societies. We now specialise – big time – in the supine, at the expense of the sturdy and the stout, and in practice this means that we have no response whatsoever to what may prove to be an existential threat to our very own presently attractive culture. This is not hyperbole. We have signed up to commitments – based on that 1951 convention relating to refugees – and our culture does not allow us to abandon these commitments, even though the convention might now be ridiculously out of date and entirely unfit for purpose. And anyway, all these poor souls emanating from the remains of dysfunctional societies have their inalienable inherent human rights, and liberalism can never countenance denying them these… even if it means that the civil rights of us in the West are essentially ignored.

Now I should say at this point that it is not my intention to be incendiary. I am simply interpreting what I see happening in the world, and my interpretation is as valid as the next guy's. So there. And furthermore, the process that is now under way (as interpreted by yours truly) does lead us to some very interesting and almost philosophical speculation. Because it is very easy to see that this cultural gradient I've referred to will continue to be climbed – by millions – until the day arrives when it will disappear. And ultimately it will disappear, not because the dysfunctional has risen to the same level as the functional, but because the dysfunctional has overtaken the functional by being 'fitter'.

Yes, a slightly novel thought maybe, but it could be that enlightened, liberal cultures have had their day, and with the world being overwhelmed by *Homo sapiens*, the fittest cultures will be those that have been hardened by suffering, intolerance, corruption and ignorance, and whose strategy for the future entails no let-up in their habits of extravagant procreation and an insidious or more obvious expansion at the expense of others. They won't even be held back by a respect for the world around them, and I doubt very much that they will keep the flame of human rights alight, and liberalism will certainly disappear. Yes, Darwinism (which they probably won't recognise) will have been proven again. Only, unfortunately for us, the fittest (in cultural terms) isn't necessarily the fittest we might have chosen…

So… we look at that house next door and we are bemused at the sight of it being trashed by its occupants. And then one day it has been trashed so much that it falls down, and its inhabitants have nowhere to live. Then we observe that they are observing us, and our own neat and tidy property, and they are maybe getting an idea. The idea then crystallises in their mind, and they climb over the fence and into our garden and then into our house. And we look on and smile. After all, we have to help them. It's in our culture.

Well, it is at the moment, and we do have our own culture at the moment, but I have to say that it seems the culture of a community attaches itself to an individual of that community very tightly indeed. This means that when any of these individuals manage to install themselves in our bit of this planet they have with them the same attitudes, views and customs that they grew up with. They retain their native cultures, no matter how reprehensible some of these might be. (And I have in mind here some of those barbaric practices generally inflicted on women referred to earlier, together with an enthusiasm for procreation.)

This really isn't good news. Discovering that one's own culture is not the fittest culture and that it has a definitively finite life is the worst news possible. It represents a slow, drawn-out death, which might make the prospect of a sudden, over-in–a-puff-of-smoke demise (courtesy of one Mr Putin) look mightily attractive.

So there you have it. One national culture that might spell our end tomorrow or a whole raft of cultures that, through their imposing themselves on our own – and through their being fitter than our own – gradually overwhelm us until we don't exist.

It's just a pity that enlightenment in our own culture spawned a degree of liberalism that robbed us of our ability to confront tyrants and our ability to be robust in the face of remorseless inundation. It makes you wonder how all those affronted liberals found so much energy and so much vehemence, and so little restraint in their use of letter openers on my person. Maybe, all this time, I have simply been misinterpreting the term 'bleeding-heart liberals'…

> There was a young fellow called Putin
> Who was much into lootin' and shootin'
> And baring his chest
> And prodding the West
> And threatening to put-in his boot-in

Or

> This one guy had learnt through his readin'
> That 'EU was Garden of Eden'
> And the best apples were
> To the north of Dov-er
> So, 'To England I go and not Sweden'

Democracy

Well, sorry about this, but before talking about democracy it's probably worth my starting by defining it. I mean, we've all grown up with it, but it's all too easy to forget what it really means. Or maybe what it should really mean. Anyway, one of the simplest definitions I can find for this laudable way of conducting our affairs is: 'A form of government where supreme power is vested in the people and exercised directly by them or by their elected agents under a free electoral system'. In the UK, if we forget about that rarest of beasts, a national referendum, we enjoy the latter manifestation of this system, as do virtually all modern democracies. We exercise our power through elected Members of Parliament. Which works like a dream...

Only, of course, it doesn't, does it? In fact, most of the time it feels as though we have no power at all, to the extent that we feel completely powerless and pretty pissed off with what our government is doing. And yet we are blessed with one of the oldest and one of the most sophisticated democracies in the entire world, a model for the democratic systems in many other countries and apparently the envy of many others. So what is going on? Why is our democracy, which promises so much, failing to deliver on these promises? I mean, why are we all so cheesed off, so exasperated and so comprehensively disillusioned with our version of a system of government that is held out as being infinitely better than any other sort of government devised by man? And it can't just be to do with our dismal weather. And it's not. No, it's more to do with a number of issues, issues that become only too obvious as soon as you start to examine its less than faultless form, and how these faults are exploited. So that's what I'm going to do, and I'll start by looking at how we choose our 'agents'. This will be my issue number one.

1. OK. You probably already know this, but an agent is supposedly chosen through the election process by his or her receiving more votes in a designated constituency than any of the other candidates on the ballot paper. It's a 'first past the post' system, and it has become deeply ingrained in our political process. Well, that's fine, but the reality is that the constituents don't choose anything other than possibly the party that they find the least offensive. The choice of agent/candidate has already been made for them by some form of constituency candidate selection panel, a small number of party activists, who will unavoidably choose the guy who they think will garner the most votes as opposed to the guy who might make a better job of representing his/her constituents in Parliament. This really

matters, because in almost 80% of all constituencies the voting outcome is a foregone conclusion. In some of these constituencies the Conservative selection panel could put forward a performing ferret and it would win, and in others the Labour selection process could provide the voters with a rubber dildo and it would have a walkover – and it would possibly do better than some of the real-life dildos who are chosen instead. Oh, and of course, the panels can only choose candidates from party-approved lists of such hopefuls, which may well not include anyone who lives in the constituency and therefore anybody who has any real understanding of the constituency's local issues, or indeed its culture. Instead the constituents will all too often be presented with a candidate who has the appropriate party approval but an entirely inappropriate motivation.

Yes, there is little doubt that our representatives in Parliament are less and less likely to be our neighbours and more and more likely to be political careerists who first decided that politics could serve them – and not the other way around – when they were pratting around with PPE at Oxford. Indeed, the norm now seems to be that one's choice of party, if one is in this brigade of toerags, is not dictated by political conviction but by the likelihood of a particular party being able to fix you up with a safe seat – probably somewhere rather unfashionable where the plebs need a PPE sort of chap to tell them what they want and what they should believe.

Alternatively, one simply chooses the party (as Euan Blair, Will Straw, David Prescott, Emily Benn and Joe Dromey have done) where there is more than just a tenuous link with its past or present establishment. This is not, of course, to suggest that nepotism is rife within UK politics or that who you know is far more important than what you know (and whether you know your arse from your elbow). But it is to state this as a firm fact.

So, just to be clear, most constituents in this country do not choose their agents. Party machines and selection panels do. And given that many of these agents will have been helped by their party connections and are nakedly ambitious, how likely do you think it is that they will vote to support the party or to nurture their own careers as opposed to voting in the interests of their dumb constituents? And no prize for guessing that only in extraordinary circumstances will it be in the interests of their constituents. Like, for example, if their constituents have occupied their London residence and are threatening to burn it down. Although I'm not sure that's a good example. As their designated second home, they could probably turn it to their financial advantage...

But anyway, I hope you now see that exercising our power through elected agents, when the choice of agent has essentially been made for us and the choice may be a very bad one, can be kinda problematical. It would be easier to exercise power if it were tied round a brick.

Alternatively, we could always challenge the role of those largely unchallenged institutions that are taking it upon themselves to make those choices for us, whether we like it or not. I mean, of course, the major political parties of this country, and these and their impact on the operation of our democracy will constitute the substance of my issue number two.

2. OK, to start with, some statistics.

- Only 1% of the electorate is a member of a political party (compared to almost 4% in 1983).
- Only about a third of the population identifies fairly or very strongly with a political party.
- The combined membership of the Conservative Party, the Labour Party, the Lib Dems, the SNP, UKIP and the Greens is considerably less than that of the RSPB.
- Party membership has been falling for years, with the most dramatic slide being that in the Conservative Party, which is down from 2.8 million in 1953 to about 150,000 now.

So one could say that the legitimacy of our principal political parties is questionable at best, and at worst that it has essentially shrivelled away entirely... and that we are now allowing what are little more than established pressure groups to have a stranglehold on the way our country is run. And if one stops and thinks about just how few party members there really are, and what motivates the majority of them, then putting our affairs in their hands is not dissimilar to a secular society handing control of itself to a tiny religious minority. In both instances real power is wielded by a few over the many, and the few have very different traits and very different objectives from the many – and they definitely have their own agenda.

If you doubt this then just consider for a moment the sort of people who join political parties. About the best that can be said about them is that they are enthusiastic activists, keen to bring about social and political change and a better life for their fellow citizens. The trouble is that what this actually means is that you have a bunch of naive and immature tosspots attempting to impose a mix of misguided and half-baked ideas on a host of other people who would rather be left to muddle through their own lives as they want. However, you can say far worse things about the sort of people who become party members, and what their character means for the parties themselves. I am sure there are lots of noble exceptions but, when you take account of the lurid stories about the three longest-established parties, you might easily conclude that they are full of bullies, just-post-pubescent tyrants, rather dim despots, pimply prima donnas, thugs, misogynists and loads of pretty well unprincipled aspirers.

Take the Conservatives, a party that is not without members who specialise in sleaze and not without a load of young hopefuls who enjoy nothing better than a pint or so of bubbly after a hard day of bullying some of their even younger associates.

Labour is just as bad. Here we have a bunch of earnest poor souls who are not unacquainted with some of the less laudable practices of trade unions, with internecine warfare and, latterly, with the intimidation tactics of both true Trotskyists and the very worst sort of sociopathic Internet trolls. But maybe the worst of all are the Liberal Democrats, that band of principled warriors who invariably lay claim to the highest moral ground but who, all too often, can be found at gutter level, engaging in such stuff as the groping of women or the harassing of disabled constituents for sex. Oh, and they're not too bad in the arts of hypocrisy and cover-up either. OK, maybe not at a local level, but at the national level… Well, in many ways, they really are the seedy party, and I can only put this down to the impact of 'moral licensing' (as discussed in a little more detail under 'Religion'). This is the phenomenon of people using something good (like being a member of the righteous Lib Dems) to justify something bad (like putting your hand inside an adviser's dress without her consent). But whatever the reason for their rather sordid goings-on they, like all the other main parties, are hardly ideal institutions to which we should be entrusting the safekeeping of our daughters, let alone the safekeeping of our fragile democracy. But we do. And then, to make matters worse, we let them loose on that 'first past the post' electoral system referred to above, and we end up not with a democratic outcome but with a travesty of the essence of democracy – as I will now demonstrate with some figures from the 2015 general election. So please pay attention.

OK, what I will now do is list the number of MPs elected to Parliament by party. I will also list the total votes cast for each party, with relevant percentages. This is as follows:

	MPs	Votes Cast
Conservative	330 (50.8%)	11,300,109 (36.8%)
Labour	232 (35.7%)	9,347,324 (30.5%)
SNP	56 (8.6%)	1,454,436 (4.7%)
Lib Dem	8 (1.2%)	2,415,862 (7.9%)
UKIP	1 (0.2%)	3,881,099 (12.7%)
Greens	1 (0.2%)	1,157,613 (3.8%)

Now it would take a world-class innumerate not to spot that there is something amiss here. For example:
- The Greens have the same order of votes as the SNP, but have one MP whereas the SNP have fifty-six.
- UKIP has getting on for three times the number of votes won by the SNP – and it too has only one MP compared to a whole friggin' clanful of Scots.
- It takes 3,881,099 people to elect a UKIP MP; it takes just 25,972 to elect an SNP MP. That is almost 150 times as many voters to elect a single UKIP chap as it takes to get one of those Scottish guys installed in Westminster.

There is something clearly missing here, and it has a name. It is called 'fairness'. For a democracy to earn its name, if nothing else, it requires the legislature – our Parliament – to have a make-up that bears at least some resemblance to the concerns of the people, as reflected in the popular vote. It may have done so years ago, when there were just two and a half parties fighting it out, but ever since their woeful custodianship of this nation has seen the emergence of other parties it certainly hasn't. Add in the impact of an effective 'voting closed shop' north of the border, harnessed, quite understandably by a nation that wants to leave the Union, and you've got a complete pig's breakfast. I mean, you've got about 17% of the population (those who voted UKIP and Green) effectively disenfranchised, while at the same time you've got a load of Scots, with less than 5% of the popular vote, handed a whole slew of seats and the ability to do as much mischief as they want – without any proportionate mandate. You've even got the prospect of their she-devil-in-chief (who isn't even an MP) lecturing all of us south of the border on a whole string of imaginary injustices levelled against her people – which many of us wish weren't imaginary at all.

What a mess, and what a mockery of our so-called democratic system. No wonder that many people don't bother to vote at all. In fact, it's more a wonder that so many do, especially when you consider that we haven't got to the end of the bad news yet. Because I haven't yet discussed one further outrage in our domestic democracy, nor have I touched on a fatal flaw that exists in all modern democracies. And I think I'll deal with the home-grown outrage first. And this is that other body making up our UK

Parliament, the one that isn't elected. Yes, having dealt with the dysfunctionality of the Commons, it is now time to deal with the dysfunctionality – and pure farce – of the House of Lords. This will be the subject of my issue number three.

3. OK, let's just list a few pertinent facts about this august body, such as:
   - Its purpose is to scrutinise bills that have been approved by the House of Commons, and it frequently amends these. It can also delay them and, in certain circumstances, it can prevent them passing into law. (So it's pretty powerful, really.)
   - It 'employs' as many Lords to perform this function as there are centimetres in the colons of five (male) humans added together (822).
   - Twenty-six of these Lords are 'Lords Spiritual', a reference to their positions as bishops in the Church of England and nothing to do with their ethereal nature (as far as is known).
   - A further ninety-two Lords are hereditary peers, and these guys represent the residue of a system abolished in 1999 and will, of course, soon be no more than… well, a literal residue.
   - Then there are 179 'crossbenchers', a bunch of life peers now positioned on the chamber's cross bench by a supposedly independent House of Lords Appointments Commission. These are the 'worthy' sorts: guys and gals who have actually achieved something in life and

therefore, theoretically at least, they are capable of contributing to the Lords' work. No, not the Lord's. That would be the job of those bishops...

- If my arithmetic is correct, that leaves us with 615 life peers who, save for a handful of non-affiliated peers, are affiliated with the main political parties and will have made their way into their Lordly environment by being appointed by the monarch. This would have been on the advice of the prime minister (having apparently been vetted by the Appointments Commission). I mean, the life peers will have been vetted, not the PM. As far as I know, he is not subjected to any sort of formal scrutinisation process whatsoever.

So, no problems really, other than there might be just one or two more Lords than are really necessary. Oh, and then there are all those politically appointed Lords, and the credentials of rather more than just the odd one or two of them. Ah, and we mustn't forget the mix of their political affiliations – compared to the apparent will of the electorate, as reflected in the popular vote for their representatives in the lower house. After all, we mustn't forget the electorate, must we? That's what democracy is all about.

OK, well... I will start with their total number, which is 822. This is double or triple what it should be. In the first place, because prime ministers just have this thing about appointing more peers, and in the second place, because peers don't retire, and they are living far too long. Modern medicine has all but eliminated their expiry through sexually transmitted diseases, acute gout and liver capitulation, and they now just go on and on – and on and on – in the best traditions of House of Lords' debates.

This overpopulation could be addressed overnight – through a series of simple measures. I suggest:

- Sacking all those who don't attend debates, or who just turn up occasionally for the money.
- Instituting a retirement age of seventy (max).
- Kicking out any Lord who has 'had a problem' with his or her expenses – like Baroness Uddin, Lord Bhatia and Lord Paul – but not before tarring and feathering them and tweaking their noses.
- Weeding out all those political appointees who were appointed to make up the numbers for their particular party, and whose only claim to fame was either having a job such as a 'community activist' or a position in a local authority somewhere in the north-east of England that was advertised as a sinecure but then, for the next thirty years, became much less demanding than that.
- Organising an annual half-marathon, where those finishing in the last fifty are put down as they cross the line.

If instituted, these measures would get us down to maybe just two colons' worth of peers, but I have to confess that we still might need to dispose of a few more. And here I have in mind the real undesirables, who may not have fiddled their expenses. So that's all those creeps who have bought their peerage, all those worthless, time-served senior politicians who just don't know when to call it a day, all those cheats, rotters, sycophants, opportunists and all those out-and-out bastards who shouldn't have been given any public responsibility in the first place. And that might just about do it, and all we'd need to do then would be to address that mix of political affiliations that I referred to above.

You see, the current mix of political affiliations in the House of Lords is:

Conservative	251
Labour	213
Lib Dem	111
DUP	4
UKIP	3
Plaid Cymru	2
Greens	1

I won't repeat the split of the popular vote at the 2015 general election because you will probably remember it well enough to realise that the UKIP and Green voters are as grossly underrepresented in the upper chamber as they are in the lower. Indeed, when the prime minister made a new batch of Lords after the 2015 election, he made no UKIP or Green Lords at all, but rather more Lib Dem Lords than were necessary, considering that the electorate had just rejected this party big time and that there were far too many Lib Dem luvvies in the Lords already. I mean, this party polled just 8% of the popular vote but still has 18% of the political clout in the Lords, as against essentially none for UKIP and the Greens.

It's a disgrace and, rather than fiddling around with the sort of quick fix reform I've suggested above, the Lords in its present form needs to be binned and an entirely new revising chamber introduced. This should probably be made up of a relatively small number of capable, respected technocrats who've had no political affiliations whatsoever – probably put forward by a series of professional and technical bodies on some sort of rotational basis. However, nobody has offered to pay me for my invaluable advice on the reconstitution of the House of Lords, so I shall say no more other than the present set-up is a shambles and it has about as much to do with democracy as a dirty pair of underpants in Raqqa does – and whoever might have worn them to make them dirty in the first place.

So, that means it's time for issue number four: how our democracy, like virtually all other modern democracies in the world, has a fatal flaw that will ultimately be its undoing, even without the help of all those SNP upstarts. Now read on.

4. To explore 'democracy's fatal flaw', it is first necessary to broach a sensitive topic. And this is really sensitive. Because it is nothing less than recognising that the majority of the electorate – here and in democracies overseas – are not blessed with an abundance of intellect. In fact, many of them are significantly

intellectually challenged; even more of them are really dim; and there is a whole host of others who know as little about the democratic process as they know about gravitational singularities and Schrödinger's wave equation. You can sometimes observe them on the telly – in some pavement-conducted vox pop – announcing with gobsmacking honesty that they don't know the name of the prime minister or what the House of Commons is all about (a new sheltered housing project in Brent, maybe?). And neither do they know what century they are living in or indeed the meaning of century other than possibly the sort of century that stands outside a 'century' box with a gun in his hand.

Politicians know about these people, and they also know how to win their votes. It's simple. You just promise them anything they want. Forget about political ideals and, possibly, an appeal to their sense of community or some sort of vision for the future, and instead just promise them a freeze on electricity bills, more benefits, more spending on the NHS and more spending on even more schools, and you've got them. That's what they want to hear, and by 'them', I'm afraid that the only shorthand term I can alight on is the 'have-nots': all those people who have come to expect the government – and not the 'haves' – to provide them not just with what they need but also with what they want. Rarely do they consider who might have to provide the government with the resources it requires to fund all these appealing promises. And they never consider that so generous have these promises become that the 'haves' can no longer provide all the funds required. The trouble is that this doesn't appear to have dawned on our democratically elected politicians either. Or, if it has, they have conveniently forgotten it or wilfully disregarded it. Because, after all, isn't it the simplest thing possible just to fund all those promises by borrowing?

Hell, it's what everybody does. You want something. You get out a credit card or you get out a loan. And the last thing you do is give any thought as to how you might eventually pay it all back. And so it is with our democratic elite. To get into power (or to retain power) they promise more than the 'haves' can possibly fund through the tax system, in the full knowledge that they will be able to borrow the money 'that doesn't exist'. It's what's been going on for years now in most democracies. Democratically elected governments borrowing not just to fund specific projects but to fund unaffordable promises. Borrowing has now become an integral part of the way a democratic country's affairs are run, and nowhere is that truer than in the United Kingdom, a country where the government can actually face criticism if it doesn't exploit low interests rates by borrowing even more than it's doing at the moment.

Well, there may be a world, somewhere next door to Alice's Wonderland, where one can borrow and borrow and then borrow some more and there are no worrying consequences. There is never a day when the borrowing costs can't be serviced, and the creditors never get impatient for their money. But that is not the real world. Sooner or later, one or two or three generations are going to have to pay for the excesses of their ancestors. Or, more likely, there will be a cataclysmic default, democratic economies will collapse into ruins... and various forms of non-democratic governments will emerge to pick up the pieces.

Yes, we have become so conceited with our sophisticated model of democracy that not only have we become blind to its drawbacks, in terms of its encouraging short-termism and a focus on what would be 'nice' as opposed to what needs to be done, but we have also completely failed to notice that there is a time bomb within it. And only when that time bomb goes off, when our country is irredeemably and finally bankrupt, will we realise that democracy as a form of government has within it the seeds of its own demise. We might be evangelical about it at the moment, and keen to press it into use in any number of backward and authoritarian states around the world. But I bet we never point out to them that it has a finite life. And if you do kick out your local tyrant and replace him with a votes-at-any-cost democracy you will ultimately find yourself with maybe a worse tyrant than before, and probably a huge load of unpayable debts.

Yes, we shouldn't necessarily try to junk our democracy overnight, because there really is nothing better. But at the same time we should probably be far less self-satisfied with our 'equitable' form of governance – which, as I've attempted to illustrate, is not really equitable at all. And we should try to make it at least just a little bit better.

Alternatively, we could just take note of my closing remarks on democracy as practised in this country – which, while not designed to, will probably make you wonder why you bothered to plod your way through all my previous observations on this somewhat defective form of government.

Yes, it is time to admit to two undeniable truths. The first is that however our democracy operates in Britain, and however inept/corrupt/sociopathic are its 'operatives', we can always take some comfort from the fact that the country is not run by a democratically elected government, kept in check by a democratically elected lower house, but instead by the British Civil Service. They, as we all know, have to make no promises. And, indeed, they are not accountable to the electorate in any way at all. Furthermore, they need not concern themselves with any of that grubby party politics, and they are short-termists only in their approach to overtime.

Alternatively, of course, you might be appalled by this revelation and keen to distract yourself from the fact that you live under the yoke of an all-powerful and faceless bureaucracy… in which case you may care to dwell on the second undeniable truth. This is that the human species is incapable of devising any durable and fair system of government that works for groups of people much more than 600 at the most – or maybe just sixty at most. (And my money's on sixty.)

If we spent the next 100 years refining and polishing our UK democracy until it shone, and then populated it with cryogenically stored clones of David Attenborough, it would still be a mess… primarily because it would still have to operate with the great British public as the electorate. And, essentially, we will always end up with what we deserve. Which goes a very long way to explaining why we have at the moment no real role in choosing our representatives, an intrinsically unfair electoral system, rather more careerists than 'conviction politicians', a bunch of illegitimate political parties in charge of the political process, a blatant affront to democracy in the form of the House of Lords and a political system that is destined to lead us to our ruin. (And, incidentally, we also have a further distortion to the democratic process that I have, so far, been unable to bring myself to address, because it is so utterly depressing. And this is the increasing abuse, in elections, of the system of postal votes – designed originally to assist all those who were prevented, for some reason, from getting to a polling station, but used now on behalf of a load of other people who are… prevented from getting to a polling station.)

However, on a more positive note, we don't, at the moment, have a Home Counties Vladimir Putin. So that's good news, even though democracy still stinks.

> Democracy is all the rage
> The new religion of the age
> But as more closely one explores
> It seems it's simply full of flaws
> And flaws so large, I do declare
> We ended up with Brown and Blair

European Union

In the appraisal of any man-made institution it is vital to retain a sense of balance. For, no matter what benefits might emanate from such an institution, the fact that it is man-made will guarantee that it is far from perfect. Yes, in evaluating the institution that is the European Union, it is extremely important to give both its benefits and its drawbacks an equal billing, lest one falls into the trap of being considered overtly partisan – in either direction.

Well, that's all very fine, but it does get a little difficult when, as in the case of the European Union, there are no benefits whatsoever, other than to its army of self-serving bureaucrats, anonymous MEPs and various other camp-followers and hangers-on. And if anybody has the gall to suggest that there has been one enormous benefit, in the shape of its keeping the peace in Europe for the last seventy years, forget it. The people of (the real) Europe have not engaged each other in battle since 1945 through a combination of memory, common sense, perceived inconvenience and, to a certain degree, faint-heartedness. Oh, and then there's that set-up called NATO as well. But, believe me, the European Union can take no credit for the absence of shellfire and bombs, even though it might one day have a claim on their return...

So, this particular 'stuff' has, by necessity, been reduced to a list of everything that is wrong with the European Union... although it is not, of course, a comprehensive list. That would be an almost impossible task, and it would require the publication of this tome in two separate volumes. No, all we have here are the *principal* failings of the European Union (which henceforth will occasionally be referred to as the misleadingly concise EU). And, as you will see, they constitute more than enough reasons for an unconditional withdrawal from its clutches at the earliest opportunity, if not sooner.

OK, we'll make a start, and to begin with, our being caught in the web...

1. You see, many of us now have only a vague idea of how we ended up entangled in such a sticky mess, and many more of us weren't even born when we were. And, like those poor unfortunates who are blind from birth, we cannot possibly envisage what genuine freedom looks like or how colourful genuine national determination really is. So, just to record what actually happened – in pre-history – it might be best to start with that tall ingrate by the name of Charles de Gaulle who, on a number of occasions, swatted us away from the web... and then didn't, when he saw how a skewed Common Agricultural Policy would keep his beloved France in clover indefinitely, and largely at our expense. Then the way was clear for one Mr Edward Heath to tell the people of Britain, in 1972, about all the

'prizes to be gained by common action', and the promise of peace and prosperity and other platitudes aplenty, whilst conveniently forgetting to mention that joining what was then 'just' the European Economic Community was merely the first step in signing up to a full economic and monetary union with our new 'partners' (for which a target date – of 1980 – had already been set!). And then, after that, of course, there would be full political union.

Now, this wasn't just an Arthur Daley-type con. This was the real deal. This was an example of misrepresentation on such a scale and an exercise in disingenuousness of such unparalleled proportions that Edward Heath's entry in Wikipedia should first and foremost be as history's greatest flimflammer – and not as a politician. Furthermore, in describing his pre-eminence in this role, full credit should be given to the British national press who, without exception, acted as his accomplices in deceiving the British public. For example, the *Daily Mirror* informed its readers that they would become 'mere lookers-on from an offshore island of dwindling insignificance' (or should that be 'dwindling significance'?). Anyway, as part of the Establishment, they did what was required of them and relinquished any vestiges of journalistic enquiry before you could say, 'One great big effing stitch-up'.

Never mind. Because, in 1975, Superman appeared to save us, wearing a Gannex raincoat and smoking a rather unpleasant-looking pipe, and giving some of us a sense of the most profound unease. Yes, Harold Wilson had committed to 'usurp the sovereignty of Parliament' and give us plebs a referendum. We were to be allowed to vote on whether we wanted to stay in the EEC (as it still was then). Well, hang out the bunting! Be merry and be glad! At last, we would have our say…

Or at least we would when the Establishment, in the form of Wilson's Labour government, the Press (again) and the CBI had mounted such a positive campaign for the EEC that only simpletons, subversives, surrealists and subscribers to the cult of Perversity and Irredeemable Contrariness would have voted to come out. Yes, we were conned, lied to and generally spun into a dream that bore no resemblance whatsoever to the reality of a 'future in Europe'. And if you think I'm being disingenuous myself, I can only invite you to read the newspapers of the day and the government pamphlets issued to each household before the vote: the 'Yes' pamphlet, the underwhelming 'No' pamphlet and the 'impartial' government pamphlet – which, with its narrow focus on Food, Money and Jobs – and no mention of costs or commitments – was actually significantly more 'Yes' than the 'Yes' pamphlet. In retrospect, the 75% vote in favour of remaining in the EEC was remarkable. With all that false propaganda taken into account it should have been nearer 95%.

Anyway, our fate was now sealed. By using duplicity, deceit, dishonesty and dissimulation, the Establishment had locked us away for a lifetime, a lifetime of subjugation and subordination – in our new vassal-state status Britain – which would now not only not rule the waves but also not have a great deal of success in ruling itself...

2. Yes, one might compare our joining that EEC to an innocent little chap joining a stamp club, with the primary objective of swapping stamps with some fellow philatelists, only to find that he's actually joined a cult: the sort of cult that not only demands money all the time but one that also wants to take over every aspect of his life.

You see, what we joined, or what we thought we'd joined, was an economic free trade mechanism between sovereign states. It was something that would enable us to get cheaper French wine and maybe a taste for German bratwurst, but really no more than this. And we would still be a sovereign state, in control of our own destiny and able to tell Johnny Foreigner to sling his hook whenever we chose. In fact, there was a definitive statement made by the British government at the time that in retrospect was possibly misleading, to say the least. This was: 'No important new policy can be decided in Brussels or anywhere else without the consent of a British minister answerable to the British government and the British Parliament.' Which, with the addition of the words 'except when Brussels wants to decide' might have been a more accurate representation of the facts.

Anyway, we all know what happened. How in 1993 we no longer belonged to the EEC but instead to the new Execrable Undertaking – or the new European Union, to give it its more sanitised name. And somewhere along the way the unanimity between member states that had been required to decide policy changes was, in certain very important policy areas, ditched in favour of qualified majority voting, and bang went our centuries-old sovereignty with barely a protest... but with just a sigh of resignation. The cult was now in full control, and all thoughts of innocent philatelic reciprocation had long since disappeared.

How the hell we've let this happen is beyond me, although it may have something to do with the British Establishment being both greedy and weedy: greedy for easily won opportunities and weedy in the sense of lacking both confidence and resolution. This is especially true in the political chapter of the Establishment, where a Chamberlain-type brand of lameness, born out of years of fashionable liberalism, has completely overtaken the Churchillian courage and determination of the past.

We are stuffed. And worse, some of us on this island still don't appreciate just how stuffed we are.

3. Yes, it has to be recognised that many in Britain somehow believe that we should stay in the EU and, even if it has its faults, it would be too risky to leave it. The cult would not take too kindly to apostasy on the part of one of its principal paymasters and it would wreak its revenge by destroying our economy and throwing millions out of work. Furthermore,

and with a more positive perspective, a good proportion of these people would argue that the EU is a 'good thing' and even if we were somehow duped into joining it, because it is a 'good thing', then it really doesn't matter that we were duped. Nor does our loss of sovereignty. No, all that matters is that we belong to a successful international club that supports our well-being in all sorts of ways.

Unfortunately, however, its success is at best suspect, and one could even argue that it is better defined by its repeated failures, which leave it in no position to support our well-being at all… and, on the contrary, undermine it.

Poor economic performance is one of its primary achievements. In fact, the only real growth has been in the Union's welfare spending. Yes, while the EU accounts for 7% of the world's population and 25% of the world's GDP, it accounts for a staggering 50% of its welfare spend. And let's not talk about the mountain of red tape it consumes. No, instead we should elaborate on that poor economic performance by mentioning how this has dragged certain member states into preposterously named 'negative growth', and that with the help of the never-to-be-resolved euro disaster and the policy of indefinitely deferred national bankruptcies there are now frightening unemployment rates and criminal youth unemployment rates in many member states. And all these 'achievements' together can hardly be interpreted as a resounding success. Instead, they add up to a very good reason to unwind the

European Union tomorrow. And, furthermore, far from helping us in this country, the EU has been complicit in narrowing our focus to just this continent, at the expense of the wider view of the world we had as an independent trading state. So we are now shackled to a Continental manifestation of underperformance and constrained in our ability to seek out real opportunities further afield.

I have it on good authority that, when viewing the EU, America just shakes its head in disbelief, China laughs uncontrollably, and most of the rest of the world simply regards the whole of Europe as a has-been, as a collection of ex-colonial powers indulging in an exercise of self-ruination and fit only for decline and recolonisation by non-Europeans. In fact, any admiration of the EU is restricted to just born-again Stalinists and members of the American Mafia, both of which types of degenerate are not only impressed but also envious at the degree of control it now exercises over its captive populations, and just how much these captive populations are being screwed.

4. OK, this might be a good time to explore the next unequivocal failing of the EU, which is how it screws its imprisoned citizens by spraying their money around – in much the same way as one of its CAP-subsidised farmers sprays liquid manure around in the hope of achieving a CAP-subsidised crop from some of his CAP-subsidised marginal land. Oh, and the smell of ordure is the same, if not worse.

Let's start with the size of its discharge. This is a neat €130,000,000,000 per year. Or at least it was in 2011. EU budgetary information is, not surprisingly, a little difficult to access, and I didn't have the time to spend discovering by how much this figure has increased over the last few years. That said, it probably wouldn't be reckless to suggest that it is now knocking €140,000,000,000 or it might even be more – which is an awful lot of woven polyester St George flags (from Amazon), even if you go for the double-stitched hem.

A lot of this loot gets spent/lost/thrown away within Europe – on CAP payments for uneconomic hill farming, non-existent olive groves, overstated herds of pink llamas and the funding of 'cohesion for growth and employment', which is EU-speak for helping the poorer nations of Europe cope with the exodus of their workforces to the richer nations of Europe. Oh, and then there is a not insubstantial amount that gets consumed (voraciously) by the EU itself. But more of that later.

Anyway, that still leaves about €15,000,000,000 that gets spent outside Europe (which incidentally is about €30 for every man, woman and child within Europe). And what this goes on is international aid, 'citizenship', 'freedom', 'security and justice', 'asylum', 'education' and 'culture'. That is to say that possibly €3 of each contributor's money might just get to a worthwhile recipient, and the remainder either gets flushed down a toilet or assists Toyota in its sales of overspecified white Land Cruisers.

But it gets worse! Because not only can a citizen of Europe not prevent this ridiculous largesse, but he or she cannot easily discover the particular toilet down which the largesse is flushed – or whether all those Land Cruisers, as they emerge from their warranty period, end up in the hands of ISIS or Boko Haram.

Furthermore, in respect of that total overall blowout of €140,000,000,000, the European Court of Auditors reported in 2014 that the 'error rate' within this gigantic eructation of riches was 'just' 4.4%. That means that only €6,160,000,000 of our cash was paid out fraudulently or illegally and that the remaining €133,840,000,000 was paid out legitimately to well-deserving agribusinesses, to a host of slightly less well-deserving inhabitants of Eastern Europe and, no doubt, to a whole army of bewildered but very happy officials throughout the length and breadth of Africa and the Middle East.

Incidentally, if you are beginning to believe that I am being unduly critical of the European Union and how it operates, I can invite you to visit the European Commission's official website and its page on its accounts where it brazenly declares that, 'The European Union Court of Auditors has today given the EU accounts a clean bill of health for the 8th year in a row. Both the revenue side and administrative expenditure are free from significant errors'. Then there is a picture, and probably only ten people in the whole of the EU have then gone on to read what is admitted below this picture – which is the rather more significant information that, when it comes to the EU spend, there is, for the 200th year in a row, no prospect of a clean bill of health, but just a report that the EU continues to lose countless millions through ineptitude and fraud.

It's disgusting. In the first place the EU fraternity is claiming some sort of credit for its ability to take money from its captive citizens – without error – and pay itself – without too much error. And in the second place it is relegating the rather more important news that it is still squandering obscene amounts of the money it collects to almost a footnote. It is an exercise in deception at its worst, and it should do nothing else but draw our attention to all those people referred to at the beginning of this rant, all those for whom the European Union is a friggin' gold mine. And these guys are the Eurocrats, the MEPs and the various other lowlifes who feed from that massive, always-full-to-the-brim European trough, and are yet another reason why we should get out of the abominable EU just as soon as we can.

5. Now, before I put the knife in... I mean, before I discuss the trough-feeders in more detail, it is worth reminding ourselves that the great minds of this world, and even the not-so-great minds, tend to seek out careers in science or technology or they devote themselves to innovation and the creation of wealth through innovation. They do not seek to become officials, bureaucrats or even politicians. These are roles destined to be filled by the mediocre,

the middling or the misguided. But despite this, we provide these people with positions of power and with positions that are hugely over-rewarded... And no more so than in the institutions of the European Union. Now read on.

OK, let's start with the Eurocrats, of whom there are anywhere between 35,000 and 170,000, depending on how one distinguishes between a 'recognised' EU bureaucrat and any one of a number of other EU hangers-on. However, if there is very little clarity on their total number, it is only too clear that they are all, without exception, grossly overpaid. Their average pay is £60,000 per year (more than double the average wage in Britain), and many 'earn' over £100,000, with nearly 1,000 of them 'earning' between £146,267 and £179,703 (compared to Mr Cameron's pay packet of just £142,500). In fact, the European Commission has been described as a sort of self-service shop where officials can pick senior job grades off the shelf and then get their promotions approved during the summer recess to avoid their being spotted by the public (or even by MEPs).

Anyway, not content with this level of remuneration, these pampered bureaucrats then require a whole sheaf of allowances – including family allowances, education allowances (for their offspring, up to the age of twenty-six!), expat allowances, household allowances and ridiculously extravagant pension arrangements. Yes, while on Planet Real Europe, where even national civil servants are having to contribute more to their pensions to receive less in pension payments, on Planet Eurocrat it is just the reverse. In 2014 their contributions were cut and their benefits were enhanced, so much so that many of them are already able to claim 70% of their final basic salary as their annual pension payout. I know pensions are all very boring but, believe me, there is probably nowhere in the world, and certainly nowhere else in Europe, where the mediocre and the middling – or indeed anybody – can walk off with such an outrageous settlement for their retirement – at our cost.

It's not much better for the carpetbaggers, the opportunists, the double-dealers, the charlatans, the scoundrels and the pettifoggers – or, as they are otherwise known, the Members of the European Parliament. I mean, where does one start? Here is a collection of people who nobody knows, doing a job(?) that nobody really needs, as part of the goings-on of an institution that nobody really understands – but for which minor inconvenience to their time they are paid enormous amounts of dosh, with seemingly little or any accountability involved. They, of course, get a very generous salary, but then, like their officials, they get a whole bundle of allowances including a general allowance to cover secretarial costs (of over €4,000 per month), which they can simply keep for themselves as extra pay. The EU, if it majors in nothing else, certainly majors in not requiring proof of expenditure before it is reimbursed.

I could now go on to describe the special trough arrangements for the EU's top guys, the commissioners, but frankly I'm beginning to lose the will to live. And if I am, then I hate to think how you're getting on. So I will just close this section of my treatise on the EU by stating, without fear of contradiction, that all those 'employed' in the machine that is the EU are having an unparalleled feast – and a riotous laugh – at our expense. And we are powerless to do anything about it.

6. I suppose, at this point, I should develop that powerless point by echoing the views of countless other people in Europe that the EU is the antithesis of a democratic institution. It is actually totalitarian in nature and, like all totalitarian institutions, it not only deserves to be dismantled but, until it is, it will act with hubris, arrogance and an almost laughable degree of self-importance. Which brings me to another reason to reject the EU, in the form of a spectacular example of its vainglorious nature.

7. There is, not in *The Mikado* but in the EU, a person who holds the title of 'The High Representative of the Union for Foreign Affairs and Security Policy', and who is the chief coordinator and representative of the Common Foreign and Security Policy within the European Union.

    This role means that this person is:
    - The *ex officio* Vice President of the European Commission.
    - A participant in the meetings of the European Council.
    - The person responsible for the EU Special Representatives.

- The head of the External Action Service and delegations.
- The President of the Foreign Affairs Council.
- The Secretary General of the Western European Union (?)
- The President of the European Defence Agency.
- The chairperson of the board of the EU Institute for Security Studies.

And on Fridays she sells croissants in the morning and prophylactics in the afternoon… and in the evening she calls the numbers at the Gala Bingo Hall in the Brussels Emporium, except when she has to fill in her timesheet or collect her expenses.

Now, it is one thing to create such a ridiculous panjandrum of a position, but the EU has gone one better than that by also creating that 'External Action Service' referred to above, of which the High Representative, etc. is the head. Because this now acts (or should that be playacts?) as the EU's foreign ministry and diplomatic corps combined, supposedly implementing the EU's Common Foreign and Security Policy (budget €976,000,000) to great effect, as is apparent in its bringing the European migrant crisis under control… Well, maybe not completely under control, but when you're still busy setting up EAS delegations in such volatile hotspots as Barbados, and undermining the roles of national foreign ministers and national embassies, you can't be expected to do everything. And then, of course, there are all those meetings of the European Council to attend, to say nothing of having to chair the board of the EU Institute for Security Studies (where apparently inward mass migration is still dealt with under 'any other business').

It's a joke, and it illustrates just how silly the EU has become and just how Byzantine it has become. Nobody who pays for all this stuff has any idea what all these councils and agencies do, just as they have no real idea of how the whole European edifice works. What do MEPs actually do? What are they responsible for? What do commissioners do? How do they interact with MEPs? What do all those bureaucrats do – other than very well for themselves? And are these officials the product of natural births or are they now all cloned? We have a right to know. We also have a right to consider the guy at the very top of the European Union – and why he, on his own, represents yet another reason to run away from the EU just as fast as we can.

8. This guy's name is Mr Juncker, and his title is President of the European Commission. Now, to give you an idea of the sort of qualities that have seen this gentleman elevated to the very top of the EU, it is first necessary to take a little detour through his home country, which is Luxembourg. Now, Luxembourg is a member of the EU, and it is its richest member – by far. I mean, its GDP per head is twice that of Holland, Austria and Germany, more than twice that of the UK and about five times that of places like Romania and Bulgaria. However, this extreme good fortune is certainly not the result of

Luxembourgers being significantly more inventive, more creative and more hard-working than their European counterparts. Nor is it the result of their being lucky enough to have found themselves sitting on vast reserves of oil. No, the truth is that the Grand Duchy of Luxembourg has no measurable mineral riches of any sort and, furthermore, its innovators are as difficult to locate as any of its contributions to the advancement of mankind in general. Which means that possibly something else has made Luxembourg into Deluxembourg, and this something is, of course, the fact that Luxembourg is nothing more than a rather fortuitously placed tax haven.

Tax havens are places where one can find very low taxes or no taxes at all, together with laws that guarantee more than a soupçon of privacy and confidentiality. They are normally in exotic locations (often exotically located islands), and only in Luxembourg's case is there one of these parasitical institutions at the heart of (and part of) a political union of states, where it is these states themselves that suffer most from its egregious behaviour.

Yes, Luxembourg is in a club – the EU – and it has been enriching itself at the expense of the other club members – to the tune of billions a year. One of its favourite ways of doing this is through the use of the well-tried and well-established 'corporate tax dodge'. This is where, by using complex tax structures within its borders, which are often based on dubious transfer pricing arrangements or even more dubious mega loan arrangements, it is able to assist big corporations from around the world in reducing their worldwide tax bills. Put another way, these corporations, by rewarding their Luxembourg hosts, are able to avoid paying taxes that they should be paying in places like Germany, the UK and France – places where they are conducting the very activities that would normally generate these taxes in the first place.

It gets worse. As an embedded tax haven within Europe one can also exploit the privacy aspects of one's so-called financial sector, even if it means battling the EU's transparency initiatives for years. That way one can attract lots more business into one's grasp – even if those bringing this business might be full-blown tax evaders, as often as not from one's fellow EU member states. Oh, and then one can adopt an easy-going approach to the supervision of one's investment funds 'industry' and so add even more piles of dosh to one's already overflowing national coffers. So, just to summarise, the Grand Larceny of Luxembourg is a tax haven at the heart of the EU, which enjoys the benefits of tax-free flows of money across its borders in a way that more distant and more conventional tax havens can only ever dream of. And, through its tax haven activities, it has been enriching itself obscenely at the expense of every taxpayer in every other country of the Union. Indeed, it has been calculated by those who perform such calculations that its tax dodges alone might be costing the rest of the world as much as $1.3 trillion ($1,300,000,000,000) per year, a large slice of which will almost certainly be at the expense of its European neighbours.

I could witter on some more – about how, rather than the EU throwing this grubby little member out of the club, it has done just the reverse by situating within its borders a whole string of European institutions (like the European Court of Justice (!) and the Court of Auditors (!!)), and in this way it has gifted it even more of its neighbours' wealth along with a disproportionate amount of power and influence. But what I really want to do is point out that the chap who was the prime minister of this country from 1995 until 2013 and its finance minister for twenty years until 2009 – and therefore the chap who was responsible for much of the mugging of the rest of the EU – was one Mr Juncker! You couldn't make it up, could you? The European Union has gone out of its way to find a bloody spiv to oversee its affairs, and a spiv who's been screwing all but one of its constituent members for years. It says everything that needs to be said about the truly rotten nature of this terrible institution – except, of course, what still needs to be said about its habit of making absolutely monumental cock-ups…

9. Yes, the European Union has what might best be described as an absolutely crap record when it comes to 'big ticket' items, and I have in mind here the introduction of the euro and the introduction of the Schengen area.

The problem is that the EU Establishment does not understand that ideology on its own does not form a good basis for the introduction of radical change.

There needs also to be legitimate research, careful analysis, planned mechanisms and, somewhere in the equation, just a little bit of democratic legitimacy. Not one of these was in sight when the euro was unleashed. It was supposed to be the culminating step in the continent's economic integration. But even a schoolboy with two economics lessons under his belt could have told you that the conditions necessary for an 'optimal currency area', which has to exist before a common currency can succeed, were not even on the horizon. It was blatantly a political decision based on a flawed ideology, and in direct contravention of all the thoughtful economic analysis that was available at the time.

The consequence? First, an avalanche of money into southern Europe, which took no account of risk. And then, when the boom turned into the biggest bust since Jayne Mansfield's, and something brown hit the apparatus with rotating blades designed to create a current of air for cooling or ventilation, the debtor nations found themselves unable to regain lost competitiveness without signing up for years of austerity and a Depression-level of unemployment. You were also able to witness the European Central Bank attempting to keep the whole thing afloat (or attempting desperately to kick the problem down the road) by promising to do 'whatever it takes' to maintain the euro, which presumably means they will be quite content to see bleak austerity and crippling unemployment levels become a permanent feature of the 'European Project'. Or maybe they intend to resort to assassinations, if required, of anybody who voices dissent from the (flawed) policy orthodoxy embraced by the European elite, which as well as screwing up millions of lives is also widening the already vast gap between the governed and those who insist on governing them.

Then there is Schengen. Brilliant! Get rid of internal borders before any thought about the security arrangements for the continent's external borders, other than how to help people to reach them and then cross over them without any effective challenge. And, when we've got that High Representative for Foreign Affairs and Security and Bingo Calling as well. Or maybe nobody asked her, just like nobody considered anything other than the ideology of the whole idea. And what a crap idea it was.

Well, if you've got this far, then well done. But one cannot overestimate just how ghastly – and how damaging – this European Union really is. (And one cannot begin to imagine just how bad it will get.)

Remember, we were duped into it; it then metamorphosed into something else – and something far worse; it has proved itself to be a hopeless, profligate burden for all those it holds captive; it is driven by an indulgent ideology that has no democratic legitimacy whatsoever, and it is run by a spiv. Not exactly ideal, is it? And not within a light year of anything that might warrant our continued (expensive) involvement.

So… it is rather more than just good news that as I write this we are about to be granted a second chance to extricate ourselves from the EU's clutches. Finally we have another referendum coming – and on this occasion, even if our national Establishment closes ranks with its international friends (and it will do), it will simply not be able to dupe us for a second time. Hell, it would take a country full of stupid, misinformed wimps for that to happen, and how likely is that? I mean, we are still British, aren't we? We haven't become a nation full of frightened, spineless children, lacking in any sort of self-confidence or self-belief. Shit! That would be just preposterous! And just appalling!!!!!

> They laid a plan; they did it well
> And now, for years, we've lived in hell
> A hell of laws and rules galore
> And 'pay us this' and 'pay us more'
> No way they've not been in cahoots,
> Those crats and creeps, to fill their boots
> And all the time they've havoc wrought
> And splashed our cash with little thought
> A mix of 'daft' and gross excess
> That's left us in a dreadful mess
> But worse's to come, and very soon
> (Because we've let our borders doon)
> For now a flood is on its way
> The sort of flood that wants to stay
> And when this flood has doused our flame
> We know the cads who'll bear the blame
> The cads with whom we've had to live
> And cad-in-chief: the de-Lux spiv…

Financial Services

Let me start with an apology. You see, I should be prepared to assemble a full-blown, comprehensive critique of the so-called financial services 'industry', but I find that its parasitical behaviour is so gross, and so grubby, that I can only bring myself to discuss it in the briefest of terms. So I am very sorry, and I can only hope that my cursory examination of this massive leech-like sector of the economy serves as a sufficient exposition of its nature.

Well, that said, I will now make a start on my perfunctory undertaking by explaining, in the simplest terms possible, what I have in mind when I refer to this so-called financial services 'industry'. And it is this. It is that collection of disparate businesses, including banks, investment funds and similar institutions that together manage our money. More specifically, they are the businesses that we are obliged to rely on if we wish to do the right thing and provide for ourselves in our retirement out of the income we generate throughout our working life. Oh, and they are also the businesses that don't necessarily see this function as their primary function, or as the one that will bring them the rewards they crave within the timescale they desire.

But that is to get ahead of myself. Because it is worth pointing out that to 'store away' money, in a way that avoids it being consumed by inflation over many years, it is necessary to invest at least a chunk of it in some sort of business. And immediately there is a problem. Because the CEOs, the CFOs and the directors in general of many large businesses have now mastered the art of transferring much of the wealth invested in these businesses into their own pockets. With the help of docile (or corrupt) 'executive compensation consultants' they systematically over-reward themselves to a staggering degree, and so plunder our pension pots even before the finance guys have got out of bed. But then these guys do get out of bed, which is when the real problems start.

Now, before examining the precise nature of these problems, it is worth reminding ourselves that investing over the long term is, or should be, a relatively simple exercise for those who are trained in this art. It should involve putting people's money into a broad range of investments, holding these investments over a long period of time, and engaging in just a bit of portfolio rebalancing every now and again (with a rare bit of emergency intervention if some specific shit hits a specific fan). However, for the finance guys, this is a bit of a problem. Because... well, simplicity doesn't pay well at all. Whereas extensive and confusing choice, non-stop activity and change, contradictory signals and the need for an expert response are all far more attractive in that they offer far more opportunities to introduce complexity, and therefore much more income, into the money management process.

So, that's the starting point: unwarranted complexity. But it is only the starting point. Because the biggest problem by far with the finance 'industry' is the 'principal/agent problem' and what this means in terms of a devastating misalignment of interests.

You see, the financial world is run by people who are not the beneficial owners of businesses, and they have very different aims from those people who are the owners. These owners are the members of pension funds, endowment policy holders and wealthy individuals, who together constitute the innocent poor bastards alluded to above, and who are merely trying to preserve their capital with a view to providing themselves with an income that might be drawn upon years or even decades into the future. These owners – the principals – clearly have to depend on the people running the finance 'industry': the agents. And just as clearly, these agents couldn't give a fig about even next year let alone decades into the future – and just want the largest possible cash reward they can obtain. And they want it now!

Incentives for these masters of the universe are therefore hopelessly short-termist in that they are rewarded after just one or two years, and not over the thirty to forty years that they have their hands on their principals' cash. Their rewards are also grossly unfair, in that if anything goes wrong over this long period they and their staff are never penalised. Not surprising then, that as well as introducing needless complexity into the investment process, the agents and their staff are very happy to take all sorts of risks with this 'other people's money' in the full knowledge that it will not be them who suffer if the risks fail to pay off. Unfortunately, these same flawed incentives are common both to the banks and the investment institutions that hold shares on behalf of the principals, and they have both learnt how to get very fat indeed on a series of bubbles and bursts, which, of course, produce, for their hordes of hapless sucker-investors, no lasting benefit whatsoever.

What all this amounts to is the fact that the financial services 'industry' is a bloody great scandal. It is no more than a gigantic parasite sucking the money out of people's pockets, and at the same time sucking resources out of the genuinely productive parts of the nation's economy. 'Rent extraction' is apparently a term used by economists to describe the process of making money from useless, valueless activity. And such is the dismal performance of the financial sector in attending to its customers' needs that rent extraction is in there somewhere, and not just to a minor degree.

Of course, the real driver of the banks' and investment institutions' pernicious behaviour is the device they've employed to harness that misalignment of their and the punters' interests in the most effective way possible. And that, without a shadow of a doubt, is their pernicious reward systems, and those monstrous fucking bonuses…

Yes, the finance fraternity operates in a performance-oriented culture, where people are under enormous pressure to deliver the goods. The focus is irredeemably short-termist, as more than mentioned in passing above – and this short-termism cannot really tolerate mistakes, and it also nurtures a lack of collaboration in the workplace. In fact, it's all about as wrong as it can be, and the typical finance 'industry' environment is one that can best be described as utterly toxic.

Of mild interest is that a system of group bonuses, as opposed to the system of individual bonuses as used in the finance sector, can be highly effective in rewarding teamwork – as any employee of John Lewis will tell you. And when the same percentage bonus for every member of its workforce is announced by John Lewis it is cause for celebration, because each member is happy for his or her colleagues as well as for him or herself. Conversely, when the annual individual bonuses are announced in the finance sector it is a time for misery and distrust, as everybody believes that they've been treated unfairly and have not got as large a bonus as their colleagues. So, that's at least a little bit of *Schadenfreude*-type good news for us investors, and there is even the possibility that the finance guys might seek some reform. After all, those in charge (and the workforce itself) must all know that by introducing increases in basic pay and more reasonable, longer-term incentives, the culture in their sector could be changed to one that is more collaborative, more conducive to longer-term thinking and more tolerant of well-intentioned mistakes. And all this might lead to a far better deal for all us defenceless, worked-over punters. Heck, they could even introduce a bonus system which meant that bonuses were deferred until retirement. And at last there would be a real convergence between our interests and those of our agents…

Well, dream on. This proposal falls down on any number of counts, not least of which is that the people who enter the world of finance *never* do so for reasons of altruism, but instead to make pots of money. And very often they are out-and-out shits who would think nothing of shafting their own mothers if it meant that this year's bonus might just stretch to a Porsche.

If it were up to me I'd forget about new principal-friendly cultures, or tougher regulation or any sort of 'moral renaissance', and I'd just employ snipers. Yes, I'd position snipers on any number of buildings in the City of London and in Wall Street who, between them, would take out as many of the fat bastards as they could. And I am reasonably confident that this 'shoot to reform' strategy would eventually bear fruit, and under a white flag of surrender the leaders of the financial sector would announce that they were finally prepared to join the real world again – in terms of their conduct and their rewards – and we principals would finally get something like a half-reasonable deal. And no, just the threat of being shot would not be enough. They'd either ignore it or they'd somehow securitise it and then chop it up into some complicated financial product and sell it on at a profit… whereas I'd like to see them try to turn a speeding bullet into some new form of derivative.

Yes, shooting is the only remedy. And if this doesn't bring about the much-needed reform it is intended to bring about, then so be it, and at least there'd be fewer bankers and investment managers, and possibly a significant reduction in the second-hand price of Porsches.

And no, I am not being serious. But I was being serious at the beginning of this piece, and throughout most of it. The financial services industry is horribly grubby, and it is populated by some of the grubbiest people on Earth. It's a fact. So there.

> In days gone by, the greedy sort
> Might rob a bank – and might get caught
> But now in banks they get a job
> Cos once-robbed banks themselves now rob

Government

You may already have read my thoughts on the operation of so-called democracy in this country, and, if you have the fortitude to plough further through this book, you may have the pleasure of reading my assault on the iniquity we call tax. However, for the purpose of this particular essay I want to set aside the faults in the nature of our government and the insistence that we fund its activities, and focus very specifically on its purpose. In short, I want to question what it gets up to and what it *should* get up to. And the way I intend to do this is not by setting out a comprehensive 'job description' for this institution, because that would be intensely boring, but by listing three things it should not do and three things it should do. This, I hope, will illustrate just how much our current government is misguided in its administration of our affairs (in common, I might say, with every other democratic government in Europe).

OK. I will start with those three 'should not dos', and the first of these concerns money.

1. Yes, our government should not spend more money than it raises in taxes. Not exactly novel, this

suggestion, is it? But, as I have already discussed under 'Democracy', this is exactly what it does as a matter of course in its attempts to bribe the electorate. Only by promising more than can be afforded will a party in our democratic system first secure power and then retain it. And it's now well beyond a joke and, as already explained, its continuation will usher in a new form of government when this current one ultimately fails.

I don't wish to repeat myself a great deal more, but it is worth pointing out just how ridiculous the situation has now become. I mean, this country now owes its creditors – all those institutions at home and overseas who hold government bonds (gilts) – more than £1,300,000,000,000. That means that, as well as bequeathing unborn generations a colossal financial hangover, we already have to find well over £40,000,000,000 every year just to pay the interest on these gilts, and then issue more gilts to enable us to pay the gilts that are maturing. Well, there are two things to note there. One is that the interest payment total is more than we spend on defence in this country, and not that much less than we spend on education. And the second noteworthy item is that the practice of issuing loans in order to service maturing loans is a system of government financing that has similarities with the operation of a Ponzi scheme: a fraudulent investment operation that is, not surprisingly, illegal.

Oh, and I have one other point to make about this excessive demand for credit by our government.

It has a negative impact on the real economy. By increasing the overall demand for credit it can drive up borrowing costs and make it more expensive to finance new equipment, stock and other capital goods. And it can also actually starve the private sector of capital by enticing its potential investors away with irresistibly attractive rates on those gilt-embellished government bonds.

So all in all it is a total disaster, and to begin to address this disaster we can now examine the second 'should not do'. And this one is a no-brainer – because it concerns overseas aid…

2. Yes, this country is now fully signed up to the idea of the voluntary transfer of resources from one country to another. In fact, we are one of the most enthusiastic supporters of this idea in that we are now the second biggest aid donor in the world (after the USA). And, when the aid we provide is measured in terms of the percentage of our gross national income, we are right up there with all those saintly Scandinavian countries (and miles ahead of the USA). Indeed, it can be safely stated that we are now so generous in our overseas aid that the amounts we give away are comfortably into the 'downright profligate'.

It is nice though, isn't it? And it should give us all a warm glow. After all, we know how, by giving money to people in other countries, we can improve their living conditions and thereby effect, in a positive way, both global security and global economic growth. At least that's what that guy with the funny ginger beard said on the *Channel 4 News* the other day. And, of course, we are also supporting the UN's eight Millennium Development Goals, which include, among other things, 'making sure that the environment is protected' and 'building a global partnership for those working in development'. (Which makes me wonder whether those goals were originally drafted with the help of a BBC executive who had nothing better to do.)

But anyway, all this enormous amount of taxpayers' money shovelled into... well, something or other, must be a jolly good idea. Even if there are one or two drawbacks in showering just so much largesse around the world – which I now feel almost embarrassed to mention, but which I will anyway. And they are as follows:

- To avoid 'unnecessary bureaucracy' (!), the Department for International Development (the department charged with spraying our money around the world) makes distributions of our aid to governments and 'international organisations that have already developed suitable programmes' to let them distribute it further 'as efficiently as possible'. Errrh, such 'international organisations' include UNESCO, which has been described as being particularly weak in efficiency and effectiveness terms but is probably not as weak as all those other international organisations and governments that are in receipt of our money. Not in their ability to swallow up the funds but in their ability and their willingness to distribute these funds in a fair and effective manner. (A great deal of our aid goes to what are recognised as the most corrupt and least competent governments on the planet, and some of it is not even project- or programme-specific. It just goes into 'budget support', which means that it is just funnelled into the general spend of an overseas government – which is probably just about as effective as turning it into compost. And I mean that slimy, greeny-brown compost that stinks to high heaven and is no use whatsoever.)

- Some money does not necessarily disappear into the 'budget support' hole, never to be seen again, because some of it does go into identifiable programmes (such as health programmes). So that's OK. Except that in 2006 the World Bank reported that half of all funds donated to health programmes in sub-Saharan Africa did not reach the intended hospitals and clinics. Money was being paid into fake accounts, prices were inflated for warehousing and transport, and drugs were being pinched and then sold on the black market. They didn't include it in their report, but I have it on good authority that some of the funds were diverted away from the health programmes and into the bulk purchase of business-class tickets on flights between London and Africa. (Actually, I have just made that up. However, if you conducted a survey of business-class passengers on these flights and discovered how many of them were African 'government officials' – and how many of these hard-working chaps had carrier-bags full of London shopping – you would see that I am not being outrageous at all.)

- International aid money doesn't just disappear. Much of it does positive harm. For example, foreign aid can actually finance corrupt governments, and it can hollow out a local economy. One only has to observe how politicians in some countries distribute aid to their own tribes – and to nobody else – or to witness the impact on local produce of filched goods being sold on the black market to see that this is not an unwarranted assertion. Furthermore, large amounts of Western cash, being used to purchase the local currency, inevitably drives up the exchange rate in the recipient country. And this unavoidably damages that country's export industries, and so strangles one of the principal methods by which poor countries have become richer over the past fifty years. The introduced cash also stokes inflation in the recipient country, forcing up interest rates and making it more difficult than ever for local businesses, for people with debts and for people with little income. In fact, it is not an exaggeration to say that, through these effects, aid can add to the instability in a recipient country and it can even increase the likelihood of rebellions and civil wars. But never mind... because at least these conflicts can be funded! Yes, it has been estimated that as much as 40% of all military expenditure in Africa is financed by overseas aid. At which point you may wish to cough, splutter or shriek in amazement. But, after you have done one or none of these things, I would just like to draw your attention to one last drawback of international aid or at least one last nonsense associated with this aid – and this concerns 'context'.

- Yes, we and the rest of the West are showering money on the world's poor countries, but at the same time we are busy distorting global trade by spending US$ 360 billion a year on protecting our agricultural production – with a panoply of subsidies and tariffs (remember the EU and its CAP, for example). And this distortion is reckoned to cost the developing countries US$ 50 billion in lost agricultural exports. Which equates to a noticeably large proportion of all overseas aid. Then we have stuff like the provision of aid to the health sectors of developing countries and the training of medical personnel – so that we can then undermine this expenditure completely by encouraging all these newly trained health professionals to come and support our own teetering health service. And sod theirs.

So what's going on here? Why, in the West, is there such a blind acceptance of the effectiveness of international aid in the face of so much evidence to the contrary? And why, in Britain, have we become essentially incontinent when it comes to dealing with aid? I mean, we are absolutely pissing it away. And I say that because we have gone beyond any pretence of identifying need and then responding to it. We have, instead, decided that a fixed amount of money has to be spent – irrespective of real need. So if it were the Department of Transport taking this approach, rather than the Department for International Development, you would have them deciding to spend £1 billion on a new motorway between, say, Dover and Bognor – and then, when it became apparent that they could spend only £800 million, you would have them putting in a few loops at the Bognor end to use up the other £200 million. It's a farce, and an expensive, misdirected and counterproductive farce at that.

Well, what I think is going on is, in the first place, a 'My dick is bigger than your dick' exercise. And what I mean by that is you had Mr Blair and then Mr Brown and now Mr Cameron turning up to these G7-type gatherings and not wanting to admit that their dicks had shrunk. And one very easy and obvious way to do that was to commit to shell out an enormous amount of money as international aid. And now they've engaged in such a public boast, they cannot admit the truth – and let their aid shrink to what would be a more honest but totally embarrassing size. And no way, of course, can they countenance their dick being cut off completely – as in a termination of all overseas aid and the dissolution of the Department of International Development.

Matters aren't helped, of course, by our colonial guilt, which makes our leaders even less likely to be 'mean' to all those poor ex-colonials. Nor is it helped by the fact that there is now an 'aid industry', which has grown so large and so strong that it can insist that it continues to be fed, indefinitely and lavishly.

Well, I think it's well past the time that we should tell the aid industry to take a hike. Our government should stop giving our money to people overseas with immediate effect. And if this means that it has to confront its colonial guilt and the true size of its dick, then so be it. Because, as well as our not being able to afford all this overseas aid, it is a 'bad thing'. And it is a bad thing (a) for all the reasons discussed above, (b) because, in my mind, it reinforces the idea of 'us' and 'them' and it undermines the self-worth of 'them' – and (c) because it is totally wrong in principle. This last point cannot be stressed enough. Because, however it is dressed up, overseas aid is charity (that's why it undermines the self-worth of those who receive it), and charity is the province of the individual. You and I should choose who we provide any sort of charity to. It should not be done by any institution, and I mean any government, on our behalf and with our money. It is just so wrong.

So international aid is out as a government function. But just to show that I am not a complete and utter monster, and to pick up on the fact that aid is a charity, I don't believe it would be impossible to replace the aid with the establishment of a well-funded 'first-response' unit. We'd devote maybe a third of what we currently throw away as aid into setting up a substantial disaster response force, which would be the first on the scene after any earthquake, tsunami or cyclone – anywhere in the world. It would also act as a coordinator for any other relief coming in. And, believe me, that would achieve more in real terms and more in terms of our ex-colonial reputation than any amount of money poured into training some thug police force in Africa or equipping some non-existent schoolroom in Lahore. It would also save us the embarrassment of having a government department which claims that its goal is not only 'to promote sustainable development' (which, in practice, is generally an oxymoron) but also 'to eliminate world poverty'. And good luck with that one… although, in truth, eliminating world poverty might be just a little bit easier than getting our government to accept the third 'should not do'. Yes, terminating international aid is the easy task. Confronting and then dismantling the welfare state is going to be far, far more difficult…

3. Yes, this is the final 'should not do'. The government should not maintain the welfare state.

   Mildly controversial, this one. But bear with me, and I'll start to make my case by touching on how the welfare state was first introduced into Britain after the Second World War. Because, it is generally believed that this momentous government decision was the most noble of endeavours: the state setting out to eliminate 'want, disease, ignorance, squalor and idleness'. However, the truth is a little more nuanced, in that we had here an expectant populace who were unwilling to just pick up from where they'd been before the war – in terms of social conditions – and who were quite likely to get more than marginally belligerent if they didn't get the changes they wanted. Which means that the introduction of the welfare state was more an exercise in containing the threat of class conflict – and thereby keeping the capitalist economy afloat – than it was an admirable step forward in the development of our society. It was also very much 'of its time' – and I will return to this statement in due course.

OK, it's time to look at what has happened since the birth of the welfare state, and how much of what has happened isn't necessarily a screaming success. Indeed, how much of it is a full-blown disaster...

- The conduct of any society always involves jobs being done that nobody really wants to do. Before the welfare state these jobs were done by those who could do nothing else. Now, of course, these people *can* do something else: they can refuse these jobs and live off welfare, while at the same time we have to import people from abroad who *are* willing to take on these unattractive jobs, with all the consequences that flow from mass immigration (see below).
- Even in the active workforce, who may or may not be receiving benefits, an assumption has grown up that it is predominantly the individual's

responsibility to look after himself and his family (or herself and her family) during his or her working life, but that when retirement arrives the responsibility largely moves to the state, especially in terms of any healthcare or social care that will (almost certainly) be required. And this assumption is so ingrained in the collective consciousness that it can easily withstand the glaring fact that the majority of people are not just 'getting back what they paid in' but are getting far, far more than they ever paid in, especially now that their years of retirement might well equal or even exceed their years of employment.

- Choosing to live off the state for one's whole life or having to live off it in retirement are both, of course, a reflection of how welfare has created a dependency culture and a sense of entitlement in the population. People now believe that the state owes them a living, and that they have a right to get something for nothing. This isn't a very healthy situation.

- It is also a situation that has introduced some other far from desirable changes in our society. For example, taking pride in being in work has diminished. There is now not the same degree of stigma that there used to be in being on benefits. This is possibly something to do with the high number of people receiving tax credits and/or housing benefits. Then there is the 'not worth my working' aspect of the benefits system, to say nothing of the catastrophic impact the benefits system has on the birth rate. We actually encourage people to have more children by rewarding them financially to be prolific in their breeding habits. We must be fucking mad. Or maybe that's what *they* are, literally.

- The outcome of the welfare state is now a vast multitude of people who are unemployed, and a similar number who claim sickness benefits. Then there are countless more who are lone parents on out of work benefits, due to the creation of a 'safety net' that was put in place to reduce child poverty but that was too generous in that it now encourages people to stay on it longer than they otherwise would.
- All this stuff costs the taxpayers of Britain £220 billion a year, which is truly unbelievable as well as being of great assistance in our dash towards national bankruptcy.

It is worth, at this stage, examining 'what went wrong' and why we have ended up with such a dismal list of negatives. And I think that one of the real problems was that initially a welfare safety net was based on the idea that individuals and families were able to look after themselves most of the time and whatever assistance was provided by the welfare state would be designed to return them to a situation where they could get on with their lives – unassisted. In short, people were assumed to be responsible for themselves, and capable. But somehow this view changed – to one where it was believed that individuals had no capacity to run their own lives. Welfare provision now assumes that they need assistance with their family life, with their attempts at child-rearing and with their 'community relations', and that they cannot manage their own health and lifestyles (we've all seen those cartoon adverts on the telly, instructing the great British public how not to become lard-arses by stuffing themselves with doughnuts and spending all their waking hours on a settee). And all the time the state and its institutions are standing by, eager to advise, to train, to counsel and to educate – and the safety net has turned into a nicely plumped cushion, and a means of achieving wealth redistribution on a massive scale.

This brings me on to my next point, which takes us right back to the initial introduction of the welfare state. Because it needs to be said that when the welfare state was introduced its founders were confident it would work, because they were dealing with an ethnically homogeneous nation and a workforce with a strong cultural work ethic. Well, we know what's happened to the work ethic. That's set out above. But there have been other consequences of having a rampant welfare state, and one of these is that our economy has become less competitive (in common with those of the rest of Europe) because the high tax rates needed to fund the welfare payments have stifled economic growth. Cosseted Europe (which, as earlier reported, accounts for 50% of all welfare spending in the world) has been taken to the cleaners by China, India and a whole list of other countries where self-reliance is still the order of the day. But it gets worse. Because that ethnic homogeneity has been replaced by 'diversity', and some argue that it is 'the wrong sort of diversity'. They claim that dynamic emigrants tend to travel to countries where they pay little tax, so that they can retain the fruits of their efforts, whereas we tend to attract more than our fair share of the less than dynamic brigade, who just want to piggyback on a generous welfare state.

This isn't sophistry, and it isn't racist. It is supported by research in Denmark that has looked at the cost of immigration into that country – and has made the point that all European welfare states are being squeezed by two opposing forces of globalisation. One is the success of those 'unburdened' Asian countries knocking us off our economic feet, and the other is the failure of the Islamic world and Africa, both of which have been sending us their 'excess' population for years and who are now sending us even more.

So we have a welfare state (in the process of a long, slow decline due to its inherent flaws) that is now facing a rapid disintegration due to the introduction of lots of people, many of whom do not share any group loyalty with the nation state and who do not have the sort of cultural background that is necessary to sustain a welfare system. Essentially, a welfare state can only work in a country with high levels of 'national trust' – such as those that were in place when our welfare state came into being because of the prevailing ethnic homogeneity. However, a system like this will not work when this trust has been removed through the process of mass immigration.

In many ways, therefore, it can be seen that the welfare state really was a product of its time, and that it is pretty obvious that its time has now passed. The government should not do 'welfare'. It should put it out of its misery and save us all a bundle of cash at the same time, to say nothing of giving us a real chance of avoiding becoming a Third World state – ultimately eligible, no doubt, to receive some well-intentioned but inevitably destructive international aid... So, just to reiterate, a welfare state:

- Creates a dependency culture and an unjustified sense of entitlement.
- Robs many people of the pride that comes with having a job.
- Infantilises people by undermining their self-responsibility.
- Encourages breeding (as a result of how it currently operates).
- Costs an unaffordable amount of money, and is open to huge amounts of abuse.
- Handicaps our industries to the point of their ultimate future obliteration.
- Creates a false sense of security in a dog-eat-dog world.
- Leads to not necessarily advantageous mass immigration.
- Raises my blood pressure on far too many occasions.

So, with the welfare state disposed of, along with international aid and overspending, it is now time to run through the three 'should do' jobs for the government, the first of which I will introduce with a Ronald Reagan quote. Yes, he was a good deal smarter than you might think, because he once said: 'Government's first duty is to protect the people, not run their lives'. And he was spot on, as I will now explain.

1. The world is full of shits and, increasingly, they are dangerous shits. We need protection from them. And for individuals to try and organise this protection themselves is just unrealistic. Few of us could afford a ballistic missile, and even fewer would run to an aircraft carrier. We have to accept that only by pooling our resources and getting the government on the job can we acquire the security we need. Of course, some shits need things other than missiles and aircraft carriers to deter them, and threats to the serenity of life in Blighty come in all shapes and forms. So it's good to know then that our government is already on the case and, while the only aircraft carriers we currently have are unfinished and unencumbered with aeroplanes, it has at least identified the most serious threats.

    In 'Tier 1' (the most serious threats of all), we have:
    - Acts of terrorism
    - Hostile attacks on our cyberspace
    - A major accident or natural hazard (like a flu pandemic)

- An international military crisis between nation states that would draw us into conflict.

There are plenty of other threats as well. These are the Tier 2 and Tier 3 threats. And these range from the inconsiderate use of chemical and biological weapons through a surge in illegal immigrants trying to come here to a bit of a major whoopsie at one of our nuclear power stations.

So, we're all OK then, aren't we? Well, no, we're not. Because it's one thing to identify threats but it is quite another to ensure that all these threats can be countered and overcome… especially when, rather than spending money on the security of the realm we send it overseas or we fritter it away on stuff of secondary importance. Or we pour it down the giant plughole of welfare. So, while our government is actually already doing this 'should do', it is not doing it anywhere near enough.

I reiterate: 'The government's first duty is to protect the people…' Well, it could be argued that this should be its only duty but, even if this it is not accepted, it is beyond dispute that it is its primary duty, and therefore it should not stint in what it spends in discharging this duty.

We should have the best-trained and best-equipped armed forces imaginable, preferably with a couple of working aircraft carriers and some of those planes that we used to have for finding submarines. We should certainly retain a nuclear deterrent (in a world that is not on its way to universal peace and love). We should have a border force modelled on the resolution of the British forces at Rorke's Drift, and a pursuit brigade for illegal immigrants modelled on the determination of the BBC licence fee enforcers. Our intelligence services should be so well funded that they are the envy of the world, and all their operatives should obviously be given a double '0' designation. Our 'cyber army' should be similarly indulged, although maybe not given Walther PPKs to play with. Our forces of law and order should be reinforced, along with our sentencing policies. And, finally, we should insist that the government makes not a single decision – about trade, health, international cooperation, immigration or the choice of indoor house plants for Number 10 – without making the consideration of the security implications of these decisions the primary and overriding consideration. If that oversized yucca plant could harbour an undersized ISIS savage, then go for a split-leaf philodendron instead.

So I hope I have succeeded in demonstrating that our government should make the protection of its citizens its top priority, not just in PR terms but in real terms. And that if this requires a huge redirection of funds from their present destinations, then so be it. I mean, hell, I would be more than happy if our government didn't spend anything other than what was needed to guarantee our security, even if it meant that it couldn't even afford that split-leaf philodendron…

That said, I wouldn't object too much to its

spending just a little of our cash on 'should do' number two, which is 'should eliminate religion from every aspect of public life and, in particular, from the education of our children'. Now read on.

2. Religion, apart from being a dubious choice, is also a personal choice. Or at least it should be. It has nothing to do with the public affairs of the country and it certainly should have no call on public funds, many of which are inevitably provided by people who are indifferent to religion or who are positively against it. So, if there is one thing that a government should do, apart from protecting its citizens, it is to go out of its way to ensure that religion does not insert itself into any aspect of public life. And the area of public life that should be shielded from the clutches of religion above all others is the education of our kiddiewinks: the *state-funded* education of our young 'uns that is designed to implant facts and logic into their malleable minds, not a bunch of disreputable myths.

Unfortunately, we appear to be marching in quite the other direction at the moment, with a significant growth in the number of 'faith schools' in this country, as successive governments have allowed various religious groups to get an even tighter stranglehold of our funded-by-everybody-including-committed-atheists education system. This is not good. In fact, it is abominable. Not only does it introduce questionable legends and fables into the education system, but it also does for community cohesion what Piers Morgan has done for journalistic decency. And community cohesion is maybe a little more important than journalistic decency.

You see, parents have an explicit right (under the European Convention on Human Rights – what else?) to indoctrinate... sorry, to bring up their children in the religion or belief of their choice without interference from the state. However, they do not have the right to state funding for religious teaching or the provision of 'faith schools' that are in line with their own beliefs. But that's what they've been given – under a specific exemption from the Equality Act 2000: a load of schools that are allowed to choose their pupils on the basis of religion – which is, of course, a discriminatory act in the provision of a public service that should be open to all. Furthermore, these institutions are even able to select their teachers, their other staff members and their governors according to their religion – which, when certain 'believers' tend to come from certain ethnic groups, is not an award-winning recipe for integration and the assimilation of 'new' cultures.

In fact, faith schools are a crap idea. Some faith schools are a menace not just in terms of reinforcing segregation within our society but also in the way they inculcate in their victims (pupils) all they will ever need to drive them even further away from those of us who have a different faith or no faith at all. I mean, religious schools are permitted to teach their own syllabus of religious education, and this RE is not specifically inspected by Ofsted but by someone chosen by the governors! Not surprising, then, that this sort of RE does not necessarily cover other religions, other than possibly to trash them, or give a fair account of non-religious views. It will probably also fail to address ethical issues such as abortion, assisted dying and homosexuality with an open mind, and it is highly likely that it will introduce what might considerately be described as misinformation. Indeed, this misinformation might even extend to the assertion that the Earth is just 6,000 years old, that Darwinism is bollocks and that the only true science is to be found in creationism. I mean, it's the fucking twenty-first century, and in some state-funded schools in this country we are allowing the promulgation of the bunkum that goes by the name of intelligent design. This is not only a grievous denial of real science but also a betrayal of our indigenous culture, and a steamin' great disgrace! We've seen how successful faith schools have been in Northern Ireland. But that is nothing like the success we will achieve throughout the UK if we allow faith schools, and certain of them in particular, to lock up the minds of our youth before stoving in those minds with some of the worst prejudicial instruction imaginable. Our success in driving people apart and establishing a fractious and miserable society will be immense.

So, that's why I think that our government should get on with the 'should eliminate religion from every aspect of public life and, in particular, from the education of our children', which will then leave it with only one more 'should do'. And this one would be a doddle and it would cost us nothing at all, because all it entails is removing something…

3. Yes, the final 'should do' is that the government should terminate all telephone links between the UK and India. By doing this we would be able to eliminate 95% of all nuisance calls, and we would also force all those UK banks and utilities to repatriate their callcentres to Britain. It would lead to the ultimate win–win situation and a rise in the popularity of the government that would be comparable only to its surge in approval when it introduced a tax break on dirty weekends and a reduction in VAT on all sex toys, including mint-flavoured whips. Or was I just dreaming that…?

Anyway, take note, our government (and all other governments), and learn what to do and what not to do. It really isn't that difficult.

> Governments should take their cue
> From 'those who don't', not 'those who do'
> And not forget that what they're for
> Is 'guarding' us, and little more…

Human Rights

Where would we be without human rights? They're essential, aren't they? In fact, they are more than essential. They are, according to the Universal Declaration of Human Rights made in 1948, rights to which all human beings are inherently entitled.

Ah... well that might mean there's a problem. Because, as laudable as this declaration was, one must always be suspicious of anything that employs the word 'inherent' – in the sense of existing in something as a permanent and inseparable element – when that something is a human, especially when one recalls how a human arrives. Yes, he or she plops into this world as a pretty much helpless, fleshy blob, and there is as much sense in suggesting that it takes its first breaths already fully equipped with thirty specific and detailed rights as there is in suggesting that, there and then, it is a Hindu, a Christian or a Muslim. No, what happens is that the society into which it is born immediately confers on it a certain number of *civil rights* and, of course, unless it is one of the lucky few, its parents then sign it up to a particular religion.

Now, I have just introduced the term 'civil rights'

there, as opposed to 'human rights', and what I need to do now is explain the very important distinction between the two. This I will do by using a convenient metaphor, and this metaphor will be taken from the business of manufacturing cars…

What I want you to imagine is the end of a production line in a car factory, where coming off the line are cars that have been sprayed in any number of colours. Now, these colours will have been selected in accordance with the wishes of those people who have ordered the particular cars. That is to say that they will reflect those people's colour (i.e. religion) of choice. And note that this is their choice, and certainly not that of the car itself. It is just fortunate that some of the paint used is highly questionable in all sorts of ways and that, for many cars, sooner or later, the paint will thankfully wear off.

OK, now what will also be apparent is that there will be a certain 'specification level' in these cars, and as this car factory is in England, this spec level will be very high. The car will have been equipped (by the national factory) with air-con, satnav, power steering and even heated front seats. It doesn't come much better than this, and the car will be fortunate indeed to have all these desirable bells and whistles.

Indeed, it will be infinitely more fortunate than all those cars produced in the Middle East that lack even windows and a full set of gears… or those others produced in North Korea, which are little more than engines with wheels (and the engines don't even work).

OK, not a prize-winning metaphor, but I am just trying to underline that there is nothing inherent in 'the rights of humans' and any rights they possess, in reality, will have been conferred on them by the society into which they were born. And, as we all know, there are all sorts of societies around the world, and some of them confer on their citizens hardly any rights at all. And this, despite the best intentions of all those who made that declaration all those years ago, as well as those today who are not prepared to see universal human rights as a series of aspirations but who instead view them as a series of intrinsic rights, located somewhere between the pancreas and the bladder, and inextricable from any human being even with the most dextrous use of a surgical knife.

Anyway, does this matter? Does this focus on inalienable rights that don't actually exist, rather than recognising that rights are created and endowed by individual human societies, really affect anything? Or could our worship of human rights not be a good thing but instead in some way detrimental, especially if we live in somewhere like Britain where law and order has prevailed for some time and where the vast majority of its citizens were inducted into the cult of human rights only very recently?

Well, yes, it could, and I will set out a little list of what I believe are the negatives associated with the embracing of human rights at the expense of the more traditional and infinitely more tangible civil rights. So…

1. The Universal Declaration of Human Rights is beginning to look more and more like a worthy but futile empty gesture. If one reads its constituent articles one is struck by just how many of the rights

they include are not (two thirds of a century on from the declaration) enjoyed by a majority of the world's population in a majority of its constituent states. I mean, take Article 25, which reads: 'Everyone has the right to a standard of living adequate for the health and well-being of himself and his family, including food, clothing, housing and medical care and necessary social services, and the right to security in the event of unemployment, sickness, disability, widowhood, old age or other lack of livelihood in circumstances beyond his control'. Well, try telling that to the next Syrian you meet, and also remind him that he is *inherently* entitled to all this stuff along with a whole list of other rights, and see how long it takes for him to punch you in the teeth. I'm sorry, but by being grandiose in one's approach to any sort of rights all one eventually achieves is to bring them into disrepute. One also does very little to advance them from the status of aspirations to a robust reality, as illustrated within the next point.

2. The sponsors of the Universal Declaration of Human Rights, the United Nations, has, in its wisdom, set up an intergovernmental body, the forty-seven members of which are charged with promoting and protecting human rights around the world. This body is called, rather un-controversially, the United Nations Human Rights Council. Possibly more controversial, and certainly more risible, is its membership. Unbelievably, it includes countries such as China, Russia, Vietnam, Venezuela, Qatar – and Saudi

Arabia (!), all of which, of course, are renowned for the promotion and protection of the human rights within their own borders. And if that's not incredible enough, the chairmanship of this body has now passed to a Saudi official. One can only anticipate the introduction of a new human right in the near future… concerning the right to be incarcerated, beheaded or whipped, albeit only one at a time. You couldn't make it up, could you? And, in my mind, it undermines the concept of universal rights even further, having first had a good laugh at their expense.

3. Never mind, because, despite the nebulousness – and abuse – of all these declared universal rights, they have spawned a number of international treaties that do have rather more teeth… but unfortunately they still largely suck. And this is because they still have no real connection to national civil societies, the only legitimate foundations for real rights of any sort. And now we are getting to the almost poisonous nature of the concept of unanchored human rights. Because most 'civilised' countries will already have carefully thought through and finely tuned civil rights embedded in their laws. They will therefore not need further laws, such as, 'You should not have harm done to you', if there are already laws preventing people from doing this harm to you in the first place. And what you will certainly not need is the interference in your existing laws by new laws founded 'somewhere else' and presided over by a cadre of individuals from 'somewhere else', some of

whom wouldn't know what jurisprudence was even if it came and knocked their fucking wig off.

4. We in Britain are now experiencing this very phenomenon: the upset of our own laws – and our own will – in the furtherance of some stupid notion of universal human rights – many of which, in practice, only serve to promote the sovereignty of the individual over the sovereignty of the state (i.e. us) in the most perverse manner imaginable. Nobody would vote to give asylum to individuals who had abused our hospitality. But that's what we are bound to do by human rights legislation, just as we are required to 'respect' the right to a traditional lifestyle even if the lifestyle in question is way beyond contempt. Yes, imposed human rights legislation is, as we've observed, corrosive and contrary to the well-being of any sorted-out society. Its only real beneficiaries are those who have no real connection with this society – and, of course, that army of human rights lawyers.

5. Uhmm, the Human Rights Lawyers Association in the UK has over 1,800 members. That's over 1,800 members making a very nice living (largely at the taxpayers' expense) from frustrating the will of the taxpayers and making a mockery of real nationally developed law. And, if that's not bad enough, there is a certain Mrs Blair who has made an extremely nice living out of specialising in human rights law, which on its own should be enough to convince everybody

that human rights as opposed to civil rights are a very bad thing. And incidentally, have you noticed that human rights lawyers seem to flourish in countries such as Britain where, frankly, they can get away with it – and they're not really needed – but they are hardly clogging up the courts in those countries where they might do some good? Yes, it's easier to earn that sack of loot down at the Old Bailey by proving that some obnoxious overseas rapist has established a family life and now can't be deported, rather than carting yourself off to Mauritania and making a stand against FGM, trafficking and slavery. Oh, and apparently, the wine bars in Nouakchott are absolutely appalling...

6. So too I suspect are attitudes to animal rights, if the concept of animal rights is understood at all. And that's yet another thing that's wrong with human rights. By definition, almost, they require a focus on us humans (as if we need it) and a dismissal of all thoughts about the rights – and the importance – of every other creature with whom we share this planet. Human rights breed selfishness.

7. This brings me on to the final and most damning condemnation of absolute human rights (still not to be confused with civil rights). Because by constantly emphasising the importance of human rights we successfully ignore the importance of human responsibilities. And this is because the UN breed of improbable human rights requires in reality no responsibilities on the part of those who seek to

access these rights. They should just be there. After all, they are inherent, remember. Whereas civil rights are rooted in a society, and it is the clear responsibility of all those in that society to maintain this society in order that its conferred privileges will continue to be enjoyed. In short, human rights encourage people to think selfishly about their entitlements. Civil rights promote an understanding of the responsibilities that all rights entail.

Well, there endeth the lesson, but not before mentioning another, often overlooked, aspect of human rights that makes them more questionable than ever, and this is their promotion to some sort of secular religion. Just listen to the people defending them and look at the expressions on their faces. There is something undeniably evangelical about them, even if they belong to a successful human rights practice and they've just finished deciding whether to put this year's excessive 'earnings' into property or into bonds. They're almost as repellent as some of their clients…

> A right to life, a right to peace
> A right to God knows what
> If only there was one more right:
> To junk the bloody lot
>
> And certainly within this land
> Where law and order reigned
> Until those human rights were cocked
> And on ourselves were trained

And then they took a dreadful toll
T'was like another Blitz
But not, of course, for quite a few
And none of these were Brits…

Islam

To understand Islam, I suggest you read the Koran.

'Is lamb a good thing?'
Asked the queen of her king.
The king said 'Of course.
But it does need mint sauce.'

Jury System

Not many people know this, but in England, juries originally were 'self-informing'. This meant that they had to investigate a crime themselves and uncover the facts of the case all on their own, and they were therefore not required to listen to a series of arguments made in court. Well, this approach finally fizzled out in the seventeenth century, since which time juries have been employed in our common law system to decide on the guilt or otherwise of those brought before a court only after the professional prosecutors and defence lawyers involved in the case have both earned their fees. They are therefore still a vital part of our adversarial system of justice, although it remains open to question whether they still should be. And I make this statement because the jury system as presently constituted has a number of pros but also a number of cons, as I will now set out.

Its pros include:
- It (supposedly) provides a check on state power.
- Similarly, it (supposedly) allows people to participate in our democracy, just about as much as their being allowed to vote does.

- It (supposedly) provides a sort of balance in the legal system – with the judge being an agent of the state and the jury being composed of anything but agents of the state – as in the great, unwashed British public.
- It is thought to provide a more sympathetic hearing to the party charged (but presumably not to the victim).
- It provides something called 'jury nullification', which is when an overwhelming number of 'not guilty' verdicts are returned to the judge for the same crime, no matter how persuasive the evidence – which may indicate that the particular law is unenforceable and needs to be changed or repealed.
- It (supposedly) legitimises the law by inserting us common folk, with our common community values and norms, into the state's judicial proceedings.

These (supposed) pros must now be set against a string of cons, which are as follows:
- Juries can get rather emotional, which isn't very helpful.
- Juries can be swayed by prejudice, and especially racial prejudice.
- Juries in multicultural societies such as our own, especially where there are ethnic tensions, can be… errh, problematic.
- Juries are not composed of superbright people – and much scientific or statistical evidence will be

beyond them – just as, for certain jurors, will be anything that takes place in court.
- The jury system is secret and entirely non-transparent.
- Along the same lines, a jury does not have to give reasons for its decision, whereas a judge in a civil case, say, will have to provide detailed reasons of both fact and law as to why he made the decision he did.
- It just seems a bit weird to employ a system where a person's fate is put in the hands of 'amateurs'.

Well, that's a more or less comprehensive list of the pros and cons of juries, from which you might have begun to suspect that I'm not their most enthusiastic advocate. So, for the sake of fairness, let me quote the Director of Policy at Liberty, who said, '(The use of a jury) is not only a hallowed principle but a practice that ensures that one class of people doesn't sit in judgement over another, and the public have confidence in an open and representative justice system.'

OK, so what seems to be developing here is a case for juries that is all about principle – and the assumption that the state, no matter how benign it might appear, may one day turn around and bite us in the leg – and a case against juries that recognises the very obvious and very real problems associated with their use. It is the theory of what might possibly go wrong against the practice of what is actually, very definitely, going wrong.

To resolve this issue, allow me to make a couple of further observations, the first of which is that it is an accepted fact (at least it is by me) that if you're innocent you'll want a judge, but if you're guilty you'll want a jury. And this simple statement says so much about what is wrong with the jury system. Sympathy, empathy, prejudice, incomprehension and downright perversity can all upset the outcome of a trial – to the benefit of the person charged. In other words, thousands of toerags are getting off scot free when they shouldn't be getting off scot free, and just as many policemen and policewomen and CPS sorts are left wondering why they even bothered to turn up to do their job in the first place.

The other observation I would like to make – and, for me, this goes to the heart of why the jury system is not fit for purpose – is that, as often as not, that wrong decision by the jury has been caused by the power of advocacy. The defence lawyer has been able to confuse and mislead… I'm sorry, has been able to persuade the jury more ably than has the prosecuting counsel. And that's simply effing outrageous. I mean, I can do no better than to set out that old exam question, which states: 'Either I get better justice by paying Sir Timothy Arbuthnot twenty guineas than by paying Mr Bunk two guineas, or I do not. If I do then justice is bought, contrary to Magna Carta. If I do not, the legal profession is obtaining money under false pretences. Discuss.' Well, the answer is as obvious as it is depressing. If you have a jury system that is open to the cajoling of a persuasive Sir Tim, despite the best efforts of a not-quite-as-persuasive Mr Bunk, this means that justice can be bought. And that means that justice can be evaded. Put another way, if you're rich and can afford it, you will get a better deal out of the jury system than you will if you're poor. Which isn't a particularly equitable state of affairs.

However, the problem goes deeper than this. Because in any adversarial system the path to the truth, no matter how nobly it is pursued, is through an open competition between the prosecution and the defence to make the most compelling argument for their case. And this focus on winning will often overshadow the search for the truth, which is exactly what an inquisitorial system does through extensive investigation and examination of all the evidence. It is as simple as having to rely on a potentially misleading advocacy system rather than one that is essentially scientific. And who can argue that a more accurate verdict will not emerge as a result of a careful and exhaustive investigation rather than as a result of two prima donnas hamming it up in front of their audience of jurors?

So, just to summarise, we have a jury system, the retention of which is justified largely because of its role of curbing the power of the state by involving the public in the judicial process. However, the system is riddled with real problems. Among these is its susceptibility to 'waywardness', tampering, prejudice, the power of advocacy and what this means in terms of those with the greatest financial resources having an advantage – and its reliance on amateurs, many of whom cannot understand the proceedings in court (or much of anything), and who are not obliged to explain the reasoning (or lack of reasoning) behind their decisions. On top of all that is the likelihood that the adversarial system, within which the juries are embedded, is much less likely to get to the truth than an inquisitorial system that is based on investigation rather than on the theatrical performance of two bewigged players. So why do we still have juries, and an adversarial system, when their disadvantages seem to so outweigh their advantages? Well, I think I know, and it isn't just tradition and it isn't too much to do with an eagerness to keep Joe Public involved in the administration of justice. No, it's rather more to do with Sir Timothy Arbuthnot and Mr Bunk and their thousands of fellow barristers and solicitors. After all... lawyers, if they can recognise nothing else, can certainly recognise a rich seam of rich pickings, and there is no way that they would want to do away with juries or with any of those adversarial proceedings and so see this richest of all seams abandoned.

Well, I can now hear a chorus of groans and a few shouts of 'Rubbish', but allow me to use my own limited powers of advocacy to convince you of my case. And a good place to start is with an examination of what has been happening to the legal profession in Britain over the last thirty years. Quite simply, it has ballooned. In 1980 there were just 38,000 practising solicitors. There are now 133,000 – and 14,000 barristers. That represents more than a tripling of their numbers over a period in which the total population of this country has increased by 'just' 14%. And this means that, even taking account of the development of international law services in London, the growth in lawyer numbers has far outstripped the growth in the economy and the growth in the need for their services.

So what's happened? Well, you may have heard

about something called the 'compensation culture', a dreadful phenomenon that has led to a huge increase in the number of claims for civil wrongs, many of which are either unjustified or frivolous and many more of which are simply fraudulent. Never mind, though, because 'Where there's blame, there's a claim', and lots of work for lots of lawyers. In fact, they have been extremely successful in establishing a belief in this country that all misfortunes are someone else's fault, and that any suffering caused should be relieved by the receipt of money. That's why 14,000 claims a year are made against the NHS, costing it (us) £1.3 billion a year – a proportion of which goes to relieve some suffering and probably a similar proportion of which goes to funding whole droves of lawyers who we could well do without. I don't know about you, but I find the whole idea of using a hard-pressed health service (and one that will inevitably make mistakes) as some gigantic and helpless cash cow somewhat repugnant... although the techniques employed by lawyers to cultivate a culture in which compensation is routinely and improperly sought is possibly even more repugnant. I mean, their adverts are sickening, and those cardboard kiosks they set up in shopping malls to tout their grubby little services to Saturday shoppers... Well, they should be made illegal, on the basis that they are an affront to civilised values and they could well cause an affray. Particularly if I've had a very bad Friday...

Anyway, lawyers cannot live on compensation culture alone, and they have made great efforts over the past thirty years for find other 'work' to support their bloated numbers. Stuff like interminable public enquiries, immigration appeals (thousands and thousands of them), human rights actions (to the point that there is now a human rights industry) and pushing the legal process into the employment sphere and into every aspect of commercial life. And, of course, they've hung on to what they've got: that adversarial justice system and all those performances they're allowed to make before a jury. Hell, they wouldn't want to see some sort of efficiently run inquisitorial system brought in, where their stage time was cut or even removed entirely and where a judge might not let them 'earn' unconscionable amounts of money for what they often regard as just an intellectual game – played out to satisfy their need for stimulation as well as their need for pots of money.

OK. Even if what I've set out above is true, you might now question why all these lawyers are able to indulge themselves in such a reprehensible way, and 'Why doesn't the government do something about it?' After all, it's our government, not that of just the lawyers, and surely it should be taking our interests into account. Well, yes, it should. But may I just point out that, of the current total of 650 MPs, eighty-six are lawyers. That's 13.23% of our political representatives – when lawyers constitute just 0.2% of the general population. No great surprise, then, that this profession has always been able to protect not only its own interests, however damaging they are to others, but through the legislative process it has also been able to create even more work for itself (as alluded to above with those references to stuff like immigration and human rights).

So there you have it. Lawyers rule, and as long as they rule – and they will rule indefinitely – we just have to keep them in the style to which they've become accustomed. And this will involve the retention of all those juries, all those panels of far from wise men, whose real job is to provide the courtroom lawyers with a captive audience – and lots of dosh – the judge with a decision that might otherwise have been pulled from a hat – and the odd bemused juror with an insight into human nature at its most inept. (And believe me: I've been there. It's really no less than scary…)

> A simple juror could not understand
> Why all our juries had not now been banned
> Then one day he duly learnt
> Without them then there simply weren't
> Enough jobs for all those overpaid barristers and overpaid solicitors, who together would fight tooth and nail to see the jury system retained right up until the second coming and probably for some time after that…

Kids

Somebody once said that kids should be seen and not heard. But I think he was wrong. For about the first eight years of their life, kids should certainly not be heard, but neither should they be seen, other than by their mum and dad and by other kids. That way they could be properly enjoyed by their doting parents, they could learn to socialise with their peers without any distractions... and we would all get a break.

I know that might sound a bit churlish, but I really have the best interests of kids at heart. And to prove this I will now set out some useful advice for all owners of kids that I hope might assist in their upbringing right through to the period when they are exposed to adults in general, whether this be at the age of nine or, for the more troublesome, some time at the end of their teens. So let's get started. And, to begin with, I will deal with Brussels sprouts...

1. Acclimatising kids to Brussels sprouts.

    Well, I hope I do not have to explain how important it is to educate kids in the enjoyment of a Brussels sprout, a vegetable packed with goodness and taste that has seen whole generations of Britons overcoming all sorts of adversities and the perils of trapped wind. So, on the assumption that you are already with me, may I first of all warn all parents of the inadvisability of preparing 'kid-friendly' Brussels sprouts. This would be akin to equipping their bedrooms with central heating – or, indeed, with any heating at all, and would just make them soft, ineffectual wusses who would start blubbing at the drop of the first serious flesh wound to their person.

I mean, to start with, to make this kid-friendly abomination, one is advised to cut the sprouts in half – 'to make them easier for their little mouths'!' But it gets much worse. Because one is then told to toss them in a bowl with olive oil, honey, garlic salt and a little black pepper. And when one has committed this sacrilege one is informed that the adulterated and, some might say, seriously abused Brussels sprouts are then deposited on a baking sheet, where 'to add a little more sweetness and variety' one is encouraged to add some dried cranberries – and then some Parmesan cheese!! Well, may I suggest that at this point, rather than roasting these poor, interfered-with vegetables for fifteen to twenty minutes – until 'nice and golden' – one instead commits them to the oblivion of the waste disposal and says a silent prayer for their demise. It would be better for them, and infinitely better for the hapless kiddie who was destined to receive them – and what would be a horribly distorted view of what Brussels sprouts were all about.

Yes, Brussels sprouts are all about a properly British taste, a taste that lies somewhere between bitter and disconcerting, but a taste that, once acquired, will be relished for a lifetime... and one that will equip any Brussels sprouts aficionado with the sort of resilience that he or she will require to make it safely through this increasingly dangerous world.

So, all one needs to do is avoid 'kid-friendly' Brussels sprouts and any of those newfangled sweet Brussels sprouts (which are clearly the work of the Devil) – and instead, plop some regular sprouts into a pot of boiling water and let them boil there until they are just moderately bullet-hard or maybe a little harder. Then simply decant them on to a plate, embellishing them with a cooked potato if thought really necessary, and place them before the lucky kid. He will relish this offering. Or at least he will eventually, when he realises that he will spend the rest of his life at the table unless he finishes every last one of his delicious green veggies. And, if this sounds just a tad too severe, then one can always soften one's threat by granting him access to a salt cellar and at least one shake of salt over his tempting green gems.

Believe me, this will work. And eventually that tiny kid at the table will grow up to simply adore Brussels sprouts – even if, because of that wise parental guidance, he ends up hating his parents' guts.

Or there again, he might end up loathing them because they have subjected him to Latin.

2. The necessity of teaching kids Latin.

Now, this one's serious, because, at school, I learnt Latin, and I can confirm that the following statements are absolutely spot on:
- Learning Latin helps in all sorts of ways with learning English grammar, and in understanding a huge number of words in the English vocabulary.
- Learning Latin fosters a precision in the use of words. After all, one reads Latin closely and carefully, and this focuses one's mind on individual words and their usage – in English, as well as in Latin.
- Learning Latin aids in the understanding of the Romance languages – like French, Spanish and Italian.
- Learning Latin provides an insight into the origins of Western concepts as, together with Greek, it was the language in which most of the concepts found in the Western intellectual tradition were formulated.
- Learning Latin provides an excellent training in methodical and logical thinking.

And then, of course, learning Latin opens a door to a whole new area of profanity. Yes, if one doesn't learn Latin, one may never discover that *'cacare'* means to defecate and that this is how tiny tots, imbued with Latin at a very early age, went on to adopt the term *'caca'* for you know what. Less lavatorial but much more interesting is that the Latin for 'vulva' is *'cunnus'* and the Latin for 'to lick' is *'linguere'*. And if you haven't already worked out in what form one of these words has found its way into the English language and what the composite of these two words describes in English, then you've probably got a problem. But if you want any help, I will just add that there is a Latin word *'criso'*, which has no equivalent in English, but in its original tongue (clue) refers to the actions of the female partner in sexual intercourse. So, I suppose, for most females, that might be 'grinding' or 'active riding' as opposed to the 'thrusting' and 'pounding' of their partner. And I hope that is all clear... as clear as it is that those Romans were a right naughty lot when they wanted to be... although not, of course, when they were simply putting a sword into a *'vagina'*. Because this is the entirely innocent name for a sheath or a scabbard, and a source of constant amusement for all those twelve-year-old pupils when Sir has to speak this word when reading from Virgil's *Aeneid*. But I suppose you already knew that. So, after reminding you of some of the more disreputable joys of learning Latin, I will now move on to the rather more demanding discipline, for kids of all ages, of learning how to use cutlery in an accomplished and inoffensive manner.

3. The necessity of teaching kids how to use cutlery.

We've all seen it, haven't we? The kid at the table with a level of competence with a knife and fork that makes a bunch of bananas look more dextrous. So, all I'm going to do here is set out a simple step-by-step guide to the use of just these two implements, in the hope that it might be used to good effect and lead to at least one or two fewer cases of adult consternation at the dining table. Here goes:

- Hold your knife in your right hand – for cutting – and your fork in the left.
- Use your fork with the prongs downwards.
- When eating do not use either your knife or your fork, or both together, to emphasise a point when talking – which you shouldn't be doing anyway if you're eating.
- Do not eat off your knife.
- Do not eat off your neighbour's knife.
- Do not stab your neighbour with your knife.
- Do not stab him with your fork, either.
- If you do stab him – by mistake – apologise to him immediately, even before calling for medical assistance.
- When you have done this it will be considered good manners to stop eating, at which point you should put your knife and fork straight on your plate, with the blade of the knife facing inwards (and preferably wiped clean of any blood).

Just get one's kid to follow these simple steps and one will soon find that those disapproving looks that were so common at your dining table become a thing of the past. And they may never even arise at the youth detention centre.

I should just say that kids, unless that have mastered the basics of cutlery (even if they have concluded their initial period of isolation from adults), should never be let in a restaurant.... Just as they should never be allowed to board a plane until they can afford to buy a seat for themselves or they are being sent overseas for their 'slum experience' visit. This vital part of their upbringing will now be discussed.

4. The 'slum experience'.

It is a fact that kids do not appreciate what they have. They grow up in Britain believing that what they receive they are due, and that as often as not they are hard done by. They can simply not comprehend how lucky they are – compared to many of their contemporaries in other parts of the world – and they therefore stand a real risk of growing up into thoughtless, self-centred bastards who will never appreciate what they have. This will not be the case if they are sent on a three-month visit to an overseas slum of their choice, where they will have no contact with their parents but only an uncomfortably close contact with the reality that stalks much of this globe. Through their exposure to slum life they will begin to understand how privileged they are to live in this country, and if they live through the ordeal they will inevitably grow up into considerate and contented souls who will never lose sight of the benefits of living in a country such as Britain.

There will be a list of slums to choose from: in Mumbai, Karachi, Dhaka, Mexico City – or indeed anywhere that can offer a suitable mix of substandard housing and squalor, with no reliable sanitation, no clean water supply, no reliable electricity, no effective law enforcement – nor, in fact, any basic services of any kind. Here they will be able to observe at first hand the necessity of making the best use possible of torn metal and plastic in the construction of a hovel. They will become aware of the impact of drugs and weapons on one's personal safety. And they can savour the sight of accumulated rubbish, the ever-present threat of stuff like malaria, cholera and typhoid – and the joys of sharing one filthy not-long-enough-drop loo with twenty or so families.

I have to confess that this great idea of mine might prove a little impractical, and it might also be seen as disrespectful to all those millions of poor buggers for whom slum life is, and will be for ever, their only life. But it's just that kids really do take so much for granted, and they do need shocking out of the cosy cocoon of their lives – and, by the way, they also need to be made aware of the importance of border controls and immigration quotas. So anyway, maybe we'll just have to stick to confining them in an underground cell for a few weeks without access to anything other than gruel and water and certainly without access to any electronic devices. Which leads on very nicely to my next point, because this point deals with the taming of their addiction to iPhones and iPads – in a very novel way.

5. Controlling the use of iPhones and iPads by kids.

OK. We're now at that point in a kid's life where he or she has been permitted into the company of adults but, despite our best efforts, he or she will almost certainly have failed to acquire (a) a taste for sprouts, (b) even a smattering of Latin, (c) any meaningful facility with a knife and fork and (d) any experience of overseas slums. However, one thing that he or she will not have failed to do is to develop an addiction to hand-held electronic devices. He or she will now be completely hooked.

One can observe the degree of this addiction at any gathering of relatives where, in the interests of convention or convenience, family members of all ages are brought together in a rather forced and certainly unnatural manner. Because I can guarantee that within minutes the iPhones and the iPads will be out, and young Luke and even younger Sarah will be tapping away at them and totally ignoring everybody else. They seem to find the company of grown-ups too boring for words… literally. And I'd dearly like to know how they'll respond when faced, at their first job interview, with the inevitable question: 'What experience have you had in talking to adults?' Because the truth of the matter is that they will have had virtually none.

Well, this just has to be a concern for even the most indulgent of parents, who can see only too well that their children are growing up with an addiction that will render them pretty well useless for anything other than tweeting and cheating. If their precious little darlings are forced to rely on their own skills and their facility to communicate with the rest of the world orally, then they're inevitably going to end up as cabbage pickers or even bankers. And most parents would welcome that outcome as much as they'd welcome the total scrapping of child allowance.

However, there is a solution, something I've dreamed up myself and something from which I fully anticipate to make a fortune. And the inspiration for this much-needed remedy for this terrible i-addiction is the Victorians' ingenious approach to the 'problem' of teenage masturbation.

Yes, concerned middle-class Victorians were eager to find some way to prevent their teenaged sons from masturbating, lest they became blind, impotent, sterile or in any way emancipated. It was then only a matter of time before Victorian ingenuity was brought into play – in the form of 'genital cages'. These were nifty little devices that were fashioned in such a way that, when 'applied' to a boy's whatsits, he would be incapable of even fiddling with himself, let alone getting himself excited. Indeed, there was one design that, with a spring arrangement, held the penis and scrotum securely, and with an inbuilt alarm, notified the parents if, by chance or otherwise, an erection had occurred…. Such cleverness and such imagination!

Anyway… Why, I thought, don't I use the idea of creating a physical barrier to a kid's intimate plumbing – to create a physical barrier to a kid's iPhone or iPad? I first toyed with making a cage into which the offending electronic device could be placed. But I soon realised that all those reluctant attendees at the family gathering would probably come along with spare devices, and then find somewhere else in the house where they could continue to use these and ignore their elders with impunity. So the final design involves a cage that will be fitted not around their machines but around their hands. In this way not only will they not be able to tap away at these infernal devices – and will therefore be available for 'conversation' – but the older ones among them won't be able to drink intoxicating liquor, and will therefore be available to drive home their possibly intoxicated parents. Which, I think you will agree, is a pretty splendid outcome all round, and well worth the fortune I'll be paid.

Incidentally, I've got a name for my device already. It will be called the 'iPen'. You know: from 'pen', as in 'cage'. And the beauty of this is that 'iPens', in the plural, is, of course, an anagram of 'penis', which means that the chosen name for my device will even constitute a fitting tribute to its original penis-focused inspiration. Brilliant!

Oh, and one last thing. I suspect some of you might think my solution, while exceptionally creative and unquestionably effective, is at the same time just a tad draconian – or even worryingly sadistic. In which case may I just suggest that the employment of an iPen could be accompanied with the introduction of some sort of reward system. That is to say, whichever kid is being subjected to the iPen's restraining regime could also be given access to a points-based 'early-release' programme, through which he or she could gain a premature uncaging of hands and thereby an earlier than expected return to moronic land. Such a programme might entail a commitment on the part of the restrained iPhone user to engage in, say, a whole hour of conversation without the use of the word 'like' (other than when actually called for), or possibly a whole hour of conversation that was similarly deficient in either guttural grunts or the repeated use of a mangled and mumbled 'sort-ov'.

So that's it: a simple guide for the upbringing – and for the salvation – of kids. A bit of a challenge, I know. But, compared to the agony of kidbirth, I imagine it is a complete doddle. And, if nothing else, it might just help to sustain the Brussels sprouts industry in Britain. And that certainly can't be a bad thing.

> There was a time when kids got clouts
> And smacks and slaps and Brussels sprouts
> But now they have just iPhones smart
> From mum and dad who live apart
>
> If only we could bring them back
> Those clouts and sprouts of which they lack
> And even teach them how to talk
> And how to use a knife and fork

But phones and pads now rule the day
And make quite sure there is no way
That all that stuff will now return
I mean like sort-ov wot they learn

London

I think it was Samuel Johnson, and not Boris Johnson, who said: 'You find no man, at all intellectual, who is willing to leave London. No, Sir, when a man is tired of London, he is tired of life; for there is in London all that life can afford.' Well, he may have had a point. And it is difficult to argue that London, in this modern age, really doesn't have it all.

I mean, to start with, it is the world's cultural capital. It is a city with opera and ballet venues, with forty-three West End theatres – the biggest assembly of such theatres anywhere in the world – and with a host of art galleries, libraries and museums. In addition to its hosting these physical manifestations of its cultural credentials it is also the home of the BBC, of a number of other national broadcasters and our national press, and it even holds the number one position in multimedia development and design. If that's not enough, it is a centre for fashion and retail and it is a huge education hub, having more than forty universities (which makes it the largest concentration of higher education institutions in Europe). And finally, to cement its unassailable position in the world of culture, it has within it four World Heritage

Sites (the Tower of London, Kew Gardens, the Palace of Westminster/Westminster Abbey and Greenwich) and also a few also-rans, such as Buckingham Palace, St Paul's Cathedral, Tower Bridge and the London Eye.

However, London isn't content with just its cultural prowess. It needs something else to confirm that in the twenty-first century it still deserves that Samuel Johnson accolade, and this presents itself in the form of 'finance'. Because London, in 2015, topped the world rankings in the global financial centres index – which, as it says on the tin, recognises its position as the world's pre-eminent financial centre. For here is a city that employs over 325,000 people in its finance 'industry', hosts over 480 overseas banks and, through its financial activities, is able to generate a whopping 20% of the UK's GDP – or 30%, if one takes in the whole of the London Metropolitan area. No wonder, then, that 70% of the UK's top 100 listed companies have their headquarters in London, along with 100 of Europe's 500 largest enterprises. No wonder either, that (after taking account of its financial clout and those cultural strengths) *Forbes* magazine has conferred the title of 'most influential city in the world' on this town on the Thames.

Anyway, with such a CV, it is no great surprise that London is a very popular place. Not only is it now home to more ultra-high net worth individuals than any other city on the planet (it hosts seventy-two billionaires) but it is also home to an increasing number of rather more impecunious mortals, as it now boasts a population of 8.5 million people (or 12.5% of the UK's population). In fact, if one looks at the larger London metropolitan area this figure rises to nearly fourteen million, and the city as a region has a population as high as twenty-three million. So, it's a pretty crowded place – and a place with the highest property prices in Europe, as well the second largest immigrant population in the world (after New York).

Yes, London's attractions have attracted many people from virtually every other country on the globe, and three million of its residents (37% of all Londoners) were born overseas. And they really do come from everywhere. I mean, there are 65,000 Somalis in London, 62,000 Ghanaians, 40,000 Afghans and even 31,000 Brazilians (and we're not talking dogs or grooming here.) In fact, it has been calculated that London now has fifty non-indigenous communities with a population of more than 10,000. And it certainly has a multicoloured hue, with Asians making up around 20% of its population and black people about 16%. And this colour shift away from white is even more evident in London state schools, where Asian and black children now outnumber white British children by about six to four. And I suppose it's worth pointing out at this point, that the percentages of Asian and black people in the UK's overall population are 7% and 3% respectively, making London rather more 'cosmopolitan' than the hillbilly neighbours that surround it.

So, having provided a snapshot of London's pre-eminence in culture and finance (and having given a brief résumé of its diverse populace) should we in the rest of this country be proud of London, or should we in some way resent it?

Well, before deciding the answer to this question, I will now have to mention one aspect of this great city that up to this point I have intentionally ignored, and that is the fact that it is the seat of government. The UK is run from London – by people who live in London and people, therefore, who cannot fail to see the world through a London lens. This, I contend, is why they seem unconcerned that London is sucking wealth and talent from the rest of the country and has been doing so for years. However, possibly not at a sufficient rate, which is why, rather than building a high-speed east-west rail connection in the north between Yorkshire and Lancashire, and by doing so revitalising that whole area, our leaders in London have instead chosen to build a north-south link that will drain away that region's talent, ingenuity – and will – even more rapidly than before.

Now, what I've just described is almost inevitable. If you are in something of a metropolitan bubble it must be difficult to look outside it or even to maintain even a passing interest in what's outside it. And unfortunately, it doesn't stop there. Because we are talking here about the people with power, not just in government, but in the arts and in the media as well, and if you have power you are often tempted to use it in a way that's… well, not particularly fair to all those who are outside the bubble. And what I'm alluding to here is the disproportionate amount of national resources that appear to be lavished on our capital.

There are a couple of outstanding examples of this bias in favour of London, the first of which must be spending on transport, where our government has got into the habit of spending more money on transport projects for Londoners than for the rest of the country combined. Indeed, in 2011, they were spending £2,700 per person in London and just £5 per person in the North East – which, even if you factor in what might have related to the 2012 Olympics, is still an unbelievable differential. And there's more: half of the twenty biggest taxpayer-funded projects in the country will benefit only those in London and the South East, and half of all infrastructure spending is spent in London. Those of us who are out in the sticks are being screwed. We are also getting kicked in the balls when it comes to the handing out of cash for the arts. Because since it was first created the (London-based) Arts Council has been intent on channelling its taxpayer-provided funds into the hands of the great institutions of London. A report in 2013 found that for every £10 spent per capita in London by the government on arts only 70 p per capita was spent elsewhere in the country! Why this, along with that transport spend imbalance, has not attracted more scrutiny is something of a mystery, and I'm sure it has nothing to do with our national press, the BBC and other broadcasters all being based in London as well. Perish the thought. And perish the thought also that there is anything more than a marginal bias towards London when it comes to dividing up the national cake. Even though there is.

You see, it is one thing to be ruled by an establishment that favours its own and looks after its own very local patch. But it is quite another to be ruled by an establishment that exists in an environment that is alien to many of those it rules and that must inevitably colour both its judgement and its attitude in general. Quite simply, London has more in common with New York and Tokyo than it has with a village in Worcestershire or even with the city of Worcester (a quite sizeable conurbation). In fact, the easiest way to regard London is as an entirely separate country from the rest of our nation, and a country that fosters some very alien views.

Let's look at the evidence for that statement, and the first exhibit is that cosmopolitan population already referred to. Remember, it is far less 'white' than the rest of the country, and it is also far from being representative of the entire nation in religious terms. In the UK as a whole the split of beliefs is roughly 60% Christian, 25% no religion, 4% Muslim and 1% Hindu. In London the split is 48% Christian, 21% no religion, 12% Muslim and 5% Hindu.

This exacerbated attrition of the Christian/no religion proportion of the population in London cannot fail to have an impact on metrocentric thinking in general, and it may even be reflected in the overall political flavour of the capital. Because, out of the seventy-three MPs representing London constituencies, forty-five are Labour and just twenty-seven are Conservative (and one is a Lib Dem remnant), and that hardly reflects the current political tone of the country as a whole. Of course London has always been to the left of the rest of the country, and it is no secret that it is the home of our out-of-touch liberal elite, those wonks and twots who have been responsible for so much of the damage done to Britain. But an injection of generally poor and possibly unsophisticated immigrants is hardly going to pull it to the right. Nor are they going to promote secularism or reinforce all those much talked about British values that are still the currency of life in much of provincial Britain. No, there is no getting away from it. We who are out in those provinces are being run by a bunch of tossers who essentially live in another country, a faraway place called London. And increasingly they impose upon us their foreign, un-British views and, in doing so, fuel the antagonism that already exists between the residents of Worcestershire (or any other county you care to mention) and they themselves as the governing elite. There's us, the overwhelming majority of the populace who don't live in London. And there's them, the tiny minority of 'foreign' rulers, who are tainted by the atypical environment in which they live. They, unfortunately, hold all the power and all the channels of national communication, and they are currently busy ruining our lives. Which means, I suppose, that even if we are proud of London as a city we might also be just a teeny bit resentful of it… resentful of what it has caused and is still causing every last one of us non-Londoners: an awful lot of grief.

I can think of no better illustration of London thinking as opposed to 'our' thinking than by bringing to your attention the fact that the Speaker of the Lords will quite casually spend more on a taxi for a night at the opera than will be raised by the efforts of many at a village hall jumble sale for the upkeep of the village church. I know this example is a bit trite, but it is a real example of what is going on in the mind of a London-cosseted apparatchik, and it points to London being not just another country but somewhere on another planet. And it's a planet that has no connection to Worcestershire whatsoever. Instead it is a planet that houses a distant political structure, and Worcestershire just happens to lie within the sphere of its political power.

So where does London's dominance – and London's indifference – leave us, all us poor schmucks out in nowhere land? Well, I'll tell you, and I'll explain exactly where it leaves us by first of all saying a few words about North Korea…

As you probably already know, North Korea is an abomination of a place where one tub of lard with a dreadful haircut now devotes his whole life to making a hell on Earth for the vast majority of his fellow North Koreans. Out in their equivalent of Worcestershire they struggle to find a daily meal and they are all far too well acquainted with privation, with no electricity, with no running water or any sort of plumbing in their homes, and with a transport system that consists of using one's legs to walk, pedalling a rickety bicycle or grabbing a lift on a truck. They have a miserable existence, which is just that: an existence rather than a life. Now, clearly, one tub of lard cannot impose such suffering all on his own. He needs a cadre of dedicated co-bastards to help him in his quest, and these people need to be kept close at hand and in *comparative* luxury. And what I mean by 'luxury' is what in North Korea would be regarded as luxury when compared to a diet of grass and rodents. So he houses them in North Korea's capital, Pyongyang, and he goes to great lengths to ensure they know that they live a very charmed life.

Pyongyang is not Paris and it certainly isn't London, and until recently it was something of a bleak dump. It still is, really, but apparently there is now a programme to update some of its ageing buildings and there has been some new construction carried out. Its 'loyal' inhabitants, or at least some of them, are now becoming acquainted with a vocabulary that includes 'croissants', 'Swiss chocolate', 'baguettes', 'mini golf' and even 'kiwi fruit'. The dear lard container is spoiling those he needs to maintain his despotic rule while ensuring that none of those peasants out in horrid land are ever allowed inside his showcase capital. So North Korea is actually two countries. In one resides all the power and privilege (and I do mean all). And in the other resides… well, millions of people who don't really count. And does that ring any bells?

I'm not, of course, suggesting that London and Pyongyang have a great deal in common. Or, for that matter, that Worcestershire and provincial North Korea have much in common. But what I am suggesting is that London, a city that could more easily identify with any mega city in the world than with the country it resides within, has already begun to create that North Korean 'two-country' state of affairs here in Britain. The more power it takes, and the more it uses or abuses this power to reflect London as opposed to British values, the more it will drive a wedge between itself and the rest of the country… until one day, in real as opposed to metaphorical terms, it will become a 'proper' foreign presence in this land. And when it does I hope we charge it an appropriately exorbitant rent.

That said, it is quite a place. It's just not quite the sort of place with quite the sort of people who you'd ever choose to run your life. Not if you lived in Worcestershire, anyway.

London's quite a funny place
With lots of things – except much space
In fact, it's 'got it all' – and more
At least for those who aren't too poor

And so it's grown as more arrive
To taste its fruits or just survive
And we all help, us country folk
This engine huge, its fires to stoke

And in return it rules us all
The thin, the fat, the short, the tall
The trouble is, it doesn't see
It's not like you and not like me

No, London's not just funny now
But foreign too, and so I vow
To see it cleaved from England fair
And shipped to where I do not care

Yes, London is another state
A place from which to separate
So let's get on and ship it off
Without or with a blonde-haired toff…

Men

Before I talk about men I need to talk about the 'essence of men', which is otherwise known as testosterone. Because this steroid hormone, which is secreted by the testicles of males, is (as well as being their sex hormone) responsible for rather too much of their behaviour.

To start with I suppose I should concede that testosterone is somewhat essential for men. It plays a key role in the development of their wedding furniture and it provides them with all those man-type physical characteristics: things like increased muscle strength, the growth of body hair and a deepening voice. Without it I imagine they'd all be like girls. Although, there again, because testosterone is also important for health and well-being, and it prevents osteoporosis, women produce it as well. Not in their testicles, obviously, but in their ovaries. Nevertheless, as the metabolic consumption of testosterone in males is so much greater (presumably to allow them to indulge in their favourite male pastimes), their daily production of this hormone is about twenty times greater than that of females.

Anyway, a hint of something else that testosterone is responsible for is that when a man falls in love his testosterone levels drop while those of the object of his love rise. This is in order, it has been suggested, that the differences between the sexes will be decreased to facilitate their pairing (and there might be a bit of preparation for parenthood going on there as well). Needless to say, the differences referred to here are those that we all recognise, in that while a woman will tend to be caring, nurturing and risk-averse, a man will typically be less empathetic, more competitive and often heedless of risk... and all thanks to testosterone. Yes, this vital hormone has a rather darker side, in that it is associated with a number of aspects of men's behaviour that we could well do without. Because not only is there a link between testosterone and men's competitiveness and risk-taking but there is also a link to verbal aggression and actual violence. And while testosterone might not be guilty of making men aggressive per se there is solid evidence that they are much less likely than women to back down from a challenge, and if they live in an environment where challenges are common there *is* a positive correlation between testosterone and aggression. (And, as testosterone peaks in a male at the age of about twenty, one only has to bring to mind present-day Syria and its complement of gun-toting jerks to see that this correlation is spot on.)

Testosterone has been shown to have a link to criminality as well. And it plays a major role in the (catastrophic) risk-taking in the finance industry, as we all know to our cost. Furthermore, it is intimately related to a desire on the part of men to be dominant in all situations, a feature of this special 'poison' that causes all sorts of problems – and one begins to despair. I mean, OK, have a hormone thing that gives a guy his balls and his whatsit, but why on Earth have this same hormone equipping him with so many antisocial and potentially dangerous traits? Well, the answer's easy, isn't it? And it concerns our biological history and a time when the name of the game for all men was to survive in a harsh environment and attract and copulate with as many women as possible. And you couldn't do that if you were an empathetic wimp with not a shred of aggression in your make-up. No, you had to be a muscular brute who would readily risk an encounter with a mammoth, wrestle it to the ground and then go off and pulverise any other man who came close to your harem. And you would almost certainly not have been be into macramé or the threading of beads.

So originally testosterone was a *good thing*. It endowed men with their tackle and with both the physical and mental equipment they needed for their own survival *and* for the survival of their women partners. And if we still all lived in caves we wouldn't now have some of the problems that we do.

Yes, we moved on, didn't we? Once mammoths were replaced by maize plants and manioc, all that risk-taking and all that aggressive desire to dominate and control wasn't needed quite as much. Or at least not for survival. But no matter, because men found a brand-new, extremely promising outlet for all their pent-up testosterone-fuelled pugnacity, and this was called 'continuous conflict'. Brilliant! Generation after generation of men could go off to war, take risks, be as aggressive as they liked, and all with the possibility of gaining some real dominance over their rivals and, with this dominance, then grabbing some power. What could be better, and what could be a greater justification for their existence? In fact, this outlet has proved so popular that it has continued to the present day, and in parts of the world it is what life is all about. Forget forging some sort of peace or righting some terrible wrong. As far as those nutters in Afghanistan and the Middle East are concerned, the fighting is an end in itself. It gives them thrills, spills and an opportunity to display the very worst aspects of male behaviour, while at the same time defining their status as the ultimate red-blooded, arse-kicking, thick-headed *man!*.

Of course, as some of the world has become a little more civilised, war as an outlet for men's gender ambitions has been largely removed, and men have had to look elsewhere for a release valve for all that testosterone. And they've been successful in their search. Because many of them now attend football matches – to shout, to scream, to indulge in a bit of vicarious aggression by observing the players on the pitch – or maybe in some real aggression by beating up some of the opposition's supporters. Then there's actually playing a sport, of which the contact sports are clearly the best, or participating in an extreme sport or maybe climbing a mountain. And if you can't do any of this stuff then you can still make do by watching some extreme violence on your laptop or by playing some mindless violent video game. The opportunities for testosterone-release are endless.

So that's all settled, then. Testosterone might be something of a throwback to our cave-dwelling past but it can be 'contained', and all those men who may have lost their traditional role in life can be dealt with and tamed. Only, of course, that ignores the most egregious effect of this hormone and the one that makes life hell on Earth for all those without it, or at least for all those who don't possess it at the level it occurs in men. Yes, who cares if men beat up other men at football matches or kill themselves in pursuing one or other of those extreme sports or get blasted by some other idiot in some miserable village in ISIS land? In fact, in that last instance, it's a case of 'the more the merrier'. But I'm afraid we can harbour no such indifference when we observe the part that testosterone plays in men's treatment of... women.

The trouble is, you see, that testosterone makes men potentially aggressive – and power-hungry. Inevitably, this has meant that in virtually every society on this planet men have insisted on taking on the high-status roles and have demanded that women should occupy only the low-status roles and be entirely subordinate. At which point I should warn you that we are now embarking on the main theme of this particular 'stuff': the outrageous treatment of women by men, which is still the norm in most of the modern world.

It isn't new, this situation. One only has to observe what went on in (civilised) ancient Greece or (civilised) ancient Rome to see that women were treated not just as second-class citizens but as little more than property. In ancient Greece, for example, women had no property or political rights, and they were forbidden to leave their homes after dark. That said, they probably had it easy compared to women in ancient Assyria, where the punishment for rape was the handing over of the rapist's wife to the husband of the victim to be used as he desired. And then there were all those cultures that demanded the death of a widow, at her own hand or otherwise, shortly after the death of her husband. This 'tradition' was common throughout India and China right up until the twentieth century, and it may still happen occasionally even now.

What certainly still happens now – in Middle Eastern countries, for example – is the maintenance of systems that deny women any influence over the political, religious or cultural lives of their societies, and also any ability to own property or to inherit land or wealth, or to be treated as anything other than some sort of commodity. In some of the countries in this region women live as essentially prisoners of men, unable to leave their houses except under the guardianship of a male guardian. And even when they do they are obliged to imprison themselves in a head-to-foot shroud to emphasise their captive situation. They really are just pieces of property – and males, as their owners, can do what they like with them. Indeed, in that most progressive of all countries, Egypt, where a man can demand sex from his wife whenever he wants it, a recent survey showed that the vast majority of Egyptian men (and women!) believe it is acceptable for a man to beat his wife if she refuses him this pleasure. This finding is probably not unconnected with the appalling treatment of women at mass gatherings in Egypt where, as a woman, if you are merely groped rather than raped then you've probably had a pretty reasonable day. (And similarly, as a German or Swedish woman, if you've survived a New Year's Eve celebration without coming to any harm.)

OK. Time to draw breath. Because I've laid the universal subjugation of women very firmly at the door of testosterone. But this subjugation is much more than their being given a second-class role. It also involves them being actively despised by men, who then go on to inflict as much degradation and humiliation on them as they can. But why? Why, as members of the same species and, significantly, those members who bear the next generation of this species, are they not revered for their life-giving and nurturing role but instead treated with disdain and even contempt?

Well, for what it's worth, I think it's all to do with that demand by men to be top dog (because of testosterone) and, most significantly, their desire not to be challenged in this role. And they can be challenged – quite successfully – by women. Because, despite their ability to enslave and control these awful hussies, these awful hussies have always been capable of arousing powerful and uncontrollable sexual urges within them at any moment. And that means a loss of control by the men, and a reason to despise women and treat them as whores.

Yes, men are on a constant quest to increase their sense of significance and status. But at the same time they are conscious that they are vulnerable to women, and they don't like it. Consequently, most cultures have had within them a noticeable antagonism towards women. They have viewed them as impure and intrinsically sinful creatures, who have been placed among men to lead them astray. And guess what? The major Abrahamic religions – all run by men, of course – have gone out of their way to reinforce this belief. For them sensual desires were (and still are) base and sinful. Where men are associated with the 'purity of the mind', their second-class neighbours – all those terrible women – are associated with 'corruption', as in the corruption of their temporal form.

If you doubt this deep-seated prejudice within our principal religions, then let me elaborate just a little on how they all major in what is actually nothing less than a nauseating adherence to misogyny in its purest form.

Let me start with Christianity, and its promotion of the belief that Adam was created first and that Eve popped out just 'to serve him and obey him'. She also, of course, did what all women do, which was to be disobedient if given half the chance, and she went off and scrumped an apple. No surprise, then, that the Church taught that women were inferior to men and that this meant that they needed to observe strict obedience, not only to their husbands but to their fathers and brothers as well. Indeed, girls in this country, until only a few centuries ago, were indoctrinated by the holy fathers in the belief that they were irredeemably inferior and not much more than instruments of the Devil. They were viewed as despicable, wanton creatures, whose principal role was to lure men away from God and into sin.

I'm sure they were made well aware of Genesis 3:16,

which states that, 'Thy desire shall be to thy husband, and he shall rule over thee.' They may even have been made aware of Saint Paul's epistles, where he reinforces the guilt of sex, the need for female subjugation and the need to be aware of the female desire to seduce men. And, if they were very lucky, they may have been introduced to some of the writings of Tertullian, a second-century Christian author who wrote, among other things, that a woman was 'the gateway of the Devil', and that she was 'a temple built over a sewer'. He clearly had a sewer for a mind himself, and can probably lay claim to being one of the first and one of the nastiest of all recorded misogynists. There again, his views on the cosmos included the belief that the heavens and the Earth intersected at various points and that it was by no means impossible that there couldn't be sexual congress with supernatural beings. So maybe we should just write him off as a loony, and move on from Christianity's oppression of women to that promoted by Islam.

Well, where does one start? Maybe with the observation that this religion is not noted for its libertarian or egalitarian views. But, more pertinently, it is worth pointing out that the vast majority of the (subjective) interpretation of the Koran has been conducted by men. This fact, combined with a preponderance of mullahs who are misogynistic by nature and regressive sharia law in many Muslim countries, has made Islam synonymous with misogyny in some of its very worst manifestations of all.

And let's not forget Judaism – and the sort of references it makes to 'Women are evil, my children…

they use wiles and try to ensnare (men) by their charms. They lay plots in their hearts against men…' and I'll let you fill in the rest. Because it's the same story as it is with Christianity and Islam: women stink and they need to be kept down – at all costs. And they never deserve to be treated like the human beings they are. So there.

It's all pretty appalling, this men over women thing. But there is a ray of hope, something that might yet bring down the empire of man. And, by way of introducing this new hope for the future, I will just mention a common belief in 1600s Britain. This was that sperm contained the seed of an entire person and that the woman was merely a place where this seed could get on and grow (such was the disdain for women and for their part in the creative process).

Well, how things might change! And to examine just how they might change, I want first to state something in the defence of men. This is that, as a gender, they do think rather differently to women, and that this different way of thinking has been very bountiful for the whole of mankind. They have proved themselves hugely imaginative and creative, particularly in the arena of science, where the advances they've brought about and the technical innovations they've introduced have transformed our world. Indeed, by being responsible for the domestication of animals for food and so eliminating the need to hunt – and, more recently, by replacing the need for muscle with the introduction of all sorts of machines – men have been instrumental in making themselves somewhat redundant. Unfortunately for them, this knack they have for scientific and technological advancement has now reached the point where quite soon they will not be just somewhat redundant but entirely redundant. Because, believe it or not, they now appear to have been successful in using stem cells to produce artificially created sperm. And that means that not only will they no longer be needed to catch mammoths or beat off hordes of foreign cavemen but they now won't necessarily be needed for that all-important impregnation stuff. The female gender, equipped with laboratory-produced semen, can get on and do its own thing, and men will be of no more use than a prayer for world peace.

This isn't just nonsense. If technology does away with the need for men then their position vis-à-vis women reverses, and they become the weaker 'species' within mankind. Men will be like human tails. These were no longer needed and were therefore done away with, other than a vestigial coccyx. And, if evolution follows its natural course, that is what will happen with men. Only there won't even be a coccyx to mark their demise.

There are of course a few arguments against the inevitability of their disappearance, the first of which is that in our human societies we are now not following a Darwinistic path (as discussed elsewhere in this book) and instead we keep our weaker strains alive. Similarly, women might decide to keep (some) men alive. Although, given how they've suffered at their hands for millennia… there again, they might not. In fact, I can only imagine that they might still want them around for some cuddles or for some real, hard-core interactive sex. But on the other hand the Japanese are already creating 'cuddly robots' and I also believe there is already a plethora of devices for women that provide a sexual experience without the presence of men. And they don't make quite the same mess, either.

Ultimately, though, I suspect the best chance for men's continuation is the need women have for love. Or, if they can manage without this, then they will still want someone to unblock the drain, touch up the eaves, risk his life with a chainsaw, pull the car from a ditch – and tell them that they've chosen the right dress. It will be a bit of a demotion from all that killing of mammoths, and it will be difficult to see how men will find any authorised outlets for their testosterone stuff at all. But it will be life – just not how we've known it, Jim.

Perhaps men will have to learn to adapt to a Sir Isaac Newton sort of life. I don't know what his testosterone levels were, but here was a guy who did all sorts of remarkable things in physics – and established the principles of gravity – but who also drew the following comments from Voltaire when he died. Sir Isaac, Voltaire said, 'Was never sensible to any passion, was not subject to the common frailties of mankind, nor had any commerce with women – a circumstance which was assured me by the physician and surgeon who attended his last moments.'

Yes, it seems that this eminent scientist not only never married, but that when he passed away he was still a virgin. This is possibly not the most attractive role model for one of those ISIS jihadists, but if they don't think about some serious reform to their male personas pretty soon then they may be the first to be given a P45 by that new monopoly of women. And God, they'd deserve it. In fact, I wonder whether subconsciously they already know that they'll soon be superfluous to requirements, and it is this knowledge that is stoking their animosity to women. I mean, most women get a shit deal in that part of the world, but these mad zealots appear to be taking the shit treatment to an entirely new level. And how else do you explain their horrific actions and their unbelievable antipathy towards women in general?

So men have lots not to be proud of. Equally, in the Western 'civilised' world, they have quite a lot to be proud of. Because many of them – in Europe, America and the Antipodes – by dismissing the misogynistic messages of religions, have come to terms with their equivalence with women and, while far from perfect, they have modified their behaviour significantly. And many of them have overcome their biological enslavement by testosterone and have become almost reasonable, even if they still take risks when they're driving.

Whether this will be enough to save them when sperm can be bought at Boots is another matter. So too is whether or not testosterone will survive its increasing redundancy. And if its levels start to decrease in line with its utility, whether the differences between men and women will disappear almost entirely. Although I suspect she'll still take longer to get dressed, and he'll still have problems with the cling film…

> Some men are fat and some are thin
> But all these men have stuff within
> A stuff we call testosterone
> A stuff we wish they'd now disown

To start with it was quite OK
And helped all men in every way
From hunting down the food they ate
To picking up a decent mate

But 'T' it worked by making men
A bit like monarchs of the glen
And this was bad because it meant
They often turned belligerent

They'd fight in wars to gain control
With winning power their constant goal
And with their strength they'd also seek
To subjugate the mild and meek

This meant, of course, their own sweet wives
'The Devil's work that blights our lives'
Yes, men are thick as well as strong
And can't tell right from what is wrong

But do not fear, you women dear
For ersatz sperm will soon be here
And when it is, my female friends
Man's reign on Earth will surely end…

NHS

Dinosaurs are extinct. Only, of course, they are not. The modern world is full of them, in the shape of thousands of species of modern-day birds. And then, of course, there is the NHS.

Now, just by making that observation, I can already detect the drafting of some sort of secular fatwa. The NHS is, after all, the ultimate sacred cow, and it deserves only our respect, our admiration – and more and more of our money. So please allow me to make a second observation on the NHS that is uncontroversial and entirely positive. This is that it is a readily available example of the correct pronunciation of the letter 'H'. After all, one never hears even the most educationally challenged (Radio 1) DJs referring to something called the N 'Haitch' S but instead to the entirely correctly pronounced N 'Aitch' S. However, why they then revert to 'Haitch' on all other occasions remains a mystery. Maybe it's something to do with their believing that 'disinterested' is a posher way of saying 'uninterested' and not knowing that it means something completely different. Or maybe it's more to do with their being completely uninterested in any of the niceties of the English language (but definitely not disinterested).

Anyway, I seem to be getting off the point, and the point is that the NHS *is* a dinosaur... and while it is not yet extinct it is in the critically endangered category, and no amount of conservation work is going to maintain it indefinitely. Remember, even sacred cows are not immortal, and this sacred cow can now hardly stand on its feet.

Right, well I seem to have veered off again into a discussion of disparate forms of four-legged animals, but I will endeavour to get back on track by making a few comments on the context within which we should examine the life chances of the NHS. The first of these is that the whole concept of a health service that is free at the point of delivery is dependent on the raising of tax, and if you have the fortitude to make it to my piece on taxation you will see that this rather torpedoes its existence without further debate. (I present an irrefutable argument in that piece for a no-tax society, of course.)

However, I am enough of a realist to accept that our cherished dinosaur will be around for a little while yet, and that there is therefore some merit in examining how it might be prevented from wheezing and coughing for the rest of its short life. Yes, I have dedicated more than a few minutes to considering how our cash-strapped, overused, near-to-breaking-point NHS may be given a draught of relief-giving oxygen – whilst, for the moment at least, suspending my assertion that it should never have been given life in the first place (an assertion that will probably earn me another even more vehemently expressed fatwa).

OK... here's the oxygen – in a series of gaseous bullet points:

1. Our police forces operate on the basis of being immune from claims of negligence. I don't know for certain, but this seems to be a sort of common-sense approach to the provision of a service by a bunch of people who will inevitably make mistakes – but a service that could not possibly bear the financial burden of legal claims, most of which would probably be made by toerags and thieves. And most of which, taking account of the appalling claims culture in this country, would probably be successful. And it works. So why on Earth don't we apply the same provision of service basis to the NHS? One gets one's treatment free, but on the condition that one accepts that things might go wrong – in which case... tough. Life, after all, isn't fair. And what's more, the NHS isn't there to provide a livelihood for thousands of lawyers and bonus holidays for initially misdiagnosed but now completely healthy punters. And to forestall yet another fatwa I will concede that there will, of course, always be cases of *serious* negligence, and these should certainly be pursued. However, I would anticipate that there would be no more than five such cases a year and they would involve such matters as being exposed for the length of a sandwich break to X-rays or being the subject of a head amputation when it should have been a leg. Oh, and it would be the radiologist and the surgeon respectively who would be obliged to pay damages, not the N 'Aitch' S.

2. Over seven million hospital appointments are missed each year. So charge £100 for each of these,

with a multiplier for repeat offenders, and you've got yourself a cool billion pounds without really trying. Simples! Oh, and your next appointment, sir or madam, will be in two years' time or after your demise, whichever comes later…

3. It has been calculated that there are 1.6 billion unnecessary antibiotic prescriptions made each year by NHS doctors, costing us all about £7billion as well as posing a serious threat to our lives (through the impact of this overprescribing on the drug resistance of bacteria). So charge £20 for every antibiotic prescription, rising by £20 a throw for repeat drongos, and over-prescriptions would fall off a cliff, as too would the costs involved. Simples again! Oh, and that third unnecessary antibiotic you've just laid out sixty quid for would actually be a laxative…

4. Then there are all these people whose procreational activities are entirely out of control and who look not only to everyone else to fund the consequences of their activities but also to the NHS for a free-at-the-literal-point-of-delivery service no matter how many times they use it. Well, that can be stopped overnight. Just institute free maternity services for the first two visits, but for those who haven't grasped that just two offspring is both reasonable and quaintly English, they will have to pay through the nose. Nipper three will cost them thousands, nipper four even more thousands… and if they are stupid enough to go for nipper five then they will end

up bankrupt, and very probably with the surname 'Pariah'. I mean, they have got to be made to realise that any society operates most effectively when its adults have the number of children they can afford, not the number they can claim for, having first had them handled by a same-day, first-class delivery service (and all free of charge). In short, being fecund is one thing. Taking the fecund mickey is quite another matter...

5. OK, 14% of all NHS spending – about £16 billion – is on management. Well, just to be clear there, it isn't necessarily on *management*, but it is on *managers*, that peculiar breed of parasites living in the entrails of the dinosaur who, because of their disagreeable situation (?), believe they deserve to be paid enormous amounts, and so enormous that droves of them scuttle off home with more money each year than the PM earns. And, whatever you think about him, he earns it, whereas the jury is out on whether this is anything like the case with our invisible NHS aristocracy. So the NHS could save at least £8 billion, say, by a round of intense hard bargaining backed up as necessary by an outbreak of drug-resistant bureaucratosis. If you can't beat 'em, infect 'em... (Only kidding. I don't want another bloody fatwa – and certainly not one drafted by an NHS manager. It would be far too expensive.)

6. Talking of which, the cost to the NHS of alcohol misuse and drug abuse is astronomical. In the absence of an ability to deport these misusers and abusers to

Australia (although I know not why) I suggest that they are all exiled to a non-NHS Britain, where they would find themselves free to get plastered and high but then have to pay for any required post-partaking treatment themselves. Tough stuff, but no doubt character-building as well… especially if their non-NHS treatment is backstreet and dodgy and recorded for a Channel 5 reality TV series narrated by a Simon Cowell soundalike (but definitely not by a lookalike).

7. Talking of which… there must be enormous scope for reality TV in the NHS itself. And I don't just mean the sanitised bits, but all the other stuff that goes on – and which would definitely appeal to the devotees of some of those more obscure TV channels along with the Twitter brigade and all those Internet trolls, and for which they'd all pay very richly indeed. In fact, there is even scope for a high-income premium service, where the punters don't sit down in front of a TV but stand right next to the surgeon in the operating theatre. It could be called something like *Ghoul Drool*, or maybe *We're Just Close Fiends*.

Uhmm, there again, maybe this last bullet point is a bullet point too far, and maybe I should now abandon my doomed attempts to save the doomed dinosaur and explore what might take its place in the process of natural and very sensible selection. If nothing else it might help you to forget that I was proposing that our current health service should seek to profit from the dismemberment of its patients in an operating theatre. I can only claim overwork and a tendency to confuse the abdominal with the abominable...

So... to start with it might be sensible to set out why I believe that the NHS is a dinosaur, and why it will soon be extinct. And, of course, it is all to do with money. It is preposterous to expect an institution that has been lumbered with an open-ended, almost infinite responsibility to its clients but which will, necessarily, always have fixed and finite resources, to survive for very long. This is particularly so when its clients' demands and expectations increase almost exponentially, but both their willingness and their ability to fund it start to flatline.

However, many of the clients of the NHS have received such a good service from this institution, and consequently hold it in such high regard, that they are simply unable to see it for what it is: an institution that cannot survive. Yes, this is that 'sacred cow' status of the NHS that I've already alluded to and the status that means it can do no wrong (even though it does), that its failings must always be overlooked and that its existence can never be challenged (at the risk of a fatwa or worse).

Well, I think it's time to get real and time to recognise that if people want a comprehensive health service then they have to pay for a comprehensive health service – directly, and in a way that reflects their likely demands on this service. Which is beginning to sound not only a little technical but slightly boring. But bear with me, because what I'm going to suggest is a very simple model. This would require every adult citizen to pay health insurance premiums into a fund of his choice, which would then be used by that fund to buy the healthcare that he or she (or their children) might require – from a private healthcare supplier of their choice. And two important points to make. First, these adults would be able to afford the premiums because they would now be paying far less tax (there being no NHS to fund any more). Second, their premiums would not be dependent on their age or their occupation, but they would be dependent on their lifestyle choices and their BMI!

Well, a suggestion like that will probably earn me more than a fatwa. I'll probably get a brick through the window. I mean, the idea of suggesting that individuals should accept the financial consequences of their bad habits and that all those others who exercise and eat sensibly shouldn't pick up the tab for their irresponsible drug-taking, booze-swilling, fag-puffing and mouth-stuffing ways it clearly outrageous. In fact, it is no less than heresy and it is probably an assault on their human rights – their human rights to be grossly irresponsible human dickheads, intent only on syndicating the output of their dickhead behaviour to all and sundry.

Tough. The reality is that a self-insurance approach would be workable, equitable and eminently reasonable, and it would also act to encourage people to take rather more responsibility for their own heath than they do now (when they know that under our current and unsustainable arrangements they can act as they choose and others will pick up the bill). Shit, they may not know how to manage themselves, but they're all bloody experts when it comes to handling our national dinosaur – and, in the process, pushing it ever closer to extinction. So in conclusion may I just say that, as dear as the NHS is to all of us, it will not be here for ever, and it would be kinder to put it out of its misery as soon as we can, and let natural selection take its course. That is to say that we should allow the survival of the fittest in the shape of a sustainable self-insured system of healthcare that will outlive us all.

Oh, and if you do want to send me a fatwa or even a brick, just bear in mind that if you've read this far then you've probably already accepted that I'm essentially right. Annoyingly, I generally am. The only drawback to the dismantling of the NHS would be the fact that it would rob us of that readily available example of how to say 'aitch'…

> Aneurin Bevan had a plan
> For every miss and every man
> Yes, pills and jabs (and all for nowt)
> To cure yer mumps and piles and gout
>
> At last we'd have a healthy land
> With ills and sickness duly banned
> All thanks to what he'd ushered in
> An NHS – which then was thin
>
> But as time passed and people saw
> Just what that NHS was for
> It had to grow at quite a speed
> To 'meet demand' and 'meet the need'
>
> And so the NHS is now
> A monster fat (and sacred cow)
> But monsters fat become obese
> And so much so they then decease…

Officialdom

Officialdom is simply another not-exactly-flattering term for bureaucracy. However, my favourite definition of this never-welcome feature of our life is 'The *domain* of officials'. To me that says so much: not only about how officialdom is a discrete and self-contained area within our society but also about how this area is controlled by the officials themselves, generally for their own benefit.

I wasn't terribly keen to write anything about this particular 'stuff', but officialdom is so damn intrusive I decided that I couldn't avoid it. I knew I needed to reflect its intrusive nature in this book, and that I had to do this by giving it a thoughtful and impartial going-over, as you will now discover. And this going-over is going to commence with a brief review of the four principal characteristics of officialdom – with references, as necessary, to the plethora of bureaucracies we have here in Britain. So here goes:

1. Well, as already referred to in the discussion of the BBC's bureaucracy, the most frightening characteristic of officialdom is its propensity to grow. And not just to grow slowly, but to grow like some

supercharged buggery. Yes, that desire on the part of all officials to have other officials beneath them leads inevitably to an exponential growth in their numbers – and a growth which has little, if any, connection with what they might be called upon to do.

One only has to look at how many civil servants were employed in Britain when Britain ran about a third of the world, and compare those numbers with what we have here today, to see that there is no real relation between the size of officialdom and its supposed workload. Some say that there were as few as 4,000 civil servants running the British Empire and they were all crammed into just one building: Somerset House. However, I am prepared to concede that there were also lots of colonial civil servants, and a fairer number might be as many as 100,000. But that was at the height of our imperial days, and 100,000 is less than a quarter of the number of civil servants we apparently need now to run just one fairly compact, self-contained country.

Yes, we now have 450,000 civil servants in this country – and a shedload more in local government and in various quangos, and one does have to wonder what they all do. I mean, take the Cabinet Office. This is just one government department that, from what I can gather, exists solely 'to support the PM and the Cabinet (in its collective decision-making)' and to deliver, to implement, to drive coherence, and no doubt to drive forward generally. So that's nothing specific, then – which isn't a disaster, because it's obviously just a few guys stuffed away in some corner of Downing Street who can be called upon as needed. Only, of course, it isn't. The Cabinet Office employs nearly 1,700 people and has an annual budget of nearly £2,500,000,000! Well, I can only imagine that with those sorts of resources it could probably support the whole bloody country, not just the PM and the Cabinet, and it would also be in a position to deliver and implement just about anything we wanted.

It is quite extraordinary. There are whole armies of people doing who knows what, and it's not just the Cabinet Office. The Ministry of Defence employs 49,000 people; the National Offender Management Service (which I believe operates through the prison service and the national probation service) employs over 42,000. And, given that we have only 85,000 people in prison in this country, that just seems an awful lot. Probably because it is an awful lot.

Yes, there is no getting away from it. Officialdom is like some greedy bacteria let loose in a Petri dish, a dish full of a nutrient agar (our taxes) which is then placed in a nice, warm environment (our acceptance of the clearly unacceptable). And surprise, surprise, it then grows at a bacterial rate and soon becomes completely out of control. Furthermore, as I will now go on to explain, it has a concern only for its own (bacterial) self.

2. Officialdom is not only indefinitely expansionary, it is also irredeemably self-serving. Yes, the officials making it up are concerned only with their own

well-being and how to maintain their cosy, feather-bedded existence right up to their retirement. After which, with gold-plated pensions, they will seek to maintain it until they finally expire.

This is not a slander. It is true. Why else does officialdom seek to maintain the status quo whenever it can, while at the same time stifling any sort of innovation, creativity or even reasonable change? Machiavelli once said 'There is nothing more difficult to take in hand, more perilous to conduct, or more uncertain in its success, as to take a lead in the introduction of a new order of things. It seems that every objection has to be overcome, thus nothing is done, and those vested in the status quo prevail at huge social cost.' I don't know whether he'd just finished a spell of work shadowing at the Home Office or maybe he'd been on secondment to the Treasury, but it does sound as though he'd had first-hand experience of what goes on in any government department you care to mention.

Letting go of that status quo could spell danger – for any official – and who would want to see any sort of change that might just risk that generous salary, more days off a year than you know what to do with, and that ironclad retirement deal when you'd filled in your final expenses form? They do get rewarded very well, considering what they do. And if you doubt this I invite you to examine the payroll details of the local government officials in your nearest city. And if that local city is, say, Bristol, you will find a whole string of 'strategic directors' 'earning' £120 to £130 K a year, even more 'service directors' on £80 to £90 K a year, and more 'service managers' than there are parking places in Bristol on £50 to £60 K a year. And no doubt the majority of these hard-working souls will be in line for a defined-benefits pension when they retire – which is now so costly that fewer than 8% of workers in the private sector can secure this arrangement. These poor sods just have to make do with a defined contributions scheme, the sort of scheme that can never be anything like as good, as it has to somehow cope with the increasing volatility of world markets and, unlike publicly funded defined benefits schemes, it can't rely on the almost empty pockets of taxpayers for as long as is needed. I won't depress you with how much public pensions are now costing us all and by how much this cost is set to rocket, but rest assured it is an eye-watering sum. It makes the Cabinet Office budget look like a mere bagatelle…

Anyway, officials do pretty bloody well. Which is a little ironic because they so often do their job so badly – as I will now touch on.

3. The third characteristic of officialdom is its incompetence. In Britain this stems from a tradition of maintaining a Civil Service full of generalists, people who can turn their hand to ordering aircraft carriers one day and then rejuvenating city centres the next, and probably establishing some strategic priorities for the metrification of allotments the day after that. The trouble is that few of these generalists have what is known in the real world as skills, and

they quite often make a complete balls-up of what they're doing, followed by a further balls-up when they engage the services of expensive but useless consultants who then make matters even worse. IT is an area where all these inadequacies have been honed into almost an art form, and you might not know this, but there is even a Turner prize equivalent that is awarded to whichever abandoned project has eaten up the most millions of pounds.

To be fair, there are a few things that they are capable of – like making questionable and even completely misguided decisions. For example, a clique of anonymous officials meeting somewhere at some time thought it would be a good idea to provide free translation services in our courts and in our health service. The fact that this would cost taxpayers untold millions of pounds and discourage all those who are unable to speak English from ever learning this language was clearly never taken into account. Nor was the offence that this would cause to all those English-speaking taxpayers. But why should those anonymous officials worry? After all, as well as being anonymous, they are bulletproof. Even if they were identified – for this or for any other egregious nonsense, or for some monumental cock-up – they know they'd be safe. Which leads me to my last characteristic of officialdom: its capacity to protect its own.

4. They always get away with it. There is never any comeback, and no matter how badly they perform

they are retained, sometimes in a different post. Or they are even promoted... and promoted and promoted.

I can think of no better example of this than a 'famous' civil servant, whom readers of *Private Eye* will be aware of, whose whole career appears to have been defined by failure and then by repeated promotion. For those of you who are not aware of her I will endeavour to summarise her career path. It goes something like this...

After qualifying as a lawyer and spending her formative years in local government she was eventually made the chief executive of a major English city. Her time there will be remembered not for whatever sterling work she performed in that post but for her achievements as the city's returning officer in a national election. In short there was a scandal surrounding the rigging of postal votes involving Labour candidates, and she drew some criticism from the Electoral Commission along the lines of her being responsible for overseeing an election process that 'would have disgraced a banana republic'. Not something one would want to put in one's CV. But never mind, because this remarkable civil servant was soon made the director general of a national directorate and, after a reorganisation, she was made the first chief executive of the UK agency that concerned itself with the security of our borders. Here was an opportunity for our heroine to redeem herself, which she nearly did... apart from earning herself a minor criticism from the House of

Commons Home Affairs Select Committee, which talked of 'catastrophic leadership failures'.

So with that success under her belt she was then made a Permanent Secretary at a government department, where her only mishap was being accused by Richard Branson of being one of those senior officials at this department who ignored his concerns about the bidding process for the West Coast Main Line rail network – which ended up costing us taxpayers approximately £100 million. This was why she was then elevated to the leadership of a well-known revenue-raising operation, where her reign was punctuated with various ill-informed criticisms by MPs and the House of Commons Public Accounts Committee concerning such matters as entirely unacceptable customer service and disappointing progress on one of its principal roles, namely that of ensuring that its revenue-raising responsibilities were not successfully evaded.

Of course, with a record of public service such as that it was only a matter of time before our Teflon-coated most civil of servants was made a Dame, after which she promptly resigned, and thousands rushed to dedicate a shrine in her honour... Ah, no, that last bit didn't happen. Instead many people were just left feeling slightly bemused and wondering just what one had to do as a civil servant in the highest ranks *not* to be awarded a very high honour. There again, maybe I'm being grossly unfair, and the least I can do is repeat her defence of her position as returning officer all those years ago. Because then, in response to the criticism made by the Electoral Commission, she maintained that she had been in 'strategic and not operational control' and had confined herself to 'motivational management and firefighting'. So that's all right, then.

It doesn't, however, detract from an unavoidable truth: that officials are impervious to blame, often to the extent that their careers can progress no matter how poorly they might have performed. And then they even get a bloody honour! (And incidentally, that's another outrage all on its own. I mean, just examine the New Year's Honours List and compare the number of faceless bureaucrats picking up gongs with the number of scientists and engineers who get anything at all. It's obscene.)

Anyway, enough of what might characterise officialdom. Because I'm now going to examine whether there is any way we can take officialdom on – right here in Britain. And by taking it on, make it smaller, rather less self-serving, competent rather than incompetent – and answerable for its actions on an official-by-official basis. Not an easy ask, I know, but we've got to give it a try – and first by making an almost sensible suggestion…

- Introduce the practice of 'Kaizen' into every government department, agency, local authority and quango. This is the practice developed in Japan after the Second World War (in Toyota, for example) where an organisation seeks to continuously improve all its functions by involving every one of its employees. This worked well in many industries, and there is nothing to stop it being effective in the world of officialdom. Well, in theory there isn't. But I suspect that in practice the habits of our officials are so ingrained that 'continuous improvement' would be seen by them as an exercise in continuously improving their own situation and not that of their department... in which case we might have to move on to remedy number two, which concerns the adoption of a particular zero.

- Yes, it is well known that most government institutions go from one year to the next simply asking for a bit more than they had the previous year. This process should be abandoned, and in its place should be introduced zero-based budgeting. This means that one essentially starts from scratch, not with what you had last year, and everything has to be justified. In fact, to start with, everything has to be remembered. And one wonders whether, at the Department for Communities and Local government, any of the officials will be able to recall that they are nominally responsible for 'neighbourhood planning', 'integration and faith', 'high streets', 'city deals' – and 'deregulation'! And if they can't remember these 'portfolio responsibilities', then they can't get a budget for them, and even if they can remember them, it doesn't follow that they should get a bigger budget than the year before. Although they probably will, which means that we'll at least have to make the officials more productive... with glasshouses.

- Officials are not noted for their work rate. No surprise, really, if they are able to just amble along through the day – hidden behind brick and stone walls. However, if those substantial, solid buildings they now inhabit were sold off and the proceeds used to construct elegant, glass-clad structures – in locations open to public gaze – it might just encourage all those officials to actually do something at their desk other than indulging in social media activities or periods of shallow meditation all day. This idea was actually implemented in Georgia, of all places (only to combat corruption there, not idleness) but it did work. And presumably the corollary of less corruption is more productivity. So it's definitely worth a try, and if it didn't work then we'd have to think of something else – something modelled on the activities of the Stasi…

- The Stasi was the name by which the Ministry of State Security in the old East Germany was known. At its height it was able to conduct a massive spying campaign on all the unfortunate people of that country through the use of a huge network of citizens turned informants. If you lived in a grim block of East German flats anywhere in that benighted country then it was odds-on that somewhere in the block there would be scores of informants, and some of them might be in your own apartment, as they might be members of your own family. Well, such a system has nothing to recommend it... other than it worked. It kept a lid on East German society by keeping everybody in line. Well, you may be there already, but would it be so wrong to introduce a formalised snitching programme into the Civil Service – of which everybody would be aware and of which everybody would take note, because of its accompanying consequences? That is to say that if (through the internal informant network) it became known that you were the biggest shirker in the office you would be out, along with maybe the rest of the worst performers in any year. I mean, it sounds rather unpleasant, but in fact it's not much more than the ultimate inclusive appraisal process, where all your colleagues get a say in how your performance is matching up to their own. There again, it's not very British, is it? And not very nice. Which means we should maybe consider how to reduce numbers not in qualitative terms but in quantitative terms – and the bigger the quantity the better.

- To start with, what we could do is organise a national campaign within the Civil Service whereby each department and agency was required to update its contingency planning – to take account of a dramatic fall in the number of its employed officials as a result of some devastating natural disaster. They would actually welcome this because it's just the sort of thing they like to do: sitting around in meetings discussing which of their department's functions would have to be reduced or abandoned because of its limited resources and which are the functions that would have to be retained at all costs (and without which the operation of the department would be senseless). Then, when all the contingency plans were finalised, the departments would be required to adopt them immediately and operate in accordance with their terms indefinitely, and as many as 70% of their officials would be made redundant. After all, it would be they who had defined what the core functions of their departments were and which of them were subsidiary and therefore dispensable. Simples!

- If this didn't do the job, then what I would suggest is a relocation programme. Shift most of the Civil Service out of London and situate it in locations that might not be seen as entirely attractive to all those metropolitan mandarins. There are plenty of such locations, and I have already identified one for the Department of Culture, Media and Sport. This is in one of the attractive self-contained buildings on the Glasshouse (!) Business Park, a new business park situated in a prominent position off the Warrington Road, Wigan, and conveniently close to Junction 25 of the M6. This would be ideal. It would be inexpensive, big enough to take the 10% of the department's officials who would be prepared to move – and close to (The Road to) Wigan Pier (culture), close to the media courses at Wigan and Leigh College (media), and, of course, close to the home of Wigan Warriors (sport). I'm sure other appropriate sites could be found for every other department, with the result that Britain's Civil Service would be located throughout the length and breadth of Britain and not just concentrated in London, and it would be a (very small) fraction of its current size, despite the attractions of places such as the Glasshouse Business Park near Wigan.

- However, such a relocation programme should not stop us exploring the benefits of automation within officialdom. Because, without a doubt, much of what goes on in officialdom is rather incestuous and only involves officials communicating with other officials – in a way that could be replicated on a modern computer. And I mean a big, modern computer with an appropriate algorithm which, for example, could replace the whole of Her Majesty's Revenue and Customs, other than maybe for one guy who would ensure that a generator kicked in to keep the computer going during a power cut. I mean, just think: it really could do everything, and do it rather better than all those current officials who make all those mistakes with your tax and then who you can't get to talk to. With a robust algorithm there would be no mistakes in the first place, therefore no need to talk to anyone – and no opportunity for unscrupulous big businesses to cut any special deals with the Revenue, like they've done in the past. And there would be no need for a chief executive of HMRC either.

- Right. One last idea to contain officialdom. Just disband it. I don't mean in its entirety, but department by department, agency by agency, and quango by quango. And then just see what happens. Wait to see whether anybody even notices it's not there. In fact, a good place to start would be with something like Ofgem – which is, as I'm sure you all know, an agency that exists 'to protect the interests of electricity and gas consumers'. To do this it requires a budget of £50 million and over 750 employees, who are housed in a nice office block in Millbank in London. Now, I don't know about you, but it seems to me that all that these 750 people ever do is kick up a fuss occasionally about what the electricity and gas suppliers have been doing or not doing, and then the electricity and gas suppliers just carry on and continue to screw everybody, make piles of dosh and pay out piles of dosh to their executives. Which, as far as I'm concerned, isn't much in the way of protection, and frankly, that £50 million would be much better spent if it were simply given as a direct rebate to every electricity and gas user in the county rather than it being lavished on what is no more than a great big official waste of space. And then those 750 officials could go off and get themselves a proper job. You may scoff, but I really would like to see this move put to the test, and I'm sure the electricity and gas suppliers would too…

Anyway, that's my review of officialdom, and a few of the ways we might seek to bring it under control, none of which will ever work, because officialdom has one last characteristic that I failed to mention at the start of this piece. And this is its indestructibility. It is a blight on our lives, but there is no way to remove it. Other than by maybe setting up a central directorate to look at the whole structure of Britain's Civil Service – equipped with a generous budget, probably a complement of 400 to 500 staff, rising to 800 as the directorate moved from its research phase to its planning phase – and probably with an oversight agency, with its own independent establishment, to say nothing of a liaison body which would provide a channel through to all government departments, itself subject to review by another body, the primary role of which would be to…

And you can make up the rest yourself.

> Not what we'd want or what we'd choose
> On life's sweet fruit, an ugly bruise
> A bruise that spreads with startling haste
> Then deep within to spoil life's taste

Population

Imagine for a moment that there are some seven-eyed inhabitants of a planet called Gussitbust in the Crab Nebula, who have been observing the development of human life on our planet for the last ten millennia. And, if you've managed that minor feat of imagination, now try to imagine what aspect of our 'development' might have occupied their attention the most. Would it have been the emergence of settled communities? Would it have been the abandonment of hunter-gatherer cultures in favour of cultures based on agriculture? Would it have been the Teflon qualities of certain religions – in the face of enlightenment? Would it have been the choice of driving on the left or on the right in different countries? Or would it have been the almost universal desire to eliminate unwanted body hair? No. It would be none of these things, because it would be first and foremost the slow-(but not that slow)-motion explosion in the total number of humans on the planet. And it has been an explosion. How else can one describe a population of humans on Earth that has grown from maybe just four million 10,000 years ago to nearly 7,000 million now? And, maybe of more interest to those handsome seven-eyed chaps on Gussitbust, the pace of expansion in this explosion has itself been explosive, with the human population increasing sevenfold in the last 200 years and more than doubling in the last fifty.

Right. Well, the purpose of my introducing these faraway aliens into this particular 'stuff' is because I have become increasingly convinced that, while most people are aware of a growth in the number of people on this planet, most are too close to the phenomenon to appreciate just how 'explosive' this growth has been and continues to be. They therefore need to adopt the same sort of dispassionate perspective that distant aliens might have before they themselves can fully get to grips with the scale – and with the implications – of a species of dominant mammals currently multiplying at a bacterial rate. And there are implications, which make 'Population' as a topic in this tome the most important topic of all. Even if only a few of us will want to admit it…

OK. I can't claim that what I'm going to set out next is particularly stimulating or even mildly entertaining. But it is, I'm afraid, necessary. Because what it is is some figures. And these figures are important because they amplify those population stats referred to above – enough, I hope, to provide the perspective of a seven-eyed alien to you all. I mean, if you think I'm in any way exaggerating the significance of our ballooning as a species then just look at how the balloon has been expanding and how it is predicted to continue to expand.

I'll start with global human population figures which, while inevitably not 100% accurate, are as follows:

Year	Millions
10,000 BC	4
1000 BC	50
1000 AD	400
1804	1,000
1927	2,000
1959	3,000
1974	4,000
1987	5,000
1999	6,000
2011	7,000
2024 (est)	8,000
2037	Pop!

Now, it doesn't need seven eyes to spot that it's taking us very little time these days to pile on another billion – when it took us an absolute eternity to make it to our first billion. I mean, for *that* billion it took us all the time from when we emerged as an identifiable species right up until when Napoleon Bonaparte was proclaimed Emperor of France by the French Senate (in 1804 – which, incidentally, is the same year in which Alicia Meynell became the first woman jockey – in England, of course). Anyway, I hope these figures have adequately illustrated just how explosive/bacterial the expansion of humanity has been, and will continue to be. But, unfortunately, this is not the extent of the unnerving news.

You see, many countries in the West have begun to understand that for life to be good it doesn't necessarily need the lady of the house to be permanently pregnant. In fact, far from it. One, two or even three children actually make for a desirable existence and, for the family's nation, make for the possibility of a stable population. It might even represent a limit on the size of that global balloon, or it would if there weren't a majority of other countries where the male of the species still appears to measure his worth in his ability to inflate both his wife's tummy and his country's already vast population. He may not be able to add too much to the world's store of knowledge, but he has no trouble whatsoever in adding to its stockpile of humans. Anything up to five is good, but nine or ten would be even better...

Which I think means that it's time for some more figures on some of these 'other' countries. These are as follows (with the population figures in millions):

	1950	1985	2015	2050 (est)
Afghanistan	8	13	32	64
Bangladesh	46	102	169	250
Egypt	21	50	88	137
Ethiopia	20	41	99	228
India	369	759	1251	1656
Iran	16	48	81	100
Iraq	5	16	37	76
Kenya	6	20	46	70
Nigeria	31	85	182	391
Pakistan	40	102	199	296
Syria	4	10	17	31

One can make just a few observations about these national statistics, and the first comment might be in a strangled voice and it might entail the use of one or two expletives. However, in the interests of (mostly) profanity-free book-writing, how about just observing that some of these population increases are nothing less than scary? I mean, take Iraq, on course to take just a single century of human history to multiply its human headcount by a factor of fifteen! Not that there aren't other alarming examples in that table – not least Afghanistan, which despite having some of the highest maternal and infant mortality rates in the world, still manages a norm of about seven children per family, which might not be completely unconnected with the rocketing of its number of citizens. Then there is Ethiopia; clearly learning the lessons of its terrible famine in 1985 by increasing its population since that date by 150%, which I suspect isn't necessarily the right way to go about making yourself more resilient to the impact of the next famine…

Another observation that might be made is that those estimated 2050 figures in the statistics might not be borne out, as clearly the compilers of these figures have not factored in the current popularity of emigration in some of these countries. As already discussed under 'Cultures,' and as is apparent on the news every day, burgeoning numbers of these countries' burgeoning numbers are simply relocating themselves to other countries where, for years, the procreation habits of their inhabitants have been more restrained, and as a consequence they are not in the shit – yet. Although, as they are now being obliged to absorb more than their fair share of the current boom in the world's population, they very soon will be.

However, to dwell on the movement of people and the consequences for individual countries is to miss the overriding significance of the out of control population growth on this planet, which is the prospect of a great deal of shit for the whole world and for everything in it.

It cannot be denied that humanity, by expanding to its current level of billions, is already 'infecting' the planet and making it decidedly ill. How else can one characterise the state of this globe when it has had huge swathes of its flora burnt, removed, built on or otherwise destroyed and when every single non-human species of fauna – that we don't eat, milk or use for transport – is at risk of being destroyed as well. Some, of course, have been obliterated already, and tens of thousands more are critically endangered, or their numbers are a fraction of what they were before we started to smother them. And no great surprise. When our focus in all discussions of population growth is on how many humans the world can sustain, it is inevitable that all other 'non-useful' life, whether of the vegetable or the animal variety, will be pushed to the margins – and then over the edge. Quite simply, the Earth can sustain a finite amount of life. The more we grab as our share the less there is for anything else, as any orangutan who has just had his forest nicked to make way for a palm oil plantation will tell you.

Yes, our infection of the world has resulted in that terrible disease called 'impoverishment', a dreadful affliction where diversity and the beauty that comes with diversity both shrivel into non-existence. And, this infection also has a terrible side effect: the spread of despoilment and disfigurement. We may have a store of pretty villages and some nice market towns in Britain, but visit most other countries in the world, and the dominant features of human settlements are concrete, corrugated iron, potholed, litter-lined roads, piles of rubbish and various forms of squalor. 'Ugly' has become our trademark, and along with the thoughtlessness, selfishness and arrogance of our actions it has now scarred the world.

Well, quite an indictment, but I'm afraid that I have to point out that there is another unwelcome symptom of there being too many people on this planet, and this is that much of the conflict that is currently consuming so many countries is a function of too many humans trying to live with too few resources. Whether it's a shortage of water, agricultural land, land for houses, jobs, or indeed any meaningful opportunities, scarcities are now causing people to become belligerent in all sorts of ways. And if you doubt that, I can only advise you to re-examine that table above and consider whether it is conceivable that the meteoric increases in the populations of certain of those countries are not unconnected with both their chronic and their acute troubles.

And finally… we mustn't forget that on top of what we have already done to the Earth there is also the small matter of what we have yet to do. Because it would be remiss of me not to mention global warming, continued deforestation, increasing pollution, accelerated species extinction – and maybe a point in time when the life support system on our single spaceship finally packs up. Oh, and that's our life support system, not the life support systems formerly available to a whole range of beasties and which we long ago switched off.

Bit of a bummer, all this, isn't it? Which does raise the question of whether or not we should do something about it. I mean, shouldn't we try to avert more damage – and if not for the sake of the world's flora and fauna, then for our own sake? So that we aren't left with just the prospect of an empty spaceship drifting through space.

Well, we can do something about it. And here I have changed into absolutely positive mode, because there are indeed some genuinely sensible and genuinely realistic ideas that can be adopted. In the form of a list they are as follows:

- Provide people – of both sexes – with cheap or even free contraception, so that when he wants it for the third time tonight there will be no risk of the third child thereafter.
- Provide education for all – especially for girls – so that they postpone bearing children, ultimately have fewer children and are not intimidated by the current hegemony of testosterone in this world.
- Provide sex education – so that he knows the consequences of his erections.
- Provide, within education systems, instruction on what population growth is inflicting on the world and how it might be better to adopt something other than a gonad-centric perspective in the conduct of one's life.
- Get rid of gender bias in the world's legal systems, in all areas of health and culture and in economic

opportunities, thus giving more power to women and an emphasis to the second point above.
- Put a stop to all policies that reward parents financially on the basis of the number of children they produce (just like we've failed to do in Britain).
- In any tax system, put a price on the environmental costs and impacts of multiple children (just like we've failed to do in Britain).
- Put population growth at the top of the agenda in all national and international deliberations and debates.

So that's sorted – only, of course, it isn't. I mean, can you imagine some of those education and women's rights solutions even getting off the ground in some of our 'problem' countries, and can you imagine even a dominant Conservative Party in Britain abandoning the present ludicrous funding of intemperate sexual habits in favour of penalising all our serial propagators? And furthermore, even if, against all the odds, you were able to implement all these solutions everywhere on the planet, all you would do is slow down the bloating process or maybe arrest its progress entirely and remain at an entirely unsustainable level of ten to twelve billion souls. And frankly, that's not going to cure the patient. It will just defer its demise, and it will make its demise no less painful in the process.

Oh dear, my positive mode seems to have evaporated already. But how can it not, when all I've done is illustrate how the most obvious, sensible solutions are no more than a series of unattainable aspirations that wouldn't work even if they graduated from aspirations? Which only leaves us with the task of looking for some rather more radical solutions. And I think one of the best ways to track down such solutions is first of all to examine how we arrived at our present inflated condition and then to devise how we might not only arrest our 'distendinitis' but put it into remission.

Well, in that case, I think it's really not that difficult to identify the two principal culprits for our ailment. The first of these is a huge increase in agricultural productivity (based on the use of fossil fuels). The second is a lessening of mortality rates due to the improvements made in sanitation and a host of medical advances. So, both ostensibly innocuous little chaps, but working in concert they have been transformational, and quite devastating in their impact. They are also very difficult to deal with, to achieve that remission in our condition that we so desperately need.

Take agricultural productivity. I mean, you could seek to ban fertilisers derived from natural gas and pesticides derived from oil and even ban the use of hydrocarbon-fuelled irrigation and hydrocarbon-fuelled agricultural machinery, but all you would achieve is your suspension from a lamp post. Nobody would consider your plan for a population-slimming pan-famine other than monstrous and deserving of ridicule (and then your deserving of a lamp post). And quite rightly too. So too would any proposals you made to counter the impact of improved sanitation and medical advances, such as placing a moratorium on drug production and giving the NHS and its international counterparts a well-deserved sabbatical so that, for a year at least, diseases were allowed to take their course. And as for reinforcing this measure by removing all safety features in cars, suspending the maintenance programmes for all aircraft, trains and buses and making mandatory the wearing of papier mâché crash helmets... forget it.

Yes, it's no good. Even if people might accept that there are too many of their kind in the world, few, if any, would be prepared to see their numbers reduced in such a heartless and indiscriminate fashion (which might just include them as well).

So, we either have to throw in the towel or we have to become seriously imaginative. In short, we have to think not just outside the box but also outside the box in which that box was delivered – or even outside the container...

Anyway, what we have to think of is not only a way of stemming the rise in human numbers but also how to shrink their numbers, but in a way that won't immediately fall foul of Jon Snow or any other similar unbiased, right-thinking zealot.

Well, I've done some thinking already, and what I've come up with is a short list of practical, compassionate measures that should see the population of humans on this planet entering a period of sustained contraction, even if we're still failing to bring down the birth rates. So, we have:

- An 'exit strategy' based on the techniques adopted by businesses when they need to shed staff. This would entail an offer to anyone prepared to leave this mortal coil of a generous financial package for his or her survivors together with an intensive 'preparation course' where the benefits of oblivion for all eternity would be explained in detail. For example, there would be no more *X Factor*, no more Keith Vaz, no more excessive parking charges – and no more bastards phoning you to sell you double glazing just when you've 'committed to take-off' in the loo. Oh, and there might even be a 'going-away party' as part of the package.

- A new National Lottery offering where, for the opportunity to win much-enhanced prizes, the lottery player signs up to the risk of being landed with a 'losing ticket' – where the 'losing' would refer to his or her life. Of course, this would only stand any chance of being accepted if the terms included the loser's funeral costs being paid, and him or her also getting their face on a batch of the following month's scratch cards.
- On the basis that people will do anything to get on the telly, the introduction of a *Finite Life* programme on Saturday nights (to replace the current dreadful options) where a person's fifteen minutes of fame would be their last fifteen minutes on this Earth. There could be a number of formats for this programme, and to make its whole concept more digestible for the viewing public it would probably need to be featured as the lead item in the first available Children in Need extravaganza.
- The introduction of an honours system based on people's willingness to…

No. They're not going to work, are they? Jon Snow will have a fit – again. And *The Guardian* will have apoplexy. Even the *Daily Mail* will probably have a wobbler. It's futile. We and the rest of the world are doomed by our numbers… unless, of course, we on our own are doomed.

Yes, enough of all this levity. It is time to recognise that as well as our posing a terrible threat to all life on this planet we are also ourselves under threat, and through our own actions.

The most dramatic threat is nuclear annihilation. This would not be very nice – for us or for the rest of the planet – as we devastated everything in sight. Objectively, our extinction through global warming/multiple crop failure/resource depletion/etc might be preferable. But the extinction route that would probably get the vote of all other life forms is a comprehensive pandemic. And, interestingly, this is the route that is probably the most likely.

After all, one of the main reasons for our expansion in numbers is the effective elimination of what were our major predators – through those improvements in sanitation allied to advances in medical science. Yes, we have rid ourselves of a whole host of infectious diseases that were caused by an army of invisible predators in the shape of harmful viruses, bacteria and parasites. And by doing so we have upset the 'balance of nature' and our paltry millions have become billions. That said, we have tended to ignore what is the hallmark of these various pathogenic biological agents, and that is their resilience.

They have been around for millions of years –

compared to our own rather more brief tenancy on this world. This long ancestry has enabled them to learn how to survive. They might have received a bashing, but they are already working out how to fight back, and how, through mutation or through overproducing themselves, they are able to overcome the effectiveness of antibiotics. They are even able to assimilate an antibiotic gene from another bacterium to achieve the same end. And, of course, while they are successfully regrouping, all we are doing is helping them – either by overusing antibiotics on ourselves or on the animals we breed for food, or by providing them with a rapid transport system around the world, courtesy of the world's many airlines.

Well, I think it might be unwise of me to comment further on the world's excessive human population or whether, in the not too distant future, it will balloon further or collapse overnight. So all I will do is reiterate my opening remarks about the overriding significance of overpopulation in this list of various stuff, and conclude with the opinion that whether we survive or whether our ancient predators finish us off we have a tragedy on our hands either way. And I'm sure the folks on Gussitbust would not disagree…

> For eons long, the Earth remained
> A place of charm where nature reigned
> And then came men – and women too
> Not hordes of them, but just a few
>
> So years went by and all was fine
> For deer and thrush and oak and pine

Until the day the human race
Commenced a surge – at quite a pace

And with this surge it wasn't long
Before the few became a throng
A throng of such a super size
It won itself a super prize

The prize, of course, was Earth itself
A world that still enjoyed good health
But not for long, as man got round
To making off with all he found

And burning up and chopping down
And turning green to muddy brown
And trapping here and killing there
And even screwing up the air

So now the Earth is very ill
And hopes and prays and waits until
That stupid race, it starts to shrink
Or, better still, becomes extinct…

Quaggas

OK... If you've just read all that stuff about population you may be feeling just a little bit battered. Well, sorry, but you're now about to feel even more battered, more battered than a piece of haddock that's been tripled battered and then battered again in a desperate attempt to win back the battered Mars bar brigade in Scotland. And if that makes no sense, then neither does our treatment of the quagga.

The quagga, for those of you who don't know, was a subspecies of the plains zebra that lived in South Africa up until the nineteenth century. It was distinguished from other zebras by having, instead of obvious black and white stripes on its body, a partial pattern of primarily *brown* and white stripes – with its back half being brown and without stripes of any sort. In fact, it looked a little like a badly coloured-in zebra fading into a plain old donkey at its rear. It wasn't the most exotic of animals or even the most beautiful, but it was a distinct animal that had probably taken thousands of years to evolve into one of the many precious ornaments that adorn this world. Until, of course, *we* came along...

Yes, when the Dutch settled in South Africa, rather

than sticking just their fingers into dykes, they began to get the whole of themselves stuck into hunting instead. More particularly, they began to hunt the quagga because it competed with their domestic animals for food. And, being Dutch, they made a pretty good job of it, and the quagga became extinct in the wild by 1878. The last captive specimen died in Amsterdam on 12 August 1883. Presumably they'd taken him there to illustrate just how little effort was required to eliminate one single subspecies, but how much more effort would be required to succeed in eliminating a whole raft of not simply subspecies types but species types as well. In fact, it would clearly need a lot more humans. An awful lot more. And lo and behold, as explained under 'Population', that's exactly what they got.

This increase in 'human resources' didn't come about immediately, and for years mankind had to struggle on and make a really concerted effort to bring to an end the existence of even a single non-human life form. But mankind managed very well, and racked up a number of remarkable successes. One of these has to rank as one of the very best: the extinction of the 'Tasmanian Tiger' or, to give it its correct name, the Thylacine.

This was an extremely handsome carnivorous marsupial, native to continental Australia, Tasmania and New Guinea, which by the 1930s, having been 'helped' by human activity, existed as merely a remnant population in just Tasmania. Here, because of the Thylacine's inability to make friends with sheep, a bounty system had been introduced as long ago as the 1830s, which meant that this remnant population was a very small one and could easily be dealt with. Yes, with the assistance of some competition from introduced domestic dogs, the erosion of its habitat and the clever ploy of also exterminating its prey species, it was only a matter of time before Tasmanian Tigers were 'tidied up' completely. And so it was, in the latter part of 1930, that the last wild Thylacine was shot by a farmer with the most appropriate of names, one modern-day hero by the name of Wilf Batty. He, of course, was not allowed to shoot within the confines of zoos, and we had to wait another six years before the last captive poor bugger died and we could claim total victory over yet another one of our fellow creatures. But no matter. The time for hard-won eliminations of just the odd species here and there was soon to be over. With our burgeoning population we could now turn what had been a small-scale cottage industry into a full-blown factory operation. We could now eliminate species not just by the score but by the fucking hundreds…

So far we've done pretty well. It is reckoned that we've now brought the total number of species extinctions caused by humans since 1500 up to nearly 800, and the truth of the matter is that we will undoubtedly have been responsible for far, far more, but we just haven't noticed. And frankly, why would we? After all, if a species gets anywhere near extinction then it is indisputable that its final demise will have a negligible impact, and therefore it won't be noticed.

OK, it's time to get a little less flippant and to admit that extinctions are just part of the natural process. That is to say that it has been calculated that more than 99% of all species the world has hosted (since the world started to host them) are now extinct. So extinction is hardly a new or novel phenomenon. However, that process of species extermination took hundreds of millions of years, and was slow enough to allow the emergence and development of new species. This is not so now. We, with our explosion in numbers, have introduced the first-ever species-caused mass extermination of other species. Yes, we have introduced the 'Holocene extermination', a human-caused mass extermination that has no parallel in the Earth's history. And if you doubt that this is true then just suck on this:

- The current rate of extinctions is 100 to 1,000 times the 'background' rate of extinctions (i.e. the average extinction rate over the evolutionary timescale of our planet).
- This current rate is anticipated to accelerate very soon to a rate that will be 10,000 times the background rate.
- With this acceleration it is estimated that up to half of the plant and animal species that presently exist in the world may become extinct by 2100.
- There are already almost 5,000 plants and animals on the 'critically endangered' list (plants and animals facing a very high risk of extinction).
- There are even more on the 'endangered' list (plants and animals that are likely to become extinct).
- There are almost 10,000 on the 'vulnerable' list (plants and animals that are likely to become endangered unless the circumstances threatening their survival and reproduction are improved).

- There are also loads of life forms on the 'near threatened' list (likely to become endangered in the near future) and even more where there is insufficient data to evaluate their status or the evaluation process has not been conducted. But I think I'm sufficiently depressed already, and I shall not be reporting their combined number here, especially as I have already reported that we will have lost one half of all our species in just eighty-five years' time!

Well, to cheer us up I think it might be worth taking just a little time to consider how we are actually going about our wholesale eradication of life on Earth. And you can't get away from it. We have been quite resourceful, hard-working and really very imaginative in our approach.

Our major tool has, of course, been our weight of numbers and what this means in terms of our demands on the resources – and the land area – of this planet. We have had to destroy or degrade the habitat of countless creatures – to plant our crops, to provide grazing for our animals… and inevitably to build, to rebuild, to build some more and ultimately to take the art of urban sprawl to a disgusting new level. And we mustn't forget the terrible impact of our logging, our mining, our 'extractive industries' (I like that one) and even some of our fishing practices, such as the use of bottom trawling in order to utterly destroy an ocean floor and annihilate everything above it and upon it.

But we've used other tools as well, and we still do. There's hunting – and overhunting, of course. There's the elimination of animals because they get on our tits – or, at least, on to our crops or on to the land on which we keep our farmed animals, where they then steal their food. And then there's large-scale pollution, which can either kill species through contamination of their environment or more directly through poisoning them or making them sterile. And how about one of the most sophisticated devices of all: the introduction of an invasive species!

This is a corker, and there is an option to do it quite unintentionally or as a result of a thoughtless and reckless venture. It works on the premise that the introduced species will establish itself and then affect native species – by eating them, competing with them or introducing pathogens and parasites that will either kill them directly or by screwing up their habitat. Fantastic! And better still, we have even been allowed on a few occasions to play the invasive species ourselves. Yes, it's not immediately obvious, but, of course, when we arrived in places like Australia 40,000 years ago – or in North and South America, 12,000 years ago – we were barging in on an environment full of animals that had never seen us before and were therefore completely at a loss in how to deal with our particular 'predation techniques'. The result was the swift extinction of all the mega fauna in almost half of the world, and a desire on the part of mankind to repeat its success elsewhere. Step forward those mammoths in Eurasia just a little while later, and then a whole raft of critters in Madagascar and New Zealand when we got round to them. The trouble is that the only place in the world where mega fauna exists in worthwhile numbers now is Africa, and to mop this lot up we're going to have to rely not on our invading them as a pernicious species but instead on some determined poaching, backed up as necessary by the impact of human-caused climate change. And let's face it, we have got them on the run already. I mean, most of them feature in one of those endangered or vulnerable lists above, and there are more than one or two absolutely outstanding examples. Take African elephants; down from a population of maybe five million in the 1940s to just 700,000 now. And better still, black rhinos; 900,000 in 1900 to less than 5,000 now – and wild dogs, creatures that used to be counted in their hundreds of thousands and were found in thirty-three African countries, now down to just 6,500, spread across a mere fifteen countries.

Ah, but we've got those game reserves, haven't we? So nasty mankind will now be kept at bay. Or he would if all these reserves were secure, if all the elephants and their mates knew where the boundaries of the reserves were and didn't wander into the unprotected areas outside and, when constrained within the reserves, these same beasts didn't procreate to outstrip the available resources and then find themselves the unwilling subjects of a culling project.

God. What an unadulterated friggin' mess! And we can do nothing about it. OK, I do accept that there might now be a recognition of just how much damage we're doing to this world and a desire to protect what we haven't yet ruined. After all, it's generally recognised now that 'biodiversity' is good – for us. And that by retaining as many of the world's species as we can we will be maintaining a genetic resource and reinforcing the stability of an ecosystem that we ourselves rely on (indeed, the only ecosystem we've got). Oh, and quite a few of us recognise that, as the current custodians of this world, it might be our ethical duty not to obliterate all those animals that aren't of some use to us – as food or beasts of burden, say. But… all we can do is create a few reserves and embark on a few captive breeding programmes or some other sort of conservation project in the full knowledge that the overwhelming majority of humankind will still prioritise their day-to-day survival over any attempts to stem the impact of their numbers and their habits. 'My manioc is more important than those stupid macaques – and don't you know I now have seven children to feed?' (Or, to retain some balance, 'We just couldn't resist this iroko table. And the eight chairs. And the other table with the four chairs. And iroko is… errh, well… you know, sustainable. At least, that's what the man in the shop told us…')

This discussion of the impact of humans on all other forms of life on this planet should really be set on a beach in northern Denmark, with a cold, windswept sea lapping on the shore and an ominous grey sky above. Because it's all irredeemably depressing, and it isn't going to get any better.

Indeed, flippancy can get you so far. But then you have to admit that all that bad news above and all those figures quoted above for the lists of endangered species really do mean something. Like, included somewhere in those lists is virtually every iconic animal in the world. And that's iconic in the sense of chimpanzees, rhinos (of course), cheetahs, hippos, lions and... well, just about every animal you'd ever go to Africa to see, along with pangolins, lemurs, gibbons, orangutans and a whole treasure trove of other living jewels. Furthermore, the real bummer is that the havoc we are wreaking should not be measured just in terms of the extinctions we have caused and are still to cause, but also in the overall impact we have had on every manifestation of the natural world. And what I mean by that is that we may have failed to wipe out lots of species up to now but, by golly, we've wiped out lots of individual creatures and lots of individual plants. In fact, we must have wiped out billions and billions of them. Because, one cannot deny that for every acre of land we grab for ourselves that is one less acre for 'them', for all those poor creatures and plants that once occupied that patch of land and are now unlikely to find a new home and will therefore die (if we didn't actually kill them as part of the process of nicking their acre). Essentially there is a finite area of land on this world, and a finite number of resources – on that land and in the sea – and the more we take for ourselves the less there is for anything else. Yes, we are not just a mass extermination event. We are also the biggest fucking usurper there's ever been. We are busy supplanting any sort of life form that gets in our way and are well on course to reduce our planet to no more than a miserable shadow of its former self.

I know what you're thinking now. You're thinking 'Hyperbole'. And I willingly admit that as a species we don't go out of our way to exterminate other species – necessarily – and that we don't usurp every other creature on this planet. There are a number of life forms that co-exist with us very happily and there are others that thrive as a result of our worldwide domination, like tapeworms, head lice and, in those societies that have not yet embraced intimate grooming, pubic lice. I also admit that some serious efforts are being made to conserve a whole swathe of creatures, and people are even dying in an effort to protect fragile reserves and the animals who live within their bounds. In fact, I am humbled by just how many people seek to do something positive and really demanding rather than just sitting down and writing a book in the comfort of their homes. However, the fact remains that we have only an impoverished future ahead of us, and many creatures have no future ahead of them at all.

Just consider: it is virtually inconceivable that the human population of this planet will not just continue to increase. Even if it plateaus out, its constituent greedy bastards will inevitably want more 'stuff' – more of all that stuff we greedy bastards in the West already take for granted. They will also not release themselves from the shackles of a series of religions which, while retaining their confrontational differences, will continue to be in agreement on one fact alone. And this fact is that humans are all incredibly special and that the rest of life on this planet is un-special/subsidiary/incidental/secondary, and only there for us humans to make use of/remove/abuse – and, if necessary, to exterminate and ultimately make extinct. And I have to say that this human/other life distinction is now so firmly rooted in our consciousness and in our way of life that even the most generous philanthropists in the world (from places like Silicon Valley) are only concerned with humanity and not with life in general. And if I wanted to be particularly cruel and unreasonable I could even say that their laudable efforts, if successful, will only exacerbate the problems for other than humans. How can they not if they result in more of us and, by definition, in fewer of those inconsequential others – all those many members of the world's fauna and flora that don't really count?

So we're in the year 2085. Jenny, our new granddaughter, is now a sprightly young seventy and has grandchildren of her own. And when she thinks about her grandchildren's future she is even more despondent than I am. In fact, she feels desolate – and guilty. Humanity's numbers didn't plateau out quite according to plan, and this continued surge in our numbers required not just some novel agricultural developments (and some plundering of the oceans) but also every acre of dry land we could get our hands on (and that we hadn't already built on, poisoned, planted with landmines, lost through global warming or otherwise consumed). Inevitably this meant that most of Africa, South America and continental Asia went under the super-ploughs, and we had to clear a lot of forest and then a lot more forest – and we also had to nibble away at some of those game reserves and national parks.

In fact, we had to gobble some of them up completely, and where we limited ourselves to just a nibble... well, it wasn't necessarily the smallest of nibbles. Which wasn't quite as bad as it sounds – because quite a few of these places had been poached out entirely. They were virtually empty of game already.

That said, there are some reserves still in place...

although, to be honest, they are more in the nature of outdoor ghettos. And without elephants, rhinos, hippos, cheetahs and – well, anything much bigger than a jackal – they are not very inviting places. It has even been said that the tsetse flies have now abandoned them, as there is nothing for them to feed on. It was a good decision, really, to put those last two giraffes and, from Borneo, those last three orangutans, into those two zoos. So Jenny's grandchildren can at least see on their tablets what a real living wild animal looks like. I mean, when they first saw the last hammerhead shark in that aquarium in Shanghai they could hardly believe it… no more than Jenny can believe that a 'wildlife encounter' these days means a glimpse of an urban fox or a brown rat, or a confrontation with a 'sensationally lifelike' hologram at one of the many Google Virtual Game Reserves… complete with genuine tropical humidity and permanent special deals on a Big (soya) Mac and fries.

Yes, in a way, the quagga was lucky. He was dispatched quickly. He didn't have to suffer in the same way that so many other species suffered. That was a long drawn-out process of hunting and hounding and poaching and poisoning and being corralled into tiny plots of land that, as it turned out, were no more than waiting rooms for death. One by one they were eliminated. Sometimes it was a disease, sometimes the demand for a Yemeni janbiya (for which a rhino horn was essential) or, more often than not, the demand for bush meat. And of course there was also that demand in China for something to carve, for something to make into an obscene, tacky trinket – for someone with obscene, tacky tastes.

Well, all I can say is that the Danish beach with

its windswept sea and its overcast sky is now looking remarkably attractive. Compared to what this whole world will look like and how spartan it will be, much sooner than we think, it already has a certain charm. And as we sit on the beach we could contemplate in peace how we are so thoroughly denuding this world of its living wonders, how we are visiting so much pain and distress on those we have yet to erase… and how, as supposedly intelligent beings, we are acting in such a stupid fucking way.

We are just awful.

> The chimpanzees have had their time
> The pangolins have too
> And polar bears, although they're cute
> Well, they're now overdue
>
> And so it is with turtles green
> And rhinos white and black
> And as for ellies brown and grey
> They too have trunks to pack
>
> We've worked so hard for many years
> To clear these beasts away
> And some were slow to see our point
> That we alone should stay
>
> But in the end they understood
> That on this ravaged Earth
> It's just ourselves and nothing else
> That's blessed with any worth…

Religion

With this particular 'stuff' I have to issue a notice. Or even two notices. In the first place, in my critique of religions, I have ignored any aspect of their charitable activities or their involvement in such institutions as hospitals, hospices and shelters. This is because I am not a perfect human being and I have no intention of undermining the prosecution's case, no matter how strong this case might be. In the second place I have been entirely indifferent to the succour that so many adherents to religion claim they receive. This is not just because I am an imperfect specimen of mankind who does not want to scupper the prosecution's prepared assault, but also because I think that these adherents would be well advised to change their habits. They might find comfort by embracing a bundle of improbable beliefs, but would they not be happier and healthier if they confronted the reality of the world and accepted that real spirituality is all around them – in the shape of the natural world? If they did, not only would they reap a benefit but so too would that natural world, the same natural world that most belief systems regard as irrelevant other than in respect of what it can provide to man, and which is consequently being trashed.

Let me illustrate this latter point by inviting you do decide which of the following actions has the most merit. These are:

- Watching another mindless episode of *Strictly Come Dancing*
- Asking for another (selfish) favour through divine intervention
- Clearing that little pond to help next year's tadpoles
- Assaulting Ken Livingstone with a frozen cucumber
- Seeking solace by making yet another visit to Hotel Irrational
- Listening to *Faith Healer* by the Sensational Alex Harvey Band, and
- Doing anything whatsoever on social media.

Well, I'll give you a clue. It has nothing to do with favours or seeking solace but quite a lot to do with frogs (although some old rockers might just disagree). And my point is that subjugating oneself to 'faith' is not just a denial of intellect but also a positively unhealthy habit, both for the denier and for the whole of the world.

Anyway, with the above two notices delivered, it is now time to invite you to read on and to discover what religion is really all about.

So… if I had been around a few thousand years ago I would have been an animist. Having experienced rainbows, lightning, partial eclipses, the transit of the sun across the sky every day and, hopefully, orgasms (although not necessarily every day), I would have been first in the queue to ascribe all this stuff to something supernatural. And, as I would be living in very much the natural world, it is here that I would have sought the home of this 'spiritual essence' – in stuff like animals and plants or maybe in a male-genitalia-shaped rock. And who could have blamed me? In the first place I would actually have been exercising my intellect, in the sense that I was seeking answers for stuff that I could not understand – and in the second place this exercise would not have been too demanding, in that the rest of my tribe would have been practising the very same sort of 'pre-religious' existence.

However, if I had been unusually smart I would possibly have noticed that my beliefs, no matter how apparently rational they might be, were beginning to be the subject of exploitation. To start with there was that so-called shaman guy who claimed he knew which plants were the most supernatural, and therefore the most efficacious when made into various so-called 'healing infusions' – before he then went one better by announcing that he could now intercede with the supernatural powers directly (on our behalf), and for only a bucketful of millet. And then there was old Muglug, the head of the tribe who, having past his physical best, was now keen to stress that his legitimacy as our leader was very much based on his having been 'chosen' by all those spirits we believed in (and wasn't just the result of opportunism following the demise of our previous leader when he fell in the swamp).

So… it would be bizarre if, as a species, our belief in the supernatural had not endured and then developed, ultimately, into the religions we know today. For not only were we still surrounded by the inexplicable, and therefore in need of some sort of spiritual anchor in our lives, but we also had a succession of people who were only too willing to utilise our needs for their own (not necessarily spiritual) ends.

Who can argue that all those padres, pastors, preachers and priests, as well as tending to our spiritual requirements, weren't also making a very good life for themselves, and generally a far better life than that enjoyed by most of their flock? They traded in religious belief in the same way that others traded in turnips or candles, only in a much more rewarding manner. And that's true even if there were genuine good guys among their number who really put the spiritual and indeed the temporal well-being of their 'sheep' before the continued comfort they enjoyed, courtesy of their sheep's enforced generosity. Similarly, there was barely a monarch anywhere in the world who, however tyrannical, wouldn't claim that he had God on his side, that he was a fervent upholder of whatever established religion was practised in his realm and that he had a divine right to rule his kingdom. Indeed, there were many who went one better by claiming that they were actually descended from some god. Or, better still, that they had become gods themselves and now required all the devotion that had, years before, been directed to the biggest fig tree in the forest. Oh, and if the standing clergy went along with the claim they could expect an indefinite period of royal protection, increased perks, and probably a sybaritic fully funded retirement plan...

And they wouldn't have their heads chopped off.

Well, before moving on (and in the interests of impartiality), I should admit that these burgeoning religions didn't just satisfy the needs of the innocent believers, the sometimes not so innocent clergy and the very rarely innocent ruling elite. They also provided a set of beliefs concerning the nature and the purpose of the universe and of the superhuman agency that created the universe, together with an established series of devotional observances that were necessary to ensure one didn't upset this agency and end up in hell. Additionally, and most importantly, these religions provided their followers with a moral code that was designed to govern the conduct of their lives.

Now, this happyish state of affairs could have continued indefinitely. Exploitation, bigotry, intolerance, fanaticism, narrow-mindedness and blatant misogyny could have been maintained without interruption until the end of days. But, unfortunately for all those pedlars and abusers of religions (and despite their best efforts), an enlightenment emerged in at least one part of the world, and it was an enlightenment that ultimately would see such an advance in mankind's understanding of the universe that all religions would be relegated to the level of embarrassing myths – overnight. Well, if only…

Yes, we may now have an insight into the origins and workings of the universe and of our place within it that would have been inconceivable just a few hundred years ago. However, so engrained is the 'habit' of religious belief and so forcefully is it upheld by the religious establishment that these religions are still with us, and perversely, some of them have a firmer grasp of their adherents than they've ever had. It is appalling, and it is a dereliction of our human intellect of the highest order. Or, more likely, it points not to a dereliction of our intellect, or even a wanton disregard of our intellect but to a fundamental inadequacy in our intellect, or at least in the intellect of all those people who appear blind to what we now know about the cosmos and about our own tiny world.

To emphasise this point I am going to discuss some of the inexplicable aspects of 'world religions' within the context of our current understanding of our world and of the universe as a whole. But, before I do this, I wish to make clear that my discomfort is not with the existence of something or other that created the universe (although, if there is something, what created 'It'), but more with the idea that our religions are really anything to do with this 'It' in their portrayal of it/him as some nice old bearded guy who is not only responsive to our behaviour but who has also created the whole of the universe for our very own benefit. After all, mankind on this planet is supposedly the focus of his attention, and everything else in the cosmos and everything else in the world is just a very elaborate backdrop for humanity's exclusive existence.

OK. Let's start with the size of the universe. Best estimates are that it contains 100,000,000,000,000,000,000,000 stars. This means that it may well contain 50,000,000,000,000,000,000 habitable Earthlike planets. And, before you suggest that my keyboard got stuck on the zeros, I might just say that I have already discounted that number of habitable planets by three of those zeros. It is quite possible that there are a thousand times more little Earths out there than I'm claiming. And frankly, whichever way you cut it, there are an unimaginable number of other third rocks from the Sun, many of which will be equipped with the same 'Goldilocks' environment that we enjoy right here on Earth. In view of this I find it inconceivable that something out there thought it was a good idea to indulge in an exercise of such mind-boggling extravagance for the exclusive benefit of a handful of upright apes on just one of those planets, on just one piddling little pebble at the arse end of one of the less fashionable galaxies in the universe. The idea is an affront to even the weakest of intellects, but sadly, it is either accepted – or ignored – by billions of his chosen race on this planet… possibly because all those noughts are just too difficult to deal with.

So, let's now look at just the Earth, a planet now coming up to its 4.54 billionth birthday, and a planet that has had some sort of life on it for almost 4.1 billion years. However, for most of the time this life hasn't bothered too much with religion. Not being 'complex multicellular' for the first two billion years, it couldn't really cope with even the simplest of myths, and it certainly couldn't get down to kneel. In fact, even that animism I started off with didn't put in an appearance until *Homo sapiens* evolved out of *Homo heidelbergensis* about 150,000 years ago. Now, this is peculiar. I mean, who in his or her right mind would wait 4.54 billion years (150,000 years is just 0.003% of that total, and therefore gets lost in the roundings) to create his chosen children, having already waited 9.3 billion years after the creation of the universe to create their home planet, Earth? Put that script to even the dopiest BBC commissioning editor and he'd laugh his socks off, just before he decided to call security. No, waiting that long can't just be put down to a lack of a sense of urgency. It can only be put down to a wilful denial on the part of the faithful of what is clearly nonsensical. And that is nonsensical in much the same way as was a particular choice of location and timing...

Yes, we now have to address the fact that three of the world's religions were initiated in the Middle East and rather a long time ago (in our terms). Well, hold a global vote on where in the world might claim to be the most rational and orderly and honest and peaceful, and I can guarantee that nowhere in the Middle East would even register in the results. That patch of the planet is, and it has been throughout its history, a place of antagonism and open conflict and, in my mind, it constitutes the most peculiar choice of a birth channel for any religion that one could possibly imagine (unless, of course, those religions were rather less divine in their emergence than the religions would have us believe.) Then there is that timing. The world, two millennia ago, had just 300 million people and no twenty-four-hour news programmes, no Facebook and no Twitter. So why, if you'd waited 4.54 billion years (having already waited 9.3 billion years to create the Earth) would you not wait just 2,000 years more, when you could then have an audience of not just 300 million for your message but 7,000 million? Furthermore, rather than having to depend on word of mouth – and the possibility that the mouth might be permanently closed in somewhere like the Middle East – you could book yourself a prime-time slot on NBC, a syndicated hour-long interview on Al Jazeera, CNN and the BBC... and, to get through to all those younger sheep, you could easily open your own Facebook page and your own Twitter account.

OK. Some of you might well have thrown this book on the fire by now, and others of you will have begun to have some sympathy for all our world religions and all their adherents. Because, as I willingly admit, I am being a bit rude about them. However, the status of religions in our modern societies is rarely challenged on the basis of their total irrationality, as I have attempted to do above. And they do need to be challenged in this way, if we ever want to emerge into the sort of post-religious future that should have begun to spread around the world about 150 years ago – but didn't.

I'm sorry, but I don't think mankind is helping itself by clinging on to religious beliefs. Indulge in spirituality by all means, but don't continue to embrace what has now been discredited; something that has been shown to be a possibly well-meaning product of ignorance but that is now so archaic as to be ridiculous. Most of us learn to dispense with a belief in Father Christmas and fairies, but far too few of us are able to dispense with what is equally fantastic: a responsive, supernatural being known for his extravagance, his tardiness and his poor judgement in terms of timing and choice of location. And this does matter, because religions today are without question causing us quite a few problems…

Let's start with conflict. Because it is irrefutable that religions now play a primary role in just about every sort of conflict in the modern world, other than maybe the sort of domestic conflict that takes place behind closed doors when Sarah discovers that her meek and mild husband Jeremy has extended his knowledge of Deborah next door into the arena of 'carnal'. But as regards the real, bullets-flying, bombs-exploding-type conflicts, it's a pretty fair bet that it will be one set of believers trying to knock the shit out of another set of believers. Or it might even be one strand of one belief trying to annihilate a different strand of the same belief.

This is not to say that mankind is not stupid enough to engage in deadly combat in the absence of religions, as twentieth-century history has demonstrated on a number of occasions. But the truth is that 'secular rivalry' of the sort witnessed in World War II has had to admit total defeat in the face of the religion-inspired struggles that now prevail in the world. Belonging to any religion these days is tantamount to being identified as the enemy by the followers of another religion. And worse still, in the eyes of certain religious types, even those of us who have prized ourselves away from religions are regarded as foes, or possibly worse than foes: just as something to be done away with.

It's appalling and senseless and depressing, and it isn't going to get any better anytime soon. And it won't get any better before we achieve the impossible and bring to an end the widespread practice of child abuse in the form of religious indoctrination.

This really is impossible for as long as religions remain disconnected from any sort of spirituality and remain essentially a cover for a variety of traditional cultural practices that can be described as anything between rather disagreeable and totally obscene.

It is very sad; generations of children who are recruited to the cause of a particular religion before they can possibly have any comprehension of even the meaning of that religion and well before their balls have dropped – if they are boys. So, without any trouble at all, we churn out more Christians, Muslims, Jews – and Mormons, never accepting that this is no more than a molestation of an innocent mind and should rank alongside the physical abuse of children as one of the worst possible crimes in the world. To beat a child is despicable. To snare that child into any form of obsolete thinking from the past is even worse. Educate him in the survival of any number of religions, but don't recruit him to their cause – or to the cause of one religion in particular: the religion into which you were press-ganged when you were his age. It's just cruel, and it has a negative effect. Not just on the prospects for world peace and an absence of explosive devices, but also on the abused one's very nature...

Yes, I now want to address one of the very worst aspects of religious indoctrination and of religions per se, and this concerns something that I have suspected for years but which has now been proved through academic research. And this is that children brought up in religious households are hindered in their moral development compared to those who are lucky enough to be nurtured in an atheist or agnostic environment.

Difficult to believe, especially when the light, guiding hand of the Church of England, say, has been used to great effect in many English households and has led to the emergence of generations of well-balanced, relatively kind-hearted souls who quite often go on to renounce religion entirely but don't, at the same time, become highly undesirable, evil-minded psychopaths. But it's true, and it involved a study of more than 1,100 children from around the world as part of a research project ultimately reported in *Current Biology*.

This project examined the impact on the altruistic behaviour of children and whether this varied according to their home circumstances. In other words, it was attempting to discover whether children brought up in secular families were more selfish than those brought up in religious families, or vice versa. Well, the results were astounding, and clear-cut. Basically, the (impartial) researchers found that those poor sods brought up in a religious environment were noticeably more selfish than those denied the guiding light of myth, and the more often the little sods went to church or the mosque the worse the effect. Essentially there was a consistent link between the piety in a household and the youngsters in these households not putting their piety into practice, at least when it came to their willingness to share anything with others. Furthermore, it was discovered that while their pious parents believed them to be more sensitive to injustice and more empathetic in general the reverse was true. Children from religious households were measurably more judgemental of others than were their religion-starved counterparts, and they were noticeably harsher in terms of their tendency to want to punish. It is apparently something to do with what's been termed 'moral licensing'. And what this means is the tendency of children (and adults) to use something 'good' to justify something 'bad', often without even realising that they're doing so. Consequently, the religious types come to believe that they have done something good simply by being religious and that this gives them the licence to do something bad. It's as though, having done something that helps reinforce their positive self-image, they then become less concerned about the possible impact of immoral behaviour and are therefore more likely to make immoral choices.

This is pretty heavy stuff. But there again, it is no more than many of us have observed for ourselves: the unwarranted righteousness of the painfully righteous in the face of overwhelming evidence of their wrongness, and the actuality that societies that base their values on religion are far less peaceful and far less 'healthy' in general than those that utilise secular values in the conduct of their affairs. Or maybe it is more. Because, if one thinks about it, what this research is saying is that it is by no means obvious that religion – in any form – is vital for an individual's moral development. In other words, the secularisation of childhood does not lead to a reduction in human kindness, but to quite the reverse. Which, QED, means that religions are not just ridiculous, obsolescent, a cover for questionable cultural practices, counterproductive in the way we care for the

Earth and the cause of most of the deadly conflicts in the world today, but that they are also a genuinely negative force in our development as kind and considerate human beings. To which I might add that religions do not, in my opinion, assist in developing an open mind. They close things down, and some of their most extreme manifestations don't just close things down, they put them out of action completely. And they certainly don't nourish enlightenment – or kindness.

So take your pick. Join them and be part of a monstrous problem, or go and clear out that pond. You'll probably find me there in my waders.

> There were these three chaps called the Trinity
> Who owned just a lot of infinity
> This wasn't enough
> And they wanted some stuff
> Which is why there's now us and divinity
>
> A Christian man, he loathed and feared
> His fellow man with straggly beard
> The same was it true
> For the Hindu and Jew
> And the Mormons… He just thought them weird

Sex

Sex can be found in Sussex, Essex, Middlesex County Cricket Club and in just about every facet of human life. Yes, sex isn't quite ubiquitous, but it does seem to wheedle its way into more or less every feature of our existence and it certainly shapes the way we live. And, to emphasise the unique hold it has on all of us, I would like to discuss this sex stuff in just a little detail and, to start with, provide an explanation of how it really does shape our lives, as reflected in the way we organise our societies.

You see, there have been various studies to establish why, as a species, we have adopted as a societal norm the practice of monogamy. That is to say, we form a sexual relationship with just one partner (formally, at least). It was first thought that there was a biological argument to support this choice, in that the demands of parental care within an environment of scarce or unreliable resources militated against any sort of polygamy. However, that view has now been largely discounted, in that genetic evidence exists which suggests that sexual polygamy was all the rage for humans right up until 10,000 to 5,000 years ago. Or at least it was in Europe and Asia.

In Africa and in the Americas the human male was into multiple partners until even more recently. And who knows, it might still be going on in the backwoods of the Appalachians even now. Although, there again, it won't be if those Appalachian folks are now all farmers…

Yes. Quite simply, men abandoned polygamy in favour of monogamy when humans abandoned nomadism in favour of sedentary farming, and they did this, it appears, in order to keep their property (their land) within their 'nuclear family'. Indeed, it has been said that the absence of a plough is the only predictor of the practice of polygamy. And it could also be said that we now know for a fact that farmers really do prefer a tractor or maybe a nice new muck spreader to an even stunningly attractive second wife.

Anyway, once monogamy had become established for practical reasons it soon found itself reinforced by cultural expectation and then by various interested parties, such as the pedlars of nascent religions and those at the top of the pile. Yes, the elite could always spot a way of harnessing a societal development for their own ends, and the adoption of monogamy was no different, even if it meant that they had to modify their own sexual behaviour. After all, if you, as an aristocrat or a member of a royal family, were keeping the number of children you had to a minimum (to protect your legacy) that didn't mean that you couldn't still copulate with as many ladies as you wanted to – outside the partnership. And, indeed, that's what they often did. No surprise, really. Because the 'natural' behaviour of the human male must still be that of having it off with as many partners as he can find, and one only has to observe what is going on in our modern societies to confirm that this is true. In the first place the incidence of extramarital sexual congress is… well, 'healthy', and the whole concept of a singular partner for life – within a formal arrangement – seems to be melting away. Indeed, now that most of us do not have farmland to protect and neither do we have too much concern for the moral directives of those in authority, one wonders whether monogamy will soon be consigned to the dustbin of history and polygamy will become established again.

In the meantime, however, we will continue to derive all the stimulation and satisfaction we require from a single partner, and if we don't, then there are always sexual fantasies to fall back on, and these can take any form one desires. Although… I have it on good authority than men's sexual fantasies are rather focused on visual imagery with a good deal of anatomical detail involved, whereas women's tend to focus on the emotional and on 'connection'. Fortunately, whatever sort of fantasy we might indulge in, this 'secret sex' is no longer seen as the work of the Devil, which it used to be. Neither is it regarded as abnormal or the result of sexual deprivation and frustration, which it used to be only in the last century. Instead, it is seen for what it is: a natural and positive element of human sexuality, and no more abnormal than thinking about sex every seven seconds…

No. That's absolute rubbish. Nevertheless, to emphasise the significance of sex in our lives, it can be reported that we do think about sex quite a few times a day, and those of us who are men will generally think about it rather more often than those of us who are women. It's just about impossible to measure and it varies widely from individual to individual, but it's reckoned that sex overtakes the thoughts of males about twenty times per day and for females it is about ten times per day... although it has to be said that the research that has uncovered these figures has also found that men think about food and sleep even more times than sex. And coffee, personal hygiene, emails and TV also feature as common thoughts – for both men and women.

I suspect that what we have here is just some sort of tickover arrangement; some sort of automatic mental process that keeps us connected to our sexuality and that primes us for even the slightest form of sexual stimulation. Like, for example, our meeting a member of the opposite sex. I'm not sure I know what I'm talking about here, but I do recall that a certain well-known (male) news reader did confess that every time he met a woman he weighed her up as a potential sexual partner. What this tells us, I think, is that this guy is probably particularly randy (but possibly not exceptionally so) and also that such mental predatory behaviour might be more the province of men than it is of women. If it were it would reflect the greater frequency of sexual thoughts in men than in women as just referred to, and it would also underline the validity of something called 'obligate parental investment'.

Here I should hand over to a Dr Diana Fleischman, an evolutionary psychologist at the University of Portsmouth who explained this obligate parental investment very simply. Because what she said was this:

'If a man has sex with 100 women in a year he might have 100 babies. If a woman has sex with 100 men she might have one baby and a very sore bottom.' Well, Dr D might not have been spot on with her time period or with what would get sore, but she was spot on in terms of spelling out what this obligate stuff is all about. Plainly, a man's minimum investment in a child might be two or three minutes of work and a thimbleful of sperm, whereas a woman's minimum investment is nine months of pregnancy and a painful and possibly perilous childbirth. And that's before any consideration as to who might be responsible for bringing up the child. So… men are, by nature, more interested in sex, and women are much more cagey when it comes to choosing a partner. And all thanks to obligate parental investment, which I think means that it is beyond dispute that men think about sex more than women do. And they probably think about having sex with every women they meet, if only 'theoretically' and as fuel for a possible future fantasy.

Men are almost certainly the majority users of the services of the sex industry as well. And if it were ever necessary to reinforce the significance of sex in the way we live our lives then one only has to look at this industry, and at its whopping size.

It is huge. It is also extremely difficult to measure just how huge. But, as an indicator, it was calculated that the US porn industry in 2009 had an annual revenue of up to $15 billion, which was more than the combined revenue of professional sports and live music combined, and a little above the box office revenue of Hollywood for that year. Of course, in 2009, free Internet porn had not yet destroyed the paid-for porn set-up. So that total might now have diminished. But, in looking at the sex industry as a whole, that would be to ignore the growth in all its other many different manifestations. So, inter alia, that would be prostitution, strip clubs, sex toys, lap dancing clubs, sex shops, contraceptive devices, bondage equipment, Viagra, non-functional underwear and, of course, Internet-based pornography, which is now enormous in its own right. Indeed, the surfing of porn sites accounts for about a quarter of all web usage in the United Kingdom... which, given that the rest is to check out the best deals on summer holidays and what various celebs are up to, makes one think that maybe one should just shoot oneself and get it all over.

But anyway, to return to the sex industry... I'm not saying that it's all good. Far from it. And one only has to examine what it has led to in terms of human trafficking and exploitation in general to conclude that the grocery trade, for example, is rather more salubrious. However, the fact still remains that if one includes stuff such as romantic novels, certain cosmetic surgery, titillating advertising and the line costs of all that sexting, it is truly enormous. Which means that we spend enormous amounts on sex, simply because so many of us choose to.

This is understandable in one way, in that sex can be such an all-consuming pastime. But it is strange in another, in that we are so well equipped to facilitate the activation of our sexual desires without industry intervention. And what I'm talking about here is our erogenous zones, those parts of our body that are blessed with heightened sensitivity and the stimulation of which may well generate a sexual response (even in the absence of a sex toy or some celluloid action).

There are the obvious ones, of course – the ones where it all happens, so to speak. But what is remarkable is just how many more there are. And, while nobody can possibly have them all, erogenous zones are now known to include: the scalp, the hair, the temples, the eyebrows, the eyelids, the earlobes, the lips, the tongue, the neck, the shoulders, the armpits, the arms, the hands, the breasts and the nipples (obviously), the navel, the abdominal area, the coccyx, the bum, the thighs, the feet and the toes! Which, gents, means that you're probably on safe ground if you touch a woman's nose, her back or her calves. But that's about it. Yes, however we have been put together, our sexual dimension has not been neglected. In fact, it has been given overwhelming prominence, which does rather tie in with my initial comments on the overriding importance of sex in our lives. And why not? After all, sex is really good stuff. It is a life-enhancing activity that promotes pleasure, physical and mental well-being and even long-lasting loving relationships. It is all good news.

But... when we start to look at the mechanics of sex... well, they don't seem quite to measure up to its status as one of the most life-affirming aspects of our existence. I mean, close up, its 'spiritual' nature can often be obscured by its awkwardness, its 'accessories' – and by its unavoidably comical nature. I think this statement needs some explanation, and I will start with those 'accessories'. Not the prophylactics or the lubricants or the Viagra, but the 'things' that some people turn to in order to optimise their sexual gratification. Yes, I'm going to spend a little time talking about fetishism, which must rank as one of the most 'entertaining' sexual practices of all.

To start with I should state the dictionary definition of fetishism, which is 'The use of a fetish to produce sexual arousal' or 'A sexual interest in non-living objects, body parts or... secretions'. Yes, well, I imagine quite a few of us might be classed as fetishists if we admitted to the attraction of stocking tops or sexy lingerie (both non-living objects), but we would be in only a minor league in the world of fetishism. Because, after exhaustive research, I have established that fetishists are turned on by (in order of their popularity with fetishists): clothing, rubber and rubber items, footwear, body parts, leather and soft material or fabrics. But a more comprehensive list includes body size, hair, muscles, legs, nails, jackets, headwear, wristwear... and stethoscopes! And if you're interested, that jacket fetishism is usually associated with the attraction afforded by padded nylon jackets, although other jackets popular among fetishists are down jackets with a nylon shell, bomber jackets and Snorkel parka jackets. And, without wishing to be at all offensive to any fetishist, I cannot think of a sexual encounter involving a Snorkel parka jacket without also thinking that it must be mightily hilarious. Although getting all hot and sweaty at the sight of someone's hat or their stethoscope is pretty amusing too.

You see, what I'm trying to explain here is how our sexual pursuits, while they can be very uplifting in every sense of the word, are also very often laughable and even ludicrous. And nowhere is this more obvious (and even more obvious than in the practice of fetishism) than in the sex act itself. After all, what could be more amusing than two people getting undressed and then tackling the intricacies of sexual intercourse or some affiliated pursuit? I am not in the least surprised that when Rodin wanted to exemplify love in a sculpture he chose *The Kiss* and not *The Bonk*. Because, even with two nubile young bodies, representing coitus in a way that is attractive is an uphill struggle. So too is the real-life coitus attempted by the millions of couples whose bodies are far from nubile and far from well acquainted with anything other than the intriguingly named missionary position and the aptly named doggy approach. In fact, even in these positions it can all be a bit awkward, and few couples in the standard copulation pose would attract the attention of any artist other than one who was looking for a bit of a laugh. I mean, it's all so undignified, isn't it? Legs in the air, bums in the air… and everything wobbling and swinging in a way that everything's not allowed to wobble and swing normally.

Then, of course, there's a huge list of 'other positions' for sexual congress, and this is where it gets out-and-out hilarious. Alfred Kinsey categorised just six primary positions. But a guy called Alex Comfort categorised more than 600, and another guy called Legman categorised 3,780. (It sounds to me as though he was a breast man as well.) Anyway, for a little light relief, see how many of these following positions you know or have tried. (You may even want to use this list next

Christmas as a Christmas quiz. You can invite Aunty Gill and Uncle Ron and whoever else has invaded your house to illustrate in turn each of the positions, using their imagination if they don't know what they are… but, of course, always with their clothes on.) So we have:

- The butterfly position
- The stopperage
- The coital alignment technique
- The cowgirl – or cowboy position
- The reverse cowgirl – or reverse cowboy position
- The lap dance
- The spoons position
- The lateral coital position
- The Viennese oyster
- The 'pounding the spot'
- The suspended congress
- The 'Ekiben' position
- The T-square
- The modified T-square
- The pile-driver
- The rusty bike pump, and
- The 'Seventh Posture'.

Without wishing to ruin that Christmas quiz entirely, I have to tell you that the 'Ekiben' position is a standing position, and it is named after a specific bento lunch box sold at Japanese train stations, which is quite fascinating. Furthermore, I think that on health and safety grounds I should tell you that the 'Seventh Posture' is sometimes described as fit only for acrobats and it should not be taken seriously. But, for those of you who want a challenge, it involves the receiving partner lying on her side and the penetrating partner facing the receiver, straddling the receiver's lower leg and then lifting the receiver's upper leg on to the crook of his elbow or on to his shoulder... and then calling for an ambulance.

Of course, all the positions above are for couples having 'regular' sex. Non-penetrative positions, positions for threesomes and foursomes – together with whatever one needs to do for intercrural sex, tribadism and docking (look them up: I did) – will be covered in the next edition. But I can tell you now that they will be just as much a source of hilarity as all the more conventional configurations.

Yes, we seem to have been lumbered with the sort of sexuality which, from an objective perspective, can amuse as much as it can provide satisfaction for its actual participants. And the essence of the act is even a bit of a joke, in that a male will normally orgasm within two minutes while his female partner will want five to seven minutes to do the same. So, not surprisingly, faking orgasms (on her part) is just another part of this entertaining activity we call sex. And that's almost as funny as those extremely rare occasions on which nothing at all wants to work and the whole game has to be abandoned before tea without any sort of result. But undoubtedly the real *pièce de résistance* in this comedy of the absurd is... well, the intimate equipment it requires: the ever-so-strange, never-to-be-taken-seriously female and male genitalia.

Well, let's start with his first. In its off-duty condition, it is reminiscent of a second-hand gas fitting hanging off the back end of an octopus, and in its standing-to-attention condition, it looks like something one might expect to see at the cheap end of a butcher's counter, next to the pig's trotters and the chitlins, piled up with more of its kind and surrounded by a neat square of plastic parsley. And hers... well, it owes something to a hamburger, a yoyo, a purse and a padded coat hanger, doesn't it? Although, that said, from a design perspective, it is very versatile, easily accessible but beautifully discrete. Nevertheless, the fact remains that while both these pieces of equipment certainly contain a strong element of sexual attraction they are not attractive in their own right and they are never described in purely aesthetic terms. I mean, have you ever heard of a fine aquiline penis or an elegant pre-Raphaelite vulva? No, you have not. Because neither of them could measure up to a slender neck or a shapely leg, or even a firm masculine jaw. They are just two more players in the hilarious farce that goes by the name of sex; a celebration of humanity itself involving odd postures, sometimes unappealing displays of too much flesh, lots of thrusts and jerks, success or failure, depending on which way the wind is blowing... and perspiration (probably), other fluids (possibly)... and a reassuring sense of being alive, whatever the outcome.

Yes, sex is great. But it is also a scream, sometimes only too literally.

And tell me. Why haven't men evolved a splint yet?

There was a young man from Nepal
Who sadly had no balls at all

He'd started with two
But he'd worn them both through
With the help of a girl from Porthcawl

There was a young man called Legrande
Who could pleasure himself on demand
But the pleasure, it ceased
When his member he greased
And the whole thing got well out of hand

There was a young girl who'd rehearse
With a whip, and with wants quite perverse
She loved in her act
Not her whip to be cracked
But instead what was quite the reverse

Taxation

Taxation is the glue that holds together any worthwhile society. Indeed, the alternative to some form of taxation is just some form of chaos and anarchy. After all, taxation has been proven to enable the creation of an environment that fosters stability and growth. Taxation also provides essential public services and essential public infrastructure. Furthermore, taxation can be eminently fair and is rarely a real burden on those who pay it. So, taxation is clearly essential and equally clearly, taxation is something that will always be essential. In short, taxation is 'good'.

Seductive, those statements, aren't they? And let's face it, even if most of us might find difficulty in agreeing that taxation is actually 'good', few of us would argue that we can do without it. All we ever challenge, as well as maybe our own personal tax burden, is the overall level of tax. And then the argument is all about whether this should be shaved down by the odd percentage point or whether it should remain where it is. Nobody suggests that it should be reduced to a small fraction of its present level, and only an idiot would suggest its complete removal. That would be plain silly, wouldn't it? Or, there again, would it?

OK... well, to examine that last question let's start with a blank page – in a time before we had what we recognise as organised societies, and possibly before the emergence of the concept of tax. And despite our best efforts we find that this blank page soon becomes stained, and it becomes stained with something called corvée, something we definitely need to study and to understand. Because, you see, corvée was the earliest and most widespread form of taxation. It was taxation in its infancy, a particular tax levied on all those poor sods who lived in the so-called days of yore and who were just too poor to pay any other form of tax. And what it was, of course, was forced, unpaid labour.

Whoever happened to be wielding power at the time would require the peasants and the landless to work for maybe a few days or even a few months every year, either for nothing or for very little indeed. And he wouldn't even give them paternity leave, luncheon vouchers, days off for funerals or a free Christmas party. In fact, this corvée stuff only differed from honest-to-goodness slavery in that the coerced worker was not owned outright and, in theory at least, was free in all other respects. Even if that was only free to have a completely miserable life, full of completely miserable food and completely miserable teeth, before eventually dying a premature and horrible death.

Anyway, this forced labour form of taxation was soon all the rage. It helped in the building of the pyramids, for example. And much later on, in medieval times, it was widespread throughout Europe, where work would be demanded of the vassal types by their feudal lord or of the plebs in general by their current callous and cold-blooded monarch. In fact, this corvée existed in France almost up to the end of the eighteenth century, and was so resented that it played an important part in causing the French Revolution (along with the exposure of drug-taking in boules and a shortage of berets).

So, all vaguely interesting, but hardly relevant to the present-day practice of taxation. Only... of course, it is. Because corvée, as a form of taxation (and it was just one form of taxation) was unquestionably an exercise in one group of people – the ruling elite and their hangers-on – imposing their demands on another group of people against their will. Through force, they were relieving them not of their money but of their labour. But it's all just the same, whether it's money or labour. It's all still robbery.

Yes, that's right: robbery. And to illustrate why it is robbery we might refer to a wise academic, who used two scenarios to illustrate the true nature of tax. In the first scenario a certain Sam Slime wants £50 and mugs a person in the street to get it. In the second scenario Mr Slime votes for a politician who taxes someone for £50 so that this amount can be redistributed to the 'disadvantaged'. That is to say, to Mr Slime. Now, both these scenarios involve the use of force (albeit different forms of force). And what's more, our perceptive academic then went on to argue that the second scenario is actually worse than the first because, through the state, Mr Slime is now empowered to repeatedly take other people's money without even the effort of having repeatedly to mug them.

'Rubbish,' shout a chorus of other academics. Or maybe they respond with a more measured 'Specious reasoning' or 'A narrow fallacious argument'. But let me reinforce my point by inviting you to consider a bunch of heavies who demand 30 or 40% of your income every month and threaten you with dire consequences if you don't comply with their 'request' – and with the same consequences if you don't also accept their offer of 'comprehensive protection services'. You would know what was going on, wouldn't you? It would be robbery: real broad-daylight robbery – or extortion, if you like. And that's exactly what is going on in Britain today under the guise of its 'legitimate tax system'. Only, of course, it's not a bunch of heavies in the conventional sense who are the villains but a much bigger bunch of heavies who are running a state-sized protection racket. And they're also immune from the law, because they just happen to be responsible for making the law as well. However, this doesn't remove the fact that both bunches of heavies are seizing our property without our consent, which is unquestionably theft. So, just to be as clear as I can, tax is theft because it is a government transgressing the property rights of an individual by enforcing compulsory taxation. And this 'morally criminal' behaviour results in an un-free society, in which the individual is condemned to a life of tax slavery, where he has to work to enrich the government and the recipients of government largesse rather than for his own benefit. He is reduced to a modern-day victim of a modern-day corvée.

This is where that chorus of other academics points out that however 'unfair' taxation might be, it is still essential. Without it, who would pay for all those essential services and how would society operate at all? The short answers to these two questions are, 'Those who use these services out of their untaxed income' and, 'Probably surprisingly well'. The longer answers are as follows:

Throughout history there have been numerous examples of private enterprise supplying everything from schools and roads to hospitals and even law courts. Yet consistently, that big bunch of heavies (otherwise known as the state) has sought to collect to itself more and more monopolies in more and more areas of civil life, because this then allows it to 'justify' the collection of even more tax. It has to be admitted that this hoovering up of everything it can get its hands on has been a great success, in that it is now widely accepted that health, education, transport and any number of other aspects of our lives are the province of the state and, as far as possible, they should be shielded from the attentions of privateers. It's incredible really, in the first place because state control of certain enterprises is not a fundamental law of nature (Einstein never even considered it), and in the second place the state, in exercising its control of its various commandeered bailiwicks, generally screws them up big time. I mean, think of state control of any enterprise and you immediately think of inefficiency, waste (huge, huge amounts of waste), overmanning, poor outcomes, poor quality… and poor bloody taxpayer – being taken for a ride yet again.

So if we now imagine a society without a thundering great tax burden, where people were allowed to spend their untaxed resources on what they wanted and what they needed, might that not represent a better model in all sorts of ways? Hell, to start with, self-responsibility would make a comeback, just as the unavoidable responsibility for everybody else would begin to wither. With this would come a sharpening up of all sorts of enterprises as they were obliged to exist on what they offered and not on taxpayers' money, and best of all, people would start to remember that they could be free citizens of this country rather than just serfs of the state. Real emancipation would be tasted by all. After which, their charitable nature would come to the fore.

Yes, there will always be people in any society who need help from others, and it would be foolish and disingenuous to ignore their plight in this review of the iniquity of tax. So it won't be ignored, and I willingly invite you to consider how generous the people of Britain are already in terms of their charitable giving and then to imagine how this innate sense of charity would inevitably blossom when freed from the shackles of tax – when men and women in this country were left with infinitely more money to do with as they chose (rather than despairing at the prospect of more of their money being used to finance the purchase of limousines in Malawi or laptops in Vanuatu).

Now, at this stage in this indisputable case for a no-tax society, it is probably worth pointing out that it's not actually the needy who do the taxing in our present overtaxed set-up. It is the state, the same state that maintains all those state-run monopolies and the same state that forces its way into our lives and into our wallets. And guess what? It is the state and not the needy, nor indeed us peasant taxpayers, that is the principal beneficiary. And by the state I mean the government, the Civil Service, all those buggers in quangos, all those other buggers who ride on the coat-tails of the state – and the wretched Establishment in general, who, without those taxes we pay, would be among the needy themselves.

It's so blatant. They have nice cars: we have a car we can just about afford. They have an expense account: we have an empty account. They have a gold-plated pension: we have plastic one, if we're lucky. They get paid a mint: we just get the hole in the middle, and then only after tax. Indeed, one has to conclude that this state – in its widest sense – is, in essence, the same sort of beast as the one that got all those Egyptians pushing stones up pyramids. It's really no different from all those other bastards who, throughout history and through the exercise or power, have forced all those without power to keep them in the style to which they've become accustomed. Yes, the state is a modern despot and, however it may seek to conceal it, a supreme thief in the way that all despots are thieves, only worse. And in my mind, much worse because, over the years, it has *diversified*. Yes, it is no longer just a plain old robber (of billions every year) but it is now also a very, very accomplished confidence trickster. Quite simply, it has convinced virtually every member of our society, by using the sort of statements at the beginning of this piece, that taxation is a valid aspect of a modern society and not an exercise in extortion on an unparalleled scale. As already pointed out, people might question the degree to which they are taxed but they will never question whether tax should ever exist at all. And I tell you… if that isn't the result of the most successful con in the history of mankind I don't know what is. The mugger has convinced his victim that being mugged is actually OK. God, I despair…

You know, the government now robs us whenever we do anything. If we buy stuff, if we fill our car, if we gamble, if we insure our house… if we don't just stay in bed all day they're on to us with another bloody tax – having, of course, already robbed us of a good chunk of what we've earned before we've even got it. The bastards are insatiable. They dream up new taxes all the time and they will never stop, despite my having made such an admirable case for the concept of no tax at all. Indeed, I have it on good authority that Revenue officials are now exploring the merits of a 'Sam Slime scenario one' approach to collecting even more tax. Yes, they are actually considering the idea of simply mugging people as they go about their daily business – and, with the sort of egregious indifference only ever found in government agencies they intend to call this new form of taxation 'a-tax on the streets'. Well, all I can say is that I find this idea totally reprehensible. But, there again, I do have to concede that this 'a-tax (attacks) on the streets' form of taxation will, no doubt, become the most honest form of taxation ever devised…

> In paradise there is no tax
> Just cherub chaps with wingèd backs
> But in that place where Satan dwells
> They tax the lot, including smells
> Which means with taxes A to Zee
> And income tax and VAT
> We have up here, for what it's worth
> A land that's now like hell on Earth

United Kingdom

In any compilation of 'stuff', it would be wrong of me to exclude a consideration of the place we call home: the United Kingdom of Great Britain and Northern Ireland. So I won't. And I will kick off this consideration with a question, and this question is 'How can one describe the United Kingdom?'

Well, here are a few suggestions: a stronghold of ingenuity; a has-been; a put-upon donkey; an arsenal of imaginative and creative thinking; a product of a rich heritage; a lost soul; a bankrupt; a centre of excellence; a confused and dysfunctional household; a beacon of enlightenment; an invalid, or possibly a doormat.

Difficult, isn't it? One could easily argue that it is any one of these, or an untidy amalgam of them all. Indeed, if one examines this country's history, its achievements and where it is now, it is the amalgam proposal that tends to win out. Or maybe there is an even better term to describe the UK in its present state and in its present predicament...

But first let us consider some other aspects of this country – and, to start with, one that is plainly indisputable. This is that, however it might be characterised now, Britain is a country that has done things that few other countries ever have. It has had an empire, and indeed what was probably the most extensive and impressive empire that the world has ever seen. And hand in hand with imperial success came advances in science on an unparalleled scale, and technical advances that guaranteed for ever its claim to have been the pioneer of the industrial age. Yes, there was a time when this small, oddly shaped country off the coast of Europe was pre-eminent in world affairs and unmatchable by any other power on the planet, whether in terms of its industries, its commerce, its military might or its sheer self-confidence as a nation.

However, nothing lasts for ever, and this became particularly obvious at the end of the Second World War. Like a battered prizefighter, as we got to our feet, we realised we were no longer the champion we'd been. Our industries had become enfeebled, our commerce was looking shaky, our military was becoming unsustainable and our empire was rapidly disintegrating. In the new world order there was, quite rightly, no place for a colonial power, and all our colonies and possessions were queuing up to sod off. And who could blame them?

Well, we still had our heritage and our ingenuity and our inventiveness – and the remnants of our industry and commerce – but our confidence had taken a knock. We hadn't lost the war, but we had lost our standing in the world. Or maybe we had lost it a long time before, but only now was the truth hitting home.

It was a difficult time which only got more difficult as the realisation of our diminished situation had to contend with our surviving sense of entitlement and, some might say, with our surviving sense of (empire-engendered) superiority. But we managed. Indeed, even though in substantive terms our situation declined even further, we still managed to make an impact on the world, ultimately with devices such as the Beatles. We might not have been a literally great Britain any more, but we were now a swinging Britain, and some of that confidence began to return. In retrospect maybe too much confidence. So that when our decline intensified in real terms we were able to fool ourselves that things were not too bad – especially as we were learning a new way to live, a new way that has since been recognised as the condition of 'living well beyond our means'. After all, why just spend what you have when, either as an individual or as a whole nation, you could spend however much you could borrow? And especially if there was now a malignant tumour at the heart of our remaining commerce, otherwise known as banking, from which we could borrow as much as we wanted and then even more.

Could things get any better (or, in reality, any worse)? Yes, they could. Because by now our welfare state was coming of age, which essentially meant that self-responsibility and self-dependency had been so diminished by the existence of a supposedly well-intentioned but ultimately misconceived safety net that things were going downhill faster than ever. Who, after all (as already discussed under 'Government'), would choose to pick Brussels sprouts in a cold Lincolnshire field if he could stay in bed until ten and just pick up a welfare cheque instead? And the less time one spends picking vegetables the more time one can devote to polishing one's inalienable rights and one's inalienable entitlements, if not one's responsibility not to abuse a support system that is paid for by one's fellow citizens.

The rot might have been stopped if there hadn't been others who *were* prepared to pick those vegetables or to work in food-packaging plants or in foundries (when we still had any foundries) or in the hotel trade or in the care industry. But there were. From all over the world they began to arrive, in their hundreds and thousands and then in their hundreds of thousands. And then a new wave came, thanks to the lunatic thinking of the European Union, the sort of thinking that could not recognise that the free movement of labour was probably a reasonable idea decades ago when the EU comprised just six countries with similar standards of living, but that it would be disastrous when it grew to include almost five times this number – and within this enlarged family there would be countries where the average weekly wage would, in the UK, buy you no more than a decent bottle of Pinot Grigio and maybe a Lottery scratch card. For years we've experienced a tidal wave of 'new citizens' (along with a constant wash of people who have no right to be here at all) and, taking account of our vassal status within the EU, and our consequent inability to stem the tide, one is tempted to reach for just a few of those terms mentioned earlier. These are the terms 'put-upon donkey', 'doormat' and, maybe, 'lost soul'.

However, there is that better term alluded to at the beginning of this piece, a term that encapsulates for many what this nation has become; what a beautiful country with an admirable heritage, a temperate climate and, by and large, a temperate nature, has now been reduced to. And that term is 'a trampled garden'.

Everything has been trampled. The herbaceous border that had been planted with thriving secularism has been damaged beyond repair by the deliberate trampling of imported and revived religions. The carefully tended rock garden, where population stability had been cultivated for years, has been all but wrecked by the careless trampling of both net migration and a hugely increased birth rate. The rose bed, where the specimens of indigenous culture and British values flourished for so long, has now been flattened beyond recognition. And even the lawn, otherwise known as the British countryside, has been so scuffed by the demands for more housing, more infrastructure and more of everything – in order to meet the demands of the burgeoning population – that it will soon not be recognisable as a lawn at all.

So, other terms to describe the United Kingdom at the beginning of the twenty-first century are of course available, but for many of us who can remember what this garden country was once like, even if it was a bit weedy here and there and it never got all the attention it deserved, the term 'trampled garden' is probably the most appropriate term of all.

One only hopes that in fifty years' time it won't have been trampled even further, or so covered in globalised decking that it is no longer recognisable as a British garden of any sort whatsoever.

Long years passed before was built
The land of rose and leek and kilt
But soon this land, it had acquired
An empire large and much admired

But not content with lands abroad
It pushed itself until it soared
Above the rest, with mighty wealth
Amassed through work and not through stealth

With engines steamed and looms engaged
It stoked the fires of minds uncaged
And so it came to be supreme
And number one in self-esteem

Enabling it to soar some more
In science, art and even law
Until the time, it came to pass
It fell upon its mighty arse

Yes, greed and 'self' had brought it down
The mighty land had lost its crown
And then they came, the new brigade
To join us in the mess we'd made

And now together we all live
A mix of men who hardly give
A passing thought for what had been
The greatest kingdom ever seen

Vatican

You might just remember that earlier in this book I provided you with a most illuminating dissertation on religion. I also provided a signpost to enable you to seek your own illumination of one religion in particular, namely that of Islam. Well, now it is the turn of a particular religious institution. It is the turn of the Vatican. And the reason I've chosen the institution that is at the head of the Roman Catholic religion rather than the religion itself is twofold. In the first place, despite my antipathy to all established myths, I am very aware that around the world there are many good Roman Catholics who are doing all sorts of good work, and I think it would be churlish of me in the extreme to irradiate them all with the searing light of my modern-day inquisition. (I mean, I don't want to trash either their beliefs or their efforts.) In the second place I do want to put an intense spotlight on the Vatican itself and attempt to show just how dreadful this holy headquarters is. And what's more, this is personal. I was baptised as a Catholic and, for a few years, I was subjected to the sort of indoctrination that is still visited on millions of others in this world as a direct result of the Vatican's teaching and the Vatican's diktats. And well… it's now payback time!

So, if you are a normal, moderate Roman Catholic who finds solace in your religion, please look away now and move on to women... I mean, move on to the next section, which is on women. I really have no desire to cause you upset, and you *will* be upset if you don't take my advice. But if you're not, and you have your own concerns about RC HQ, then you might want to read on and discover what are my concerns about this rather insidious institution. And to make it easy I have decided to number these concerns, starting un-controversially with number one, and number one will deal with 'Original Sin'.

1. OK, this Original Sin stuff is all about the immovable doctrine, maintained by the Church, of humanity's state of sin resulting from the fall of man during his transitory tenancy of the Garden of Eden. And I'm afraid I'm going to have to interrupt myself here, because this fall from grace – as a result of eating a bloody apple, of all things – has just so much about it that is wrong.

    I mean, God had supposedly given a lecture about the wickedness of scrumping to Adam, but he hadn't said anything to Eve. He'd simply assumed that Adam would pass on the message, and that Eve would give the same weight to a message delivered by a guy she had only just met as to a message delivered by the Supreme Being himself. This was very odd indeed, and I think it pointed to a complete misunderstanding on God's part of how a woman's mind works – or, indeed, of how a man's mind works. Crikey, nobody accepts stuff from a stranger at face value, especially when what he or she has to say makes little or no sense. And in this instance it made no sense at all. Because, we have Adam and his animated rib warned off eating the fruit of 'The tree of the knowledge of good and evil'. But why? If there was a 'Tree of how to cheat at bridge or any other card game', then fine. But here we have a tree that supposedly equips humans with what they might need to conduct their lives honestly and decently: a firm grasp of what is good and what is not good. So what's the problem? I might add that the total nonsense of all this apple stuff is then exacerbated by God choosing a snake to persuade Eve to eat the forbidden fruit. I mean... how likely is it that Eve will be a woman who doesn't just act like the majority of women (and quite a few men) who will just run away from the snake or go all wobbly? And she certainly won't be in 'receiving a message' mode, no matter how enticing or otherwise the message might be. But no, we are supposed to believe that she stays and listens to the serpent, and the serpent persuades her to do the naughty deed. Well, this scenario might just work if it was a talking panda or maybe a chimpanzee with the voice of Morgan Freeman, but in no way would it work with a snake – and a talking snake, at that. No, choosing a snake to play the naughty role was just the very first example of disastrous miscasting, and was nothing to do with selecting the right beast for the job but was all about prejudice. Quite simply, snakes are not regarded with affection, and that Garden of Eden appearance was a reprehensible exercise in emphasising their totally unwarranted reputation as something bad. It did nothing whatsoever in assisting them in getting anything like a fair deal. However, all this Garden of Eden stuff did distract me from the principal theme of point number one, which is the critique of the whole idea of Original Sin.

So, to return to this... I should first of all say that there is something deeply concerning – and deeply unfair – about this Original Sin. Because it appears that the first tenants of the garden, by not adhering to the garden rules, had lost the 'original holiness and justice' that had been conferred on them by God, not only for themselves but for all those humans who were yet to be born. We are then told that this means that the very nature of humans is weakened in its power (albeit not in its power to trash the world), that these humans will be subject to ignorance (can't argue with that one) and suffering (yep), and that they will be inclined to sin (which is something called 'concupiscence' apparently, and which I think we humans would have got around to ourselves, whether somebody had eaten an apple or not).

Well, great, but what about the iniquity of communal guilt? What about 'a bit of an over-reaction'!? And what about that famous free will?

It just seems all wrong to me, but ideal for Vatican doctrine, of course, because it means that they are able to claim that we all arrive on this Earth with a terrible stain, and that this stain can only be removed, not with repeated applications of Cillit Bang, but with 'baptism'. And – surprise, surprise – only the Catholic Church can administer this stain-removing sacrament.

It's not much different from buying an iPod and then finding that, like every other iPod, it's got a serious glitch, and that this glitch can only be fixed by an Apple engineer – after you've signed up for a lifetime service deal that will dictate the conduct of your life and require you to buy other sacraments... sorry, other service visits, right up until the time of your death. Only, of course, it's not like this at all, because we are not talking about an iPod here. We are talking about a real human being, and he (or she) and his (or her) parents being subjected to one of the worst scams in the world: the 'Only we can fix it' scam, which even the most pushy of Nigerian scammers might think twice about before using. But not so the guys in the Vatican. They have no problem whatsoever in branding a newborn lump of flesh with an imperfection and then claiming that only they can scrub it clean.

It is completely reprehensible, even when the Vatican tries to defend itself by claiming that while baptism achieves the removal of Original Sin, an infant may not be guilty of any personal sin – and 'Original Sin is a sin contracted and not committed' – or it is a state and not an act. Well, rubbish. Forget the nuances and the smokescreens. The truth of the matter is that good Catholics are led to believe that their children need baptism to wash away all sin and to allow them to be 'saved'. Indeed, they are warned that delaying baptism until their child can understand the sacrament may put their child's salvation in danger, should they die unbaptised! Or, even worse, their infant might acquire just enough knowledge and wisdom to realise what a load of wicked nonsense all this stuff is and thereby take steps to avoid being successfully press-ganged by the Catholic Church by refusing to be baptised.

Now, if I haven't yet convinced you that this Original Sin stuff is an abominable racket, then let me remind you that when it suits it, the Vatican can actually make a very exceptional exception. Because, of course, its doctrine includes the 'fact' that Mary was conceived free of Original Sin. She was, after all, the product of an Immaculate Conception. She didn't need baptising. It's just us plebs who need to be 'cleansed'. Because, of course, it's just us plebs who the Vatican wants to get its hands on. Mary is history. New, pink and chubby innocents are its future. And they must not be allowed to get away. And with that shabby device called Original Sin, most of them won't…

2. Well, I went on a bit there, didn't I? So, with this number two, I'll attempt to be a great deal briefer. And it really won't take me long, because what I want to talk about now is 'limbo'.

Limbo, you see, is all about the 'afterlife'. And it's not really much more than an idea. But, there again, it is a very compelling idea, because it concerns the fate of all those pink and chubby blobs who die before their Original Sin has been washed away with a dose of good old-fashioned baptism. And the idea is that, as they can't enter heaven and it would be a little unfair to commit them to hell, they will instead spend their presumably infinite afterlife in somewhere called 'limbo'.

I am pretty sure that you cannot locate this limbo on your satnav, just as I am pretty sure that it is a place that nobody would choose to end up in, particularly if it were for infinity. I mean, without wishing to be offensively flippant, the idea of an infinite existence in the company of a host of gurgling infants – even if you're one yourself – has what might be described as minimal appeal. No fiery chambers and prods with red-hot tridents, but it isn't really what you'd want, is it? Especially as all you'd done is fail to make it to the font on time.

Interestingly, one of the assumptions underlying the idea of limbo is that its inhabitants would be unbaptised infants who were 'too young to have committed personal sins'. Which does make me wonder whether the Vatican has set down an age at which you are *not* too young to commit personal sins. I mean, is there an age for responsibility for sinning in the same way as there is one, in most legal systems, for criminal responsibility? Well, that is a question to which I do not have an answer. But I do know how the Vatican gets around this whole speculative issue of limbo, which has now become more than a little awkward.

You see, the Vatican maintains a defined doctrine on Original Sin, but it has no such doctrine on the fate of unbaptised infants. This is left to theologians to ponder on, and whatever theories they come up with can be accepted or rejected by the 'magisterium', the authority which lays down what can be considered authentic Church teaching – and which is vested in the Pope and his bishops (i.e. the Vatican).

This is just as well. Because this limbo idea was sold as a fact to all Catholics well into the twentieth century. And only in 2007 did the Church bury this idea on the basis that it was an 'unduly restrictive view of salvation'. That is to say that the magisterium, through an International Theological Commission, threw limbo on the scrapheap because, as it wasn't Church doctrine, it was able to. And this was very magnanimous of it, and to suggest that it was done for other than reasons of magnanimity would be scurrilous. However, I am writing in a scurrilous manner, and I suggest that this move was not unconnected with a 'problem in the market' – in Africa. You see, in that part of the world, where Catholicism is engaged in a battle for souls with Islam and where there are all too many infant deaths, it cannot help one's cause to offer a religion that may well consign one's offspring to an eternal, unpleasant nursery – when the competition offers nirvana for all, whether they've undergone any sort of ceremony or not. In short, Islam offers eternal salvation/happiness/grace, etc. for an infant from the moment of its birth, but up until 2007, Roman

Catholicism could only promise this after that infant was baptised. And many didn't make it to that event, and were therefore denied that eternal banquet with God. So a no-brainer. They had to get rid of it, even if it rather undermined the need for baptism at all. I mean, business is business, my son. And one can't let anything get in the way of that. Not when it might mean losing out to the competition. Especially in a market where one's ban on contraception has such amazing potential…

Ah, yes, that sounds like my next gripe: the Vatican's doctrinal and quite shocking approach to contraception. I invite you to read on.

3. The Vatican's view on contraception is unequivocal. Basically, all sex acts must be both unitive and procreative, and to use contraception is intrinsically evil because it renders the sex act unfruitful. And, of course, it chokes off the supply of new Catholics.

Now, this view has been in place since the second century AD and it is part of Church doctrine – which is a bit of a problem for the Vatican, not least because they know that about 99% of all Catholics either ignore this doctrine or wish that they could. But how can the Vatican change its view when this would contradict the dogma of papal infallibility and thereby undermine the Pope's authority? Well, it can't. But it can organise a fudge. And that's what it's done. Only it's a desperately poor fudge, and it achieves nothing other than more heartache and some valid accusations of rampant irrationality.

What I'm talking about is its 'concession' that, while artificial contraception is still intrinsically evil, 'natural family planning' is morally permissible – in some circumstances. As far as I can work out, the justification for still banning sensible forms of contraception but for allowing a dodgy and impractical one is that the former is too easy. And by being so easy, it could lead to moral infidelity, a general lowering of moral standards – and it could rob men of their reverence for women and reduce women to mere instruments for the satisfaction of male desires. Incidentally, this justification doesn't appear to take into account women's views or women's sexual desires. But, there again, what can you expect from a bunch of celibate men? After all, if they knew anything about sex, they wouldn't be proposing natural family planning as a realistic and effective form of contraception. I mean, have they even any knowledge of the female metabolism, the female form, the intricacies of female plumbing – or, indeed, who does what to whom and what gets put in where? It really does make you wonder.

So too does this acceptance by these Vatican types of any form of contraception at all. Because if all sex acts have to be procreative, how can natural family planning, which might just achieve the same outcome as condoms and things, be in any way OK? Surely it's the objective of an action that's important, not its nature. And both condoms and NFP have the same objective: to prevent the arrival of more little darlings. This is the irrational aspect of the Vatican's pronouncement on contraception that I alluded to above. It is entirely irrational, as much as it is entirely indefensible.

Yes, it's one thing to play around with people's sex lives, but it is quite another to play around with their lives, as in whether they will continue to live or instead suffer a premature death as a result of contracting Aids. It is simply appalling, putting the Pope's authority before the lives of countless people and maintaining the pretence that nothing can be done or needs to be done. Well, something does need to be done. And something is being done – by ordained members of the Catholic Church who are close enough to the problem to see that condoms are not the work of the Devil and need to be handed out to all those poor sods who just have natural urges, but not a natural immunity to Aids.

And then there's the population considerations… And all I'll say here is that, if given the ability to prevent it, how many women – and men – in developing countries would have a football team for a family? Fewer than the Vatican would like, I'm sure. But it should be their choice, and not that of a bunch of virginal antiques who don't know the first thing about desperation, survival, poverty-induced anguish – or orgasms. Anyway, time to move on to the next in this series of mild chastisements of the Vatican, which will deal with the vexed issue of homosexuality…

4. Well, when the Vatican pronounces on the issue of homosexuality, one thing is very clear. And this is that nothing is very clear at all.

In recent times there have been all sorts of nice words about the need not to discriminate against any particular group of people and the desirability of homosexual people responding to the 'call to chastity' (as in a lifelong denial of sex). And it has even been stated that being a homosexual is merely to be the subject of an 'objective disorder', as it means being 'ordered towards an intrinsic moral evil'. But, there again, it is not sinful unless it is acted upon.

So maybe the Vatican is trying. Maybe it is finally coming to terms with the views held by many in the more enlightened parts of the world. Or maybe it isn't.

I mean, one suspects that its true opinion of homosexuality is reflected in its opposition to the decriminalisation of homosexual activity in certain countries around the world and the stand it took against a proposal from the United Nations calling for a global decriminalisation of same-sex shenanigans. Then there are its guidelines concerning the suitability of candidates to the priesthood, which talk about the candidate needing to have 'sufficient effective maturity and a clearly masculine sexual identity'. Furthermore, candidates with homosexual tendencies (or at least those with deep-seated homosexual tendencies rather than with transitory homosexual tendencies?) should be shunned, as quite clearly they are not fit to receive the sacrament of Holy Orders. Because let's face it, chaps, homosexuality is a disorder and homosexual acts are contrary to natural law. (Although it should be pointed out that these guidelines might not be too effective in that it has been estimated that the homosexual penetration, so to speak, of the priesthood in percentage terms is much higher than that in the population at large.)

Anyway, my guess is that the Vatican would just like homosexuality to go away. And if it won't, then maybe what you need to do is undertake some research which demonstrates that there is no link between celibacy and paedophilia but that there is one between homosexuality and paedophilia, even though there isn't. Yes, it seems that some within the Vatican might have a desire to scapegoat gay people within the Church as a way of avoiding the responsibility for all the abuse of children at the hands of the clergy, while also further demonising gay people in an attempt to justify the Church's anti-gay stance. And just maybe these wicked people in the Vatican are themselves gay, and they are all doing the best they can to further entrench within that institution its homophobic views as a way of atoning for their own 'deep-seated' and deeply repressed homosexuality. And if you think I'm fantasising there, then be aware that the Catholic Church has an extensive history of gay priests and bishops, and there were even a handful of what were thought to be gay popes. Indeed, one of them, Pope Paul II (1417–1471) was said by some to have entered the afterlife while being sodomised by a page boy, which must have made his arrival at the Pearly Gates more than a little awkward…

Anyway, the fact remains that the Vatican has got it about as right on homosexuality as it's got it right on contraception. It is out of step with enlightened opinion. It is even out of step with its enlightened flock, as it appears that in Europe and North America the support for same-sex marriages and measures to protect gays against discrimination is more popular among Catholics than it is in the general population. And, of course, it is out of step with natural justice. Because if gay Christians believe that their sexual orientation is innately created, then to be told that it has 'a tendency towards evil' requires them to deduce that they are the work of a sadistic God. And that terrible deduction should weigh on the conscience of all those clever Dick theologians as they dream up their next ecclesiastical somersault in their attempts to 'beat back the gays'.

I fear, however, that it won't, just as I fear that I will not see a Vatican float appearing in a gay pride parade in my lifetime. Which is a real pity when you think about all those colourful vestments they wear in St. Peter's…

But never mind, because it's now time for the final chastisement of the Vatican, which has nothing to do with homosexual tendencies and everything to do with its own 'temporal tendencies'…

5. It all started a long time ago, when very rich people, having been told that their Earthly goods would act as a barrier to their getting into heaven, decided that they should hand over great chunks of it to priests

and bishops as a way of easing their passage – to heaven, that is. Well, this was all very nice for the clergy, who became wealthier and wealthier – and worldlier – and who then began to emerge as a new sort of landed gentry. However it wasn't so good for the Vatican crowd, because not only were these naughty clerics taking the view that the endowments made to the Church were effectively their own personal property, but they were mostly married clerics with offspring. And offspring were known for their eagerness to claim their father's property when said father popped off. In essence, there was a growing threat to Church property.

Step in a series of popes who first attempted to stop this threat by banning the offspring from inheriting anything, and then by declaring all offspring illegitimate. After that it was a ban on priests taking wives and mistresses, and before you knew it the clergy had to adopt the practice of celibacy.

Yes, I'm afraid the adoption of celibacy by the Church was very little to do with ascetic values or maintaining spiritual purity or to form more fully a relationship with God but much more to do with protecting assets, and thereby building up both power and wealth.

And frankly the Roman Catholic Church never looked back, and to this day the Vatican is not just influential but also powerful and it is certainly not a stranger to the temporal as well as to the spiritual. Nor, by the way, is it reticent in adopting insular and secretive practices in order to protect the temporal.

And within the Vatican's operations, transparency and openness hardly feature at all, and instead opaqueness and impenetrability are the order of the day.

Indeed, these secretive ways have become a significant problem for the Vatican, and certainly for the Vatican's bank. This is a splendid illustration of just how bad things can get when your mission statement is 'Murkiness at all costs'. Because here is an institution with lots of assets, lots of clients, lots of accounts and lots of cash transactions (from church collections and charitable donations) that operates with systems that are characterised by non-transparency and are therefore wide open to the attention of money launderers and tax cheats. So no great surprise, then, that there appear to have been links to the Mafia and that back in 2013 the bank's head honcho, who had also been head of the accounting department of the Vatican's treasury, was arrested for various naughtinesses involving moving money for organised crime.

So the point I'm trying to make here is that the Vatican has been for many years, and still remains, an institution totally distracted from its primary role as the head office of a spiritual organisation. Instead it is fixated on the worldly, for which reason it has become steeped in a culture of secrecy and insularity, seasoned with just a dash of appalling and unforgivable bigotry. Of course, it is in this state because it has within it an abundance of not just weak and fallible humans but also a good number of despicable, power-hungry creatures who wouldn't know what goodness and charity were if they found them nestling in their cassocks. In fact, I suspect you could find more 'holiness' in the deeds of a single dedicated priest in one of Brazil's poorest favelas than you could in the whole of the Vatican City, even if you counted in the efforts of its latest papal incumbent. There's so much 'negative-holiness' there, and such a dedicated focus on the temporal, that it would take at least a dozen well-meaning popes before things began to be even marginally holy.

On which observation I shall close. If for no other reason than not wanting to be accused of being completely vindictive in my appraisal of the Vatican. Even though I have been… because it richly deserves it, and I remember all too well what it was like to be on the receiving end of its contemptible brand of 'conditioning'. (And that was even before I had much of a grasp of stuff like contraception and homosexuality, and well before I had learnt to distrust all human institutions on this planet and, in particular, all those run by men in long flapping robes…)

> The Vatican is not the place
> To change folks' views on falls from grace
> And as for condoms, coils and pills
> Well, they're all seen as prime ee-vils
>
> It's much the same for poor old gays
> And, as for fair transparent ways…
> Well, they're as rare as priestly wives
> Or sex-permitted priestly lives

In fact the more one looks inside
This place whose job is to preside
One sees that underneath its skin
Its holiness is wafer thin…

Women

This is a rather delicate aspect of 'stuff'. After all, women, as we all know, are essentially perfect, and how can anyone make any worthwhile comments about anything that is perfect? Or, if you prefer just a tad less bullshit, how can a man (me) really know what he is talking about when he tries to talk about women? I might as well try to write a piece about nuclear magnetic resonance, something I failed to get my head round even after three years of a degree course in chemistry. Nevertheless, one thing that I did learn was never to learn when it's really not worth trying to do something at all. So, at the risk of a shedload of opprobrium, I am now going to address the subject of women by making some careful and considerate suggestions as to how they might improve themselves as a gender even though they are already perfect. So here goes…

1. Many of us will have noticed that women are… well, just a great deal more emotional than men. And it's true. They are. Nothing wrong in that. But when those emotions surface in a woman when a man is in close proximity, well… it can all get a bit ugly. I mean, we've all experienced it, haven't we? She gets overtly

emotional, and his response is to leave the room. He certainly doesn't want to respond in kind, and if she wants to tell him what she is feeling he never wants to admit how he might be feeling himself. There's just a huge bloody difference between the two, which can lead to all sorts of upset (and worse).

Well, you will be very pleased to know that there is a very simple explanation for the man's reaction, which all women would do well to bear in mind. You see, he's not just being an uncaring bastard, but, unlike women, whose brains are hard-wired for talking things over, men have brains that are hard-wired for action during periods of acute emotion. I don't really know why, but it's probably down to all that hunting he used to do in the past, where emotion, stress and action all got blended together. But, however it arose, it now means that to start with a man knows instinctively that his emotions can very easily boil over into anger, and to avoid this possibly leading to some regrettable violence he seeks to put a lid on it straight away – by withdrawing. Furthermore, he will want to calm down. And this is because again he instinctively knows that this will be better for his health, as staying around and letting his emotions take over will lead to his blood pressure rocketing and his risking a heart attack. Remember, his brain is hard-wired for action, and frustrating this desired action by staying put and just 'talking things over' can actually be physically dangerous.

So, in the highly unlikely event that what I have set out above is accepted (and it should be, because it is true) a man should be aware of how a woman's brain is hard-wired and, *if possible*, respond sympathetically when she wants to parade her emotions. But the woman should bear in mind the very different wiring in *his* brain. Which means that my first suggestion as to how women in general could improve themselves as a gender is by reconciling themselves to the fact that men will never respond to their female emotions as they would like, and that their men running away or clamming up is just something that they can't avoid. In fact, it would be better all round if women only ever got emotional with other women. Not easy, I know, but it really would add just a little more perfection to their already perfect selves. Honestly.

2. OK, staying with the emotional make-up of women for just a little while longer, I now want to talk about their crying. You see, when women cry they are 'connecting with their feelings' and are very probably looking for some sympathy from their male partners. The trouble is that, just as in the pure emotional conflict discussed above, men don't like it. They may interpret it correctly, as a desire for a hug. However, they might also see it as manipulative or as confusing because for them to cry themselves is a sign of weakness, and they believe that you only really cry if something is very wrong indeed.

Furthermore... according to a new study, women's tears can dramatically reduce men's testosterone levels and, to a lesser extent, their sense of sexual arousal. Quite simply, women crying can turn men off (and I very much suspect that most men will have observed this for themselves). Indeed, this phenomenon is quite understandable when one considers that tears might just dissuade a potential rapist (I say 'might') – and they could also be a regular signal to a partner that his attentions are not, for the moment, required. And what I mean by that is that it is common knowledge that women are more prone to crying when it's that time of the month and, from an evolutionary standpoint, it is just not worth his bothering until it is no longer that time of the month.

I haven't made this stuff up. It's true. Just as is the fact that women would again add to their perfection if they accepted the fact that men will always react badly to their crying. Or, even better, if they learnt not to cry at all… other than at the sight of puppies or on witnessing the decommissioning of the last flying Vulcan.

3. OK, my next topic is 'chivalry' – or let's just call it gentlemanly behaviour. But, whatever we call it, it means all those little acts that indicate that men are being polite and courteous in their dealings with women. Well, apparently some women find this objectionable on the grounds, it seems, that men are treating them differently (from their fellow men) for no other reason than their gender.

Hells bells! I mean, come on. If these women really paid attention they might notice that virtually all those men who were being courteous and polite to them were being equally courteous and polite to everyone, men included. They were just adopting that maxim that you should treat everybody else in the same way as you would like to be treated yourself. And they hold a door open for men as well as women, because they would like to think that a door would be held open for them. And frankly, even if there are a few 'sexist' chivalrous types out there who might just major in the abuse of women, what would any women really prefer: a gallant gesture or an intrusive grope? Better to spend one's New Year's celebration with a thousand old-fashioned honourable idiots than with two thousand pairs of fondling and fumbling hands.

So this is an easy one. Women, do not be affronted by chivalrous acts. If you are offended, it is you who have the problem.

4. Now, women dress up. It is a well-known fact. But, when they have done this, some of them take great offence at being complimented on their appearance by males. Extraordinary! I mean, I can't believe that when they've taken the trouble to doll themselves up – for a special occasion or just for a night out – that they've done this on the basis of getting dolled up 'just enough', just enough to be presentable without wishing to look attractive. No, they will have done all they can to appear as beautiful and as elegant and as attractive as they can. And for them then to take offence at somebody confirming that they have succeeded in this task is just amazing. Because, you know what, you ladies? A complimentary remark about your appearance can be just that, and it doesn't necessarily mean that the guy who has made it has the infiltration of your pants on his mind. I'm not

saying he won't for sure, but just that it is probably unlikely and, even if he has such intentions, he may make rather clearer signals than just commenting on your dress. And you will probably spot them.

So give the guy a break. If he says that your blouse really suits you just thank him, and don't blank him. Just accept that unless you wear dirty and stained clothes, really shapeless clothes, something by Vivienne Westwood or a burka, somebody may well compliment you on your appearance and it won't be a precursor to copulation.

5. Now, I've already strayed into the arena of a woman's appearance, and so while I'm here I might as well list a number of ways in which her appearance can be harmed, and which she should therefore go out of her way to avoid.

The first of these must be tattoos. These, however intricately applied, are simply ghastly and should remain the province of hairy sailors. They should never appear on the hairless skin of a woman – anywhere. Piercings, other than for pretty earrings, are even worse than tattoos. And the further south they are the more revolting they are (and, in my mind, entirely off-putting as well as redundant). Then, moving on from what might not be revealed in public to what is far too often revealed in public, I have to register my dismay at the sight of bulging midriffs. The term always reminds me of something geological, possibly to do with the movements of tectonic plates, and certainly there is something almost surface geological about a bulbous ring of flesh that would be much better kept out of sight or, even better, actually removed by adopting a McDonald's-free diet for a couple of months. And I must say, as often as not, the worst examples are to be found on girls and young women, and one wonders what goes on in their minds or whether, indeed, they own a full-length mirror. It's all very peculiar.

So too is the practice of stuffing overlarge bums into underlarge jeans or shorts. I can't really understand it. Although I can understand knees. Yes, I'm afraid these are often a weak point in appearance terms, except when the legs are bent. But conducting one's life with bent knees is probably impractical, in which case women should look to their knees and look to conceal them, if required. Which is probably as far as I should go before somebody accuses me of being less than chivalrous in my comments and attacks me.

6. OK, next point. Women would be well advised not to emulate certain male behaviour such as showing off, driving too fast or being callous and stupid. Leave all this to those who know how to do it best.

7. One specific male activity that women should never emulate is drinking to excess. I don't mean just getting jolly, tiddly or merry... or indeed unmerry, as in morose, sleepy or even virtually comatose. No, what I mean is getting really completely blotto to the point where displays of underwear are involved and there is even the possibility of the uncontrolled

voiding of fluids from one or more of one's corporeal orifices. This is really bad, and makes bulging midriffs seem like just a minor misdemeanour.

8. Some women get loud when they are drunk. Unfortunately, many more women manage this stone-cold sober. Yes, please turn it down. All you women whose cackling and shrieking can be heard over the noise of a heavy metal band... just be aware of how frightful you sound, and modulate and moderate your output. There will be so many people who will thank you.

9. A minor one here, but might I suggest that the perfection of women would be tweaked just a little if they thought about what drink they would like before they got into a pub. Men always know what they are going to drink, and will only delay their order by the time it takes them to discover what brand of ales are for sale. Women, conversely, appear surprised that the pub offers drinks at all, and when they've overcome their surprise they will then debate all those drinks they really don't want before settling on the one that they do... before then changing their mind possibly just once, but maybe as many as three times. Strange, really, and quite perplexing. A bit like women themselves, I suppose. As is the capacity of this habit to irritate men...

10. And finally, I have to return to the appearance of women, because I failed to mention earlier what

they might do to polish their perfection on the make-up front. Clearly, some of them need to reduce the weight of their face make-up to less than a kilo, but many more of them need to learn that one of the biggest mistakes they can make is to equip themselves with those huge false eyelashes that look as though they've been cut from a heavy-duty draught excluder. They are truly terrible and make even a pretty woman look absurd and, very often, comprehensively cheap and tacky.

So, just to recap, women would be even more perfect than they already are if they learnt to understand men's responses to displays of emotion and if they didn't cry, if they accepted chivalrous acts and compliments on their appearance, if they didn't impair their appearance with tattoos, piercings, expositions of oversized midriffs and oversized bums – and 'awkward' knees, if they didn't try to emulate male behaviour – and get obscenely pissed, if they turned down their volume, if they thought about what they wanted to drink – and if they eschewed those awful false eyelashes. Oh, and I haven't mentioned it before, but they should also stop telling men what they should or shouldn't do. After all, we *are* perfect.

> The first woman on Earth was called Eve
> Who with 'bits' was designed to conceive
> But she needed a bloke
> Who inside her would poke
> His one 'bit', or so I believe

X-rated

One of the principal features that supposedly defines Britain is its hard-won 'freedom of speech'. We are all allowed to air our views on any topic we choose and, no matter how offensive or ridiculous these views might be, we will not be silenced. No, instead, on quite a few issues, we will be ridiculed, pilloried, roundly abused or, worst of all, accused of not complying with the norms of modern liberal thinking and therefore unworthy of being listened to at all.

Well, I'll let you into a secret. The norms of modern liberal thinking are no more than a construct. They are merely a collection of largely misguided ideas that together constitute a phantasm, an illusion that there are all these widely accepted values out there which in truth are only the values held by our liberal elite, by the even more liberal media and by a bunch of people who are either immature, silly or perverse.

Yes, ignore all those talking heads on the telly, all those earnest politicians and all those even more earnest 'activists', and one can begin to see the truth. And the truth is that there are legions of people out there in normal land who hold views that might not be classed as liberal but that do have the hallmarks of both common sense and reason. The trouble is they never get heard. They never get invited into the *Newsnight* studio and they never get asked to write a leader for *The Times*. And if they do occasionally force their way through to where they might just be heard… then it's derision time, if not worse. The liberal media will pounce on them to rubbish their opinions and their ideas will be scorned or, if entirely contrary to 'accepted thinking', they might even be regarded as completely taboo and in need of a 'helpful' X-rating.

Right, so you'll now understand what this section of stuff is all about. And if you don't, I'll spell it out. It's an illustration of just some of the views that many people probably hold, but because of 'sensitivities', 'perceptions', 'accepted modern thinking', and 'the danger of causing offence' – all concocted and sustained by the liberal elite – they never see the light of day, and therefore they are thought not to exist. Well, they do exist, and if the few of them that I've set out on the following pages are ever read by any members of this elite then I truly hope that at least the majority of them are thought worthy of their X-rated certificates, or maybe even of some thoughtful expurgations.

Anyway, here goes, and I think I'll start with something that is such a taboo it rarely if ever gets an airing of any sort. And what I'm talking about is the concept of 'recolonisation'.

1. Colonialism is and was a bad thing. That's what we're told. And, to be honest, in its heyday it did have its faults.

I mean, colonisation simply means the establishment of a presence in one territory by a political power from another territory, generally with the intention of exploiting that first territory and not necessarily asking anybody's permission to do this. In fact, it typically involves what might best be described as an unequal relationship between the colonial power and the colony, and almost certainly between the colonists and the colony's indigenous people. Inevitably, in this sort of relationship, the colonial power ends up making fundamental decisions affecting the lives of the colonised people, and these will be decisions that rarely if ever favour their interests. Instead they will favour the colonial power and they will be made in some distant metropolis by people who are entirely convinced of their own supremacy and of their ordained right to rule.

However, I do not believe that we should lose sight of the fact that it would have been extraordinary if colonialism hadn't occurred in the past. It was what powerful countries did then. It's as simple as that. And if there had been African or Asian countries that had developed technologies and industries in the way we did in Europe before we did, then they would have colonised us. But they didn't, and just because we did, almost unintentionally, we shouldn't feel in any way guilty, especially as we (and I mean Britain in particular) did bring to our colonies a certain number of benefits…

Before I talk about these benefits I just want to mention that there are other relationships between powerful territories and not so powerful territories which, unlike the colonial model, are regarded as good. I have in mind, in particular, the establishment of a 'protectorate', which is where a dependent territory that has been granted autonomy and some independence still experiences the suzerainty of a greater sovereign state. (Which, in everyday English, means that the powerful state controls the protectorate's foreign policy and international relations while allowing it to exercise its autonomy internally.) This arrangement can be very favourable for protectorates, especially where the political interest of the protector is one based on historical obligation, ethnocultural ties or just a desire to do the right thing.

In fact, 'just doing the right thing' *might* have been the reason for Britain making Zanzibar a protectorate in 1890, when the prime minister, Lord Salisbury, explained his position in the following sensitive way: 'The condition of a protectorate dependency is more acceptable to the half-civilised races, and more suitable for them than direct dominion. It is cheaper, simpler, less wounding to their self-esteem, gives them more careers as public officials and spares them of unnecessary contact with white men.'

How things change, and how incredible we now find such sentiments. After all, here was a man doing what he thought was right, but at the same time displaying such... well, such outmoded and, frankly, such scandalous (to our ears) thinking. But, there again, before we consign him to an unenlightened past, should we not stop to consider why he was expressing the view he was? And should we not also consider whether this view was coloured in any way by those benefits I referred to before, those benefits we visited on our possessions all around the world? Because I think we should, and I can guarantee that by doing so I will soon clock up an unequivocal X-rating and I will probably earn myself some serious contempt as well. Let us see.

To start with, I'm going to list some former British possessions – from quite some time ago. These are: Aden, Anglo-Egyptian Sudan, Egypt, Nigeria, Southern Rhodesia and Libya. This list could be a lot longer and could include many more countries that, like the six listed, are not now bywords for peace and prosperity and are more associated with unrest and rampant corruption.

Yes, I'm sorry, but some people just seem incapable of running their own affairs (think of Afghanistan, Somalia and Libya). Others run their affairs no more than appallingly badly (think of Pakistan, Nigeria and Zimbabwe). And what do we do in response to these endemic inadequacies? We provide piles of ineffective international aid and convince ourselves that, as part of the 'International Community', it is our responsibility to continue this aid indefinitely without ever considering that a more honest solution to this whole problem might be a process of full-blown recolonisation. Now if you peer around the borders of that X certificate that's just been awarded you might see that this idea is not so shameful and not so stupid as it sounds. After all, just consider the following:

If one of these failing/incompetently run states was recolonised, its ruling elite would not welcome it with open arms, but it would soon adapt to it. Furthermore, the common man would probably be a lot keener on it than you think, particularly if he knew that he could now work in his fields without the threat of intimidation and that his wife could now shop safely (and she wouldn't starve to death or be raped or be trafficked or be hit by artillery or by a barrel bomb from above). And maybe, above all else, that common man might believe that there was now a pretty good chance that he could experience some genuine justice and see an end to all that dreadful corruption. Because, while not always getting it spot on, two of the benefits we imposed on our colonies and protectorates in the past were more or less honest government and the rule of law. Both of which are now absent in many of their current-day manifestations as sovereign states.

This is not balderdash. I have been told in two of our former possessions – by older natives of these now independent states – that they would welcome our return if it would only mean a curtailment of what they now experience every day: endemic and rampant corruption. Furthermore, when we had restored peace and tranquillity to these countries with our new altruistic rather than exploitative form of (re)-colonisation we would be able to see a number of further benefits.

To name but a few: a decrease in conflict and tension around the world; the emergence of some attractive destinations for all those millions of migrants who have left them; an ability to involve ourselves directly in local health services (including their family planning operations); an ability to limit the power of local theological forces, and even the possibility of our being able to travel to some places where we are currently prevented from travelling (on account of how we would get our heads blown off (see under 'Zealots')).

Anyway, I reckon that a recolonisation of a whole string of countries – by countries with the requisite power, good intentions and appropriate capabilities – could usher in a new era of safety, justice and honest administration wherever it was needed most. And that statement has nothing to do with Lord Salisbury's rather embarrassing supremacy views, but everything to do with what I observe on the telly. Colonialism was appalling in many ways, but compared to the status quo in much of the world now it cannot be denied that there is much to recommend its reintroduction. However, it will be denied – by all our liberal, PC-first friends, who will also have a problem with some of my views on death…

2. Ah, yes… death: the inevitable outcome of dying. Always a popular topic, and perfectly well suited for a bit of X-rated treatment. And, to get that X certificate prepared for its issue, why don't I start with what death brings to an end? Namely, a life. And, for us humans, that immediately leads us into a consideration of the principle of 'the sanctity of

human life', a principle that certainly colours our views on death and, some might say, one that distorts these views entirely.

I mean, the sanctity of human life, within the context of religion and ethics, is the belief that human life is in some way so holy, so sacred or otherwise of such value that it must be protected and maintained at all costs. Yes, we, in some way, are so precious and of such inestimable value that our lives must be preserved no matter what – even if, as a species, we are so indifferent to the death and suffering of other sentient animals. Well, sorry, guv, but that just doesn't wash with me. However wonderful and accomplished we may be, we are still all just animals, and we are in no position to claim any sort of exclusivity – certainly not in terms of having an inalienable and 'sacred' right to life that is not bestowed on any other creature on this Earth. And if one accepts that proposition it follows that one must accept that not all humans can use this so-called sanctity of life principle to shield them from their just deserts. And let me first deal with those who have committed heinous crimes against their fellow man and who, in absolute terms (and uncluttered by the considerations of sanctity), should forfeit their lives.

Quite simply, capital punishment isn't the mix of savagery and inhumanity that it has (very successfully) been made out to be. It is no more than a measured and proportionate response to a number of actions by human beings who deserve nothing else. Frankly, there are far too many people on the planet anyway, and the desire to salve our consciences by not ridding ourselves of those who have clearly relinquished their right to remain in their numbers is misguided, wrongheaded and plainly daft.

After all, the advantages of capital punishment so far outweigh its disadvantages – as I set out below, starting with the incidental disadvantages first. These are:

- Genuinely innocent people might be executed, just as one in 10,000 recipients of a life-saving vaccine might expire – which, given the advent of DNA forensics, might be a fair reflection of what proportion of people who got the chop should have been left unchopped.
- The executed might be mad rather than bad. This, I'm afraid, is merely a confirmation that life sucks.
- Execution is now regarded, at least by the Establishment, as 'cruel and unusual punishment'. (Well, sorry, but as burning at the stake, pressing to death and breaking on a wheel have now all been consigned to history, I think that this claim is more a reflection of the silly soppiness of our Establishment than it is a genuine observation.)

Which leads us on to the advantages of capital punishment. These include:

- The permanent incapacitation of the criminal. Yes, we permanently remove the threat to society, and the threat to the prison guards who might otherwise have to deal with that murderer or terrorist for the remainder of his or her life as well as to his or her fellow inmates. We also remove the threat to any one of us who might run into a lifer who has absconded from jail. This is not an insignificant consideration, especially when we are talking about any sort of terrorist or terrorist sympathiser/helper who, while in prison, is unlikely to become saintly or even less radicalised but just more dangerous. So there.

- The cost saving. There are much better things to spend taxpayers' money on than hotel accommodation for people who should not even be allowed to live. In fact, money spent on *anything else* is money better spent.
- Capital punishment is not capital rehabilitation, and it is more honest for that. And anyway, rehabilitation stinks rather too much of re-education, indoctrination and even brainwashing (in my mind, anyway). And, in the mind of the unconsidered victim's friends and relatives, I imagine it might also stink rather too much of unwarranted lenient treatment. (Permanent, rehabilitative incarceration must also rob them of any sense of closure.)
- Capital punishment might act as a deterrent. But even if it didn't it would hardly encourage the committing of more crimes that attracted the death penalty, would it?
- And just to show I'm really all heart, it can be argued that an immediate demise is a lot less

cruel than being forced to spend one's life behind bars. No matter how pampered criminals are within our prison system, fifty years of three square meals a day, interminable dominoes and licence-free TV viewing could be considered unduly cruel.

So why are we so squeamish? Why do we cling on to this antiquated notion that human life is sacred when there are more and more people in the world demonstrating the exact opposite by going out of their way to bring as many lives to an end as they can – in the full knowledge that if they follow that pursuit here or in most of the 'civilised' world they will not have to pay council tax ever again. Or work again, or be responsible for themselves again, or be cold again, or be lonely again…

Yep, there are numerous people who quite clearly deserve nothing less than capital punishment. And, if you are not yet convinced, then let me invite you to consider any of those monsters who have sought to blow people up on the Underground, to shoot people shopping at a Jewish supermarket, to beat and starve to death their own infant children or to systematically rape young girls. None of these people can ever have any 'sanctity' appended to their lives, and I'm afraid that they should just be done away with. And I'm not even suggesting burning at the stake… I might suggest, however, that we extend this little written chat to a consideration of 'extrajudicial killings'. And so I will.

You see, there have been a number of successful movies, such as *Magnum Force* and *Sudden Impact*, which owe a great deal of their success to focusing on an unavoidable feature of our modern societies. And this feature is that it is easier for a justice system to protect the rights of those who transgress the law than of those who are their victims. And, accordingly, it is a matter of some celebration when the justice system does not have an opportunity to crank into action because some hard-nosed cop has managed to settle the problem once and for all with a discharge from his oversized gun.

This reaction to 'swift justice' should not be underestimated. It reflects a desire on the part of those who applaud it for nothing more than real justice – a villain paying with his life for what he has done – without scores of lawyers feeding off his misdoings for the next seven years. In other words, these supporters of *Sudden* justice are not bad but they are just demonstrating a greater reverence for 'natural' justice than for the application of a legal process. They are also very likely identifying with the victim of crime, the poor sap who as often as not is essentially ignored by even the most enlightened justice systems on the planet.

Well, bearing in mind the X-rating of this section, it would be a dereliction of my duties if I did not go on to point out that it is not only acceptable for the forces of law and order to mete out expeditious executions. It is also, under the right circumstances, no less acceptable for a wrongdoer to be entirely undone by one of us – by any one of us – in that giant army of unconsidered victims. I'm thinking here of what might be our justified response to that guy in a balaclava who tries to rob a convenience store armed with a handgun or a knife, or to the bane of domestic Britain: the ubiquitous burglar.

Now, I know that we are allowed to use 'reasonable force' to protect ourselves against crime, but what is 'reasonable'? With a burglar in one's house, probably at night, does one invite him to sit down at the kitchen table to debate the matter or does one make a unilateral decision on the matter? And if one does, does one (a) lunge at him with a butter knife, (b) attempt to strike him with a poker, (c) do the best one can with a carving knife, or (d) shoot him dead with the gun he's left on the sideboard and then shoot him again just to make sure that he doesn't get up, wrestle the gun away and then shoot you? I don't know about you, but I think dealing with a burglar in this situation is akin to dealing with a rabid dog. One does not thwack it across the head with a rolled-up copy of the *Radio Times* in the hope that it will desist from its planned biting spree, but one tips the fridge on it, and then sits on the fridge until the dog expires. (And I might say I have a great deal more sympathy for the rabid dog than for the burglar. The dog is as much a victim as the person he intends to bite. The burglar is not a victim.) Anyway, the point is that you don't take chances, and the reality of these middle of the night situations is that if you don't use the maximum force available to protect yourself you may be in serious trouble. And if this maximum force leads to an early retirement from life on the part of the miscreant, then so be it. And the burglary rate would drop significantly as well. Which can't be a bad thing.

Recently a judge, who was commenting during a burglary trial, remarked to the accused that, 'It must take a desperate kind of courage to burgle a stranger's house'. Well, what that indicates to me is that the justice system has lost all interest in the casualties of crime, if it had any in the first place, and can offer us no guaranteed protection... just as our stretched police force cannot protect us at every hour of night and day, and especially in our homes during hours of darkness. So let's just be realistic, and accept that sometimes we will have to look after ourselves and this may or may not involve another 'extrajudicial killing'... although if a householder racks up much more than four dead burglars, then he may have a case to answer... possibly.

Right. Well having dealt with the state killing people and uncompromising cops and innocent citizens killing people, I now want to continue this deadly theme by talking about something which in itself should not attract an X-rating, but which in the way I suggest it is promoted just might. Because the something is assisted dying, and how I want to promote it is by linking it with the conduct of some civil disobedience. So here goes.

3. What is *not* contrary to *genuine* liberal thinking is the need to change the law on assisted dying. In fact,

82% of the population of Britain believe a change is now well overdue, and that this change should allow terminally ill people to be assisted in their desire to fall off their perch and so avoid what can be an extended period of dreadful and senseless suffering.

The trouble is that a majority of our MPs are spineless, lily-livered wimps who have either been nobbled by the Church or who are just naturally gutless and unwilling to support any sort of radical change, and we therefore can't get the change in the law we want. And no, even I don't think that threatening to assist these MPs in their own demise if they don't see sense will achieve what we want, whereas a little bit of organised civil disobedience might.

You see, civil disobedience is all about the active refusal to obey certain laws or the commands of the state – generally when and because the state has got it wrong. Well, the state has certainly got it wrong on this occasion, at least according to an overwhelming majority of its pretty well pissed off citizens. So, with no prospect of the state doing anything to rectify this situation, as there is no likelihood of those pusillanimous invertebrates in the Commons suddenly growing a backbone, it must be time for action. It must be time for a bit of assistive civil disobedience.

And the idea would be, first of all, to equip 100 people with any sort of pill, which taken singly would have no significant effect, but which when ingested by the hundred, would prove (promptly) lethal. The next step would be to find somebody who was compos mentis and who clearly wanted a bit of assistance to exit this world. At an appointed time, the 100 pill-carriers would then assemble at the home of whoever was seeking release, and they would all participate in the assistance process by each donating their pill. The mechanics of pill administration could be sorted out to suit the particular circumstances, but the important point would be that 100 citizens had taken part in an act of assisted dying and were prepared to admit this. It would then only need this act to be repeated about 100 times and the state would have to acknowledge not only that it could not possibly charge 10,000 people with murder or manslaughter or find prison places for them but also that, overnight, it would have to change the law.

Mahatma Gandhi made civil disobedience work when faced with a ruthless and powerful Britain. Rosa Parks did it when confronted with some of the most obnoxious authorities imaginable. So how easy would it be when all we have to deal with is a bunch of faint-hearted milksops who, when the authorities were being overwhelmed by hundreds of 'murderers', would be in an absolute panic?

And remember what Percy Bysshe Shelley said, which was something along the lines of, 'Government is evil. It is only the thoughtlessness and vices of men that make it a necessary evil. When all men are good and wise, government of itself will decay.' Well, that won't happen any time soon but, as regards its unwillingness to legislate to allow assisted dying, our government is being truly evil, in that it is committing countless people to needless suffering and sustaining the prospect of a terrible end for us all.

So, evil or just spineless? You choose. And then go off and equip yourself with a pill. Then I'll give you a call.

4. Well, that wasn't what you'd call fun, was it? So why don't I conclude this section with a quick run through some rather more upbeat X-rated topics. Like suggesting that:
   - We should stop talking about people being radicalised and instead refer to them radicalising themselves. They are not victims who deserve some assistance. They are potential murderers, who deserve only our acute contempt.
   - Following on from the above point, why is our government trying to stop radicalised monsters going off to join ISIS? They should be encouraged to do so, and never let anywhere near us again.
   - British soldiers should not be subjected to prosecution for acts committed years ago in the heat of battle in Iraq. Even if some of their actions might not have been beyond reproach, they are all far less culpable than the greedy lawyers who are seeking to cash in on the past by making spurious claims, many of them based on witness statements that have already been found to be 'unprincipled in the extreme' and 'wholly without regard to the truth'. Which isn't entirely

surprising, as many of the so-called witnesses who have come forward have been recruited from the ranks of such admirable outfits as the bloodthirsty Mahdi Army, that well-known instigator of sectarian violence. In fact, if the legal leeches really want to make money out of such a despicable process then they should be informed that all hearings about supposed outrages in Iraq will be conducted entirely in that country, with soldiers being able to remain in Britain (where they would then supply evidence to the hearings via a video link). The prospect of six nights in Baghdad, let alone six months, should discourage all but the most avaricious lawyers, and even this handful would probably not survive out there for long. I mean, the whole idea of attempting to find fault with men who have risked their lives – for a lot less than any British lawyer gets paid – is no less than deplorable. In fact, it's a fucking disgrace.

- The term 'Cannot be named for legal reasons' should be consigned to history. If someone is old enough to get into serious trouble, then he or she is old enough to be named.
- Positive discrimination should be outlawed. It demeans those it is intended to help and it is grossly unfair to all those who, by necessity, must suffer completely undeserved negative discrimination.
- A standing rule should be that 'new citizens' accommodate the habits, practices and

peculiarities of indigenous people, not the other way round.
- Piers Morgan should be a proscribed organisation, albeit with just one member.
- We should make a pre-emptive strike on Argentina before they have another go at the Falklands.
- Slavers and traffickers should be welded together.
- Ken Livingstone should be 'lent' to Venezuela for an indefinite period.
- Diane Abbot should be sent to Venezuela as a back-up for Ken.
- Mr Juncker should be sent anywhere, just so long as it's outside Europe and he can't get back from where he's sent. It would also be a good idea to tar and feather him before he was dispatched.

And that concludes the X-rated stuff, much of which, in reality, is only just X-rateable. And, of course, it is not a comprehensive list of such stuff – for safety reasons, obviously.

> Certain things, without a doubt
> No longer can we talk about
> Except with friends and with our spouse
> And only then within our house
>
> Yes, PC World has won the day
> With non-PC kept well away
> And unright thoughts we have to keep
> Inside our head and hidden deep

The thought police have won the war
To gag our thoughts for evermore
And soon there'll be a fucking app
To find and close an open trap

So come ye men of Engerland
And join me now to make a stand
And tell those twerps just what we think
By kicking up an awful stink

And what I mean, I do declare
Is give our thoughts some needed air
So don't be shy and say your piece
On Mumsnet, saints and bloody Greece!

Young people

Young people have everything going for them. And sorry, but all this talk of their being a disadvantaged generation with only the prospect of penury and suffering before them... well, I'm afraid it simply won't wash. Not least because young people, whatever their economic situation, still have the ability:

- To stay up all night.
- To ignore the disconcerting reality of the world.
- To be unjustifiably optimistic.
- To be refreshingly naive.
- To be convinced that they are right, with no room for any doubts.
- To assemble enthusiasm at the drop of a hat.
- To enjoy new experiences and not to fear them.
- To choose a hairstyle that doesn't entail a comb-over or a perm.
- To eat without necessarily getting fat.
- To talk to friends without discussing ailments.
- To happily ignore all those 'symptom checkers' on the Internet.
- To indulge in 'going commando' with complete confidence.

- To have an orgasm while waiting for a bus, and, of course,
- To have more sex than I did when I was their age…

But despite this long list of reasons to be happy quite a few of them appear to be far from happy, and even further away from being anything like reasonable in their views. Yes, while many young people are apparently entirely admirable in how they think there are others who are increasingly a cause for concern, in that their approach to both 'enlightenment' and 'tolerance' seems to be to want to snuff them both out. Furthermore, these rather misguided souls are to be found not in some snooker hall or some seedy pub, but instead on a university or a college campus. This malaise of which I speak is a malaise of purportedly well-educated young people, and all the more worrying for that.

So what forms does this affliction take? Well, at least three to my knowledge, and I shall now discus these three, starting with the treatment meted out to visiting speakers.

1. Universities and colleges should be synonymous with free speech. They should represent pinnacles of tolerance and open debate within our society, even if we sometimes have to moderate this tolerance when faced with the sort of radical views that can only be described as loathsome and the very essence of *intolerance*. (And I have in mind here a particular brand of radicalism and the words of one Karl Popper. He was the liberal philosopher who

observed that unlimited tolerance would lead only to the tolerant being destroyed by the intolerant. And amen to that.) Anyway, with that proviso, everybody should be allowed to spout their views on a university campus, if only to show how ill-informed and wrong-minded they are or possibly to convince their audience that they do have a valid point of view. It is therefore entirely wrong for (young) students to prevent somebody speaking who, in their mind, is not liberal enough, not 'inclusive' enough, not 'moral' enough – or not purple-with-blue-tinges-around-the-edges enough. This isn't just stupid. It is highly objectionable, potentially very dangerous, and a little too close to the sort of repression seen in some of the most despotic societies on the planet.

There are lots of examples of this behaviour – too many, in fact – but I will mention just one. This was the University of Manchester's Student Union attempting to ban a self-styled men's rights activist from speaking at the university's free speech and secular society because its self-righteous members had decided that he was a 'professional misogynist' and 'rape apologist'. At the same event it was planned to have a contribution from a 'feminist writer', who also fell foul of the student politburo because it considered her views on transgender people to be 'transphobic'.

Well, the good news is that, on this occasion, the free speech society pulled a flanker and outwitted the apparatchiks of the Union. (They did this by forming a new association, simply affiliated to the university but not constituted as a society and therefore beyond the clutches of the Student Union. And then they held their event – with the two invited speakers – at an alternative venue on the campus, having advertised the venue and the event on the morning of the day the event was to take place.) Interestingly, and commendably, one of the organisers of the event wrote in the university's student newspaper that he was not endorsing the invited speakers' views, but that, 'There is a perceived monopoly of righteousness held by left-leaning students at the university. This desire for hegemony of opinion is killing academic discussion.' I could not agree with him more.

In fact, it's a pity that he's not active at Goldsmiths University in London as well. Here there was another manifestation of this unwarranted repression of free speech, this time in the form of the sabotage of a presentation as it was being made. What happened was that a lecture was being given by a feminist who had fled Iran and who now campaigns against Islamic extremism. In the middle of her talk some university 'protestors' interrupted the proceedings, turning off her projector and accusing her of violating their 'safe space'. What was then amazing was that the feminist, who had been outrageous enough to express the view that it was wrong for Bangladeshi bloggers to be hacked to death or for Afghan women to be stoned in the name of religion, was then further abused by the Feminist and LGBTG Societies, who each posted statements of solidarity with the Islamic Society denouncing her as an Islamophobe! One could not make it up – and one wonders what goes on in the heads of those who posted those statements, or whether there is anything in them at all other than possibly stupidity, ignorance, vitriol and bile.

I cannot understand what is going on here, particularly when it is well known that there are some serious problems closer to home. And what I mean is… why isn't Goldsmiths Feminist Society squealing about sexual harassment on university campuses rather than standing shoulder to shoulder with a bunch of Brownshirts? Hell, there is a huge problem with the behaviour of male students on campuses these days, with 37% of women (and 12% of men) claiming that they have received unwelcome sexual advances. Laddism is rife, and well overdue for a concerted campaign by all students and all student societies to bring it to an end. However, all the National Union of Students does is call on the university authorities to do something about it, and meanwhile too many students and too many student societies don't get stuck in themselves, but instead busy themselves with the hounding and repression of anyone with whom they disagree. And they never pause for a moment to ask themselves whether it might just be them in the wrong or, whoever might be in the right, whether it is always wrong to emulate some of the worse aspects of Nazi Germany. I think it's about time they did.

They could also give some thought to their wish to impose their orthodoxies and values on figures from the past, as I will now discuss…

2. The first time I became aware of enlightenment and tolerance reversal number two was when I read what was going on not at a British university but at one in the States. This was at the University of Missouri, where the university students were calling for the removal of a statue of Thomas Jefferson (the third president of the United States) on the basis of his being a 'racist rapist'. Obviously their words, not mine.

Well, it cannot be denied that good old Tom did have slaves on his plantation, just as most people of his standing in that part of the world did at that time. Furthermore, there is more than a little evidence that he may have fathered a number of children from one of his slaves. This is not to be commended but, given the norms of that time, it doesn't really mean he was a monster and not really what many people would regard as a rapist.

I mean, here was a guy who was one of the principal authors of the Declaration of Independence and a dedicated proponent of democracy and individual rights. In fact, not only did he go on to be president of the United States but he was the guy who signed into law the act that prohibited the importation of slaves. And while this did nothing for the situation of slaves already in the country it cannot be denied that it was a step in the right direction and an act that is somewhat out of character for one's normal, common or garden racist rapist.

Well, this rather misguided campaign could be written off as just that: something that the students of Missouri had thought up as a distraction from the sticky heat of the south, and not to be taken seriously. But unfortunately it has proved not to be an isolated incident, and following on from those American bullies we now have some English bullies doing exactly the same thing at Oxford. They are bullies at Oriel College, to be precise, and their demand is that the college authorities remove a statue of Cecil Rhodes from college grounds. He was a major benefactor to the college and, in the eyes of the bullies, a terrible racist and colonialist who behaved deplorably in the nineteenth century and therefore somebody not worthy of retaining any link with their precious institution.

Jesus! Well, of course he was racist and a colonialist. And he thought the English were a master race. And he was instrumental in the seizing of great swathes of African land. And he probably wasn't unacquainted with supremacy or misogyny. Indeed, one could go as far as saying that even at the time he was seen as a little controversial. But not that different from most of his contemporaries and certainly never as 'evil'. He was a product of his time. Maybe a slightly imperfect product, but in no way was he in the Hitler and Stalin league (gentlemen whose statues *should* be removed wherever they are).

Yes, I'm afraid it's these young people again, intent on imposing today's orthodoxies on the past rather than trying to improve the orthodoxies of the present. It's ridiculous and offensive, because as well as demonstrating a wanton disregard for historical fact it also demonstrates an appalling level of conceit, in that it implies that this generation has finally got it sorted and that all those that went before were rubbish or worse than rubbish. Well, what's actually rubbish is the idea that we've all reached some sort of nirvana in our thinking, and these stupid students would do well to learn some humility before they impugn anybody from the past.

I'm not the only person to find their behaviour intolerable, and some have described it in even more extreme terms. They have, for example, likened this desire to eradicate a representation of a figure from our past to the desire on the part of groups like ISIS to destroy cherished antiquities wherever they find them. Others have pointed out that many public statues and public buildings in Britain would have to be removed if the same moral vanity being assumed by Oriel's students were adopted by us all. How stupid. And where will it end?

I mean, I don't want to be too provocative, but if student fascists get around to reading some of Winston Churchill's early stuff (and I have in mind a particular paragraph in one of his works that begins: 'How dreadful are the curses Mohammedanism lays on its votaries'), then the acclaimed greatest Briton of all time will be somewhat in the soup. And God knows how many statues of Winnie there are in the country, to say nothing of how you would go about turning a towering heroic figure of the recent past into one of the world's worst villains without, at the same time, inviting an absolute tidal wave of derision.

Well, I think there is one way to resolve at least the Oriel situation. And this is to remove Cecil's statue but, at the same time to repay his bequest – with interest. Clearly, if Oriel's students want nothing to do with his representation then they will, no doubt, want nothing to do with his money. And as, with interest, his bequest probably now exceeds the value of the fabric of Oriel College, its authorities will have to sell it off and deprive all those sanctimonious tossers of their place of learning. They would deserve nothing less. And whatever their loss, they will of course have that warm glow of righteousness to comfort them as they are thrown on the street.

They might even want to distract themselves with a bit of crusading... crusading against something like the scourge of 'inappropriately themed balls'. And, of course, I'm not commenting here on the threat posed by a new brand of perversion focused on the scrotal sac but on another manifestation of the totally idiotic desire to tick off the past. Yes, I'm afraid this desire of young people to somehow find fault with all their forebears is not limited to statue removal but it also extends to their wanting to extinguish any vestiges of our history that do not come up to their own modern-day, testing standards. Particularly when there is a social event like a university ball involved.

Yes, this time the youthful thought police made their views known when two Oxford colleges had the temerity to announce that they would be hosting summer balls based on *The Great Gatsby* and New

Orleans in the 1920s. Well, blimey, did these colleges not think for a minute how many women and ethnic minority students would be upset by what would be a very cruel reminder of a time when there was… well, far less equality. Hell, it's all very well promising 'amazing jazz', 'clandestine magic' and 'an indulgent gambling scene', but had these colleges no idea that a ball which was themed to reflect those wicked times from the past would inevitably be seen as a celebration of an era that was simply steeped in racism of the very worst kind? And what of reminding their students of a time when the colleges themselves would have been devoid of both women and 'people of colour'? How could they be so callous, and how could they be so incredibly insensitive?

Well, where can I start? By first of all reminding all those women and ethnic minority students that they *are* now in those two colleges, that they are receiving a wonderful education, and this is in large part due to the efforts of all those terrible people from the past who, maybe, harboured a number of views on race and gender that wouldn't necessarily win them any plaudits in our current supposedly liberated times? Or how about suggesting to them that it is pretty offensive to disparage what was just the normal behaviour of the time, and one that allowed the development of what we now regard as the civilised Western world? Or, on the 'ad absurdum' basis, does this mean that we can no longer hold Civil War battle re-enactments, mock medieval jousting tournaments, fifties-themed discos or

Victorian music hall nights? Because, strange though it may seem, in all these periods, there wasn't quite as much 'equality' knocking around as there is today – and all sorts of people might be offended. Or, like one Ms Arushi Garg, who complained about that 1920s-themed ball, they might at least feel uncomfortable. And we wouldn't want that, would we?

No, we'd prefer that they felt really uncomfortable by being confronted with their staggering arrogance and their appalling lack of understanding of how the world works and how it develops, and the need not to distort or to eliminate the past. And no matter how 'comfortable' this distortion/elimination might make them feel.

I mean, what are these people doing in places of learning, anyway? They certainly don't seem to be doing much in the way of learning. In fact, they are doing just as little as the next bunch of morons who have taken it upon themselves to get inappropriately righteous about something called 'cultural appropriation' – a phenomenon which, not surprisingly, I am about to discuss.

3. Yes, the last and most preposterous form of student intolerance that I want to bring to your attention concerns something most people are not even aware of, because most people live in the real world and don't spend their valuable time looking to find offence where none is intended. Because, you see, this something is this 'cultural appropriation'

referred to above, and what is meant by this term is simply the employment of elements of one of the world's cultures by members of another culture. This is a dastardly thing to do, apparently, because if the 'borrowing' culture is, say, the majority culture, this might be construed as a way of oppressing the minority culture by stripping it of its group identity or its intellectual property rights. Heaven forbid: this vicious and vindictive behaviour might even lead to the loss of meaning of the cultural elements adopted, which would, of course, be disrespectful to the members of the originating culture, or could even be seen as a form of desecration.

Well, let me say now that there are a very small number of instances where I would have at least a little bit of sympathy for the 'abused culture', especially if what was borrowed was deeply spiritual – for them – and it was then essentially dragged through the mud by those who had borrowed it. But these situations are so rare that I have not been able to think of a real example. And no, I do not believe many North American Indians would go into a steep mental decline if they caught sight of even a fully grown Caucasian wearing a replica of their traditional headdress. So when young people start to claim that this is the new front in that constant battle for a fairer, more harmonious, more respectful (and more tedious) world… well, one has to remind them that they are being just a little bit naive and a big bit fucking stupid. And if you have any problem with that statement, I invite you to read on – where I now describe two specific instances of the scourge of 'cultural appropriation'.

The first took place in one of our ex-colonies: Canada. Yes, at the University of Ottawa, a woman called Jennifer Scharf was asked by the University's Student Federation to provide yoga classes at the university's Centre for Students with Disabilities. However this was before the federation had given due thought to the 'cultural sensitivity' that existed due to the subjugation of the Indian subcontinent by the British Empire. How remiss of the federation. And how admirable that its guardians of sensitivity were soon on the case and asking Ms Scharf to desist from her egregious pursuits. Yes, she was told in no uncertain terms that yoga was just one of many spiritual practices that had been appropriated from another culture. Furthermore, was she not aware that many of these cultures are cultures that have experienced oppression and cultural genocide due to colonialism and Western supremacy? And even if the truth is that yoga is not a religion, but a form of exercise that can provide great benefits to all, one cannot let little niceties like that get in the way of one needlessly ruining what might be a really useful service for disabled students if there is the slightest possibility of any sort of 'cultural appropriation' being condoned. Yes, Ms Scharf, however far backward you bend (in attempting to accommodate the concerns of the federation's students) it will never be far enough. Because when it comes to flexibility of thinking they have as little of that as they have common sense and a sense of what is proper and reasonable.

The same could be said for the young and presumably completely daft members of the University of East Anglia Students Union who banned the handing out of sombreros at a Union event!

It was an event at which a local Mexican restaurant had taken a stall and had then embarked on what they thought was a bit of innocent marketing – in the form of distributing free sombreros – until such time as the goon squad arrived to inform them that they were being 'culturally indifferent'.

After the event the Union's 'Campaigns and Democracy Officer' (you can just imagine him, can't you?) made a statement, which included, inter alia, the following: 'At the Students Union we want all members to feel safe and accepted, so at all events we try to ensure that there is no behaviour, language or imagery which *could* (my italics) be considered racist, sexist, homophobic, transphobic or ablest.' and '...we know that when it comes to cultural appropriation, the issues can sometimes be difficult to understand and many don't realise that they may be about to cause offence or break a policy.'

Gordon Bennet! How does anyone get that far up his own arse? And how does a whole students union get to be so friggin' asinine? And do any of them eat at that wicked Mexican restaurant... and risk culturally appropriating some Mexican nachos and chilli beans?

I mean, what a pile of horseshit! And have any of these cultural-appropriation-sensitive souls ever stopped to consider what is going on in the world? And what I mean is that there are a host of cultures out there, our own included, which, far from appropriating other cultures, are having to accept them without question. Having a tattoo done that uses a piece of Polynesian iconography is one thing. Having to accommodate – and bear the burden – of forced marriages, FGM and the non-humane dispatch of animals is quite another.

Also… how far would you have to travel throughout East Anglia to find a Mexican who had been offended by the promiscuous use of sombreros? It is a complete joke. But at the same time it is worse than a complete joke because it is another manifestation of what can only be described as the growth of 'liberal fascism' on our university campuses.

Yes, I would like to end this piece by suggesting that the suppression of free speech, the desire to condemn the past and the desire to find offence in the present, where no offence is intended, are all worrying signs that something is amiss in the minds of our young ones. As I said at the beginning of this piece, young people should be busy enjoying their youth. And, in particular, they should be having lots of sex. What they should not be doing is acting as censors, acting as revisionists or acting as prats. And the more of them who kit themselves out with sombreros the better. I suspect the whole of Mexico would be absolutely delighted…

The young are quite a funny lot
They think they know what they know not
And if you have a different view
Then yours is 'false' and theirs is 'true'

It seems to me they should see sense
And not cause quite so much offence
'So just grow up. And on the way
Indulge in sex three times a day'

Zealots

Once upon a time zealots were exclusively Jewish. This is because they were the members of a political movement that sought to incite the people of the province of Judaea to rebel against the Roman Empire. They wanted to encourage their fellow Judaeans to expel the Romans from the Holy Land, by force of arms if necessary, sometime in the first century AD. So they were good guys in a way, even if what we now recognise as zealots are rarely if ever even rational, let alone good. After all, to be a zealot now means to be somebody who is fanatical and totally uncompromising, normally in his or her pursuit of some hare-brained religious or political ideal. The name says it all, really. Because its modern base is the word 'zeal', and have you ever met anybody in your life who has impressed you with a display of zeal? No, and you are never likely to either. Zeal simply means rather too much enthusiasm and it might even mean a degree of (non-sexual) passion, and that can never be a good thing.

Anyway, zealots are bad news, whatever religious or political ideal they subscribe to. That said, there is a particular breed of zealots who are streets ahead of any other zealots when it comes not just to a rejection of any real sense and any real perspective but also to a rejection of even the lowest of civilised values. I am, of course, talking about those monsters who go by the name of ISIS – and all their fellow travellers, who, as a group of modern-day barbarians, are firmly committed to their desire to propel us all into the seventh or eighth century just as fast as they can.

This Insane Sociopathic Idiots Society is almost beyond comprehension. For here is a bunch of brutes who have engaged in plain old murder, widespread extortion, kidnapping, the destruction of antiquities, the rape and gross mistreatment of women, suicide bombings, mass shootings, throwing people off tall buildings, the beheading of people, the crucifixion of people, the burning of people while still alive and even the public 'execution' of a mother by her son. It is as though they have a checklist of atrocities and they are going through it one by one in order to confirm their status as the most savage, most bloodthirsty, most shit-stinking bunch of twats that the planet has ever hosted. Or maybe somewhere in their headquarters in Raqqa, they have a 'New Atrocities' working group, a gathering of morons whose job it is to dream up ever more horrible behaviour to ensure that ISIS stays out in front in the abhorrence stakes and well ahead of all those fellow travellers alluded to above.

And before we go any further let's just consider these fellow travellers: all those other bands of bastards who practise their zeal through the use of bullets and bombs. It's quite a list, and it goes as follows:

- Boko Haram (Nigeria)
- Al-Qaeda in the Islamic Maghreb (Mali, Burkina Faso, Algeria and Libya)
- Ansar al-Sharia in Tunisia (Tunisia)
- Ansar al-Sharia in Libya (Libya)
- Ansar Bait al-Maqdis (Egypt)
- Al Shabaab (Somalia)
- Al-Qaeda in the Arabian Peninsula (Yemen)
- The Taliban (Pakistan, Afghanistan)
- Jemaah Islamiah (Indonesia), and
- Abu Sayyaf (Philippines).

This epidemic of zealots is terrible news in all sorts of ways, not least because it means that if you're one of those odd white enlightened types from the West there is now an ever increasing chunk of the world that is completely out of bounds. And frankly, along with the ISIS playground of Syria and Iraq and all those countries listed above, you can probably add bits of Turkey, the whole of the Arabian Peninsula and maybe even Bangladesh to this 'may well be killed if you go there' category. Although, to be fair, so far they've only hacked to death local (secular) bloggers in Bangladesh. So its inclusion in the no-go slice of the world might be a little premature, and we should probably put it into just the 'potentially dangerous' category, along with any European city you care to mention.

Anyway, we're stuck with all these zealots, and it might be worth asking why there has been this recent outbreak of deluded tosspots and whether there might possibly be some justification for their zeal. Because it has been argued that bad governance is at the root of their emergence, in that virtually all of them have organised themselves in countries with corrupt oppressive regimes where dissent is not allowed and economic progress is normally stuck in reverse. Therefore, if you are a young disadvantaged youth in one of these countries who has also convinced himself that he is being discriminated against because of his religion or that he is losing out just because of his criminal record, his small brain or his small penis, it is no great surprise that he responds to the call, and becomes a despicable savage.

Well, that might be part of the explanation. But it occurs to me that there are many corrupt regimes around the world (in fact, the majority of regimes around the world are corrupt) and equally, there are tens of millions of disadvantaged youths with an axe to grind – but that axe is all they grind. They don't sharpen a knife for the purposes of cutting off hands or a meat cleaver for cutting off heads, and they don't organise themselves into what are essentially death cults intent on world domination. So maybe what is really behind this odious contamination of the world is a range of cultures that are, if not odious themselves, then far from perfect. And they are cultures that, furthermore, cannot cope with a surge in the number of their adherents. Put another way, there are a whole string of countries out there embracing cultures that stifle enlightenment and progress but conversely that appear to nourish the out-of-control growth in their populations. The result is inevitable: a tripling and quadrupling of their populations in the last forty years (as already discussed under 'Population').

And, as a consequence, the exhaustion of their resources, an explosion in the number of their unemployed youths, a sizeable exodus of these youths (to richer pastures in Europe) and the birth of a credo of hate.

It was interesting to see that ISIS finally decided that it would ban the watching of TV because it promotes 'wizards and rationalist philosophies'. It is apparently full of propaganda that 'is insulting to Allah and makes fun of his religion and his allies via television series and vile dramas, which lead people to develop a taste for such things'. Indeed, 'it propagates sorcery, charlatanism and rationalist philosophies that poison the minds with ideas of atheism and boldness against Allah'.

Well, I have to confess that I did think that one of the recent plot lines in *EastEnders* was pushing rationalism a bit too heavily, but I also think that all those lunatics strutting around Raqqa would do well to give rationalism a second look. (Incidentally, they might also spend some time tidying the place up. I was in Raqqa in 2012, and it was a shithole then. And I hate to think what a crap place it is now.) But anyway, they should take some time out to get to grips with the fact that rationalism, far from being really bad, is merely the practice or principle of basing one's opinions and actions on reason and knowledge rather than on religious belief or emotional response. And, by taking a rationalistic approach to life, most of the world has at least been able to distance itself from the Dark Ages and is not floundering in the swamp of ignorance, along with all those frightful places I've referred to above. Yes, they should put away their meat cleavers and their bombs, brush those fucking great chips off their shoulders and give some proper thought to what might most effectively drag them out of that stinking swamp. And they might just decide that it is not a journey back through the centuries and a futile attempt to obliterate all those who don't wish to join them on this trip.

There again, that would require a brain, wouldn't it? And I see little sign of activity (let alone intellect) in their particular organs, and I suspect that ISIS and all the rest of those zealots will just carry on as the most aggressive manifestation of evil on this planet we've ever seen, until such time as we decide to squash them underfoot. And in the meantime I can offer no remedy for their behaviour but only a little humour, which might just puncture their terrible zeal. This is in the form of a second list, a list of their most popular music choices as they sit in their Raqqa bunkers polishing their AK 47 millimetres. And this list is as follows:

- 'Road to Nowhere'
- 'Lipstick on Your Collar' – means death!
- 'Give Peace a Chance' – ha!
- 'I Love the Sound of Breaking Glass' – and crumbling masonry, etc.
- 'Boom Bang-a-Bang'
- 'Eve of Destruction'
- 'I Shot the Sheriff' – among others.
- 'Baby's in Black'
- 'First We Take Manhattan'…
- 'World Without Love'
- 'Pictures of Macho Men'
- 'Never Look on the Bright Side of Life'

- 'Love Don't Live Here Anymore'
- 'Dancing in the Street' – is punishable by crucifixion.
- 'Mama Weer All Crazee Now'
- 'Something in the Air' – could be an Apache helicopter.
- 'Even the Good Times Are Bad'
- 'What's Love Got to Do With It'
- 'Red Red Blood'
- 'This Wheel's on Fire' – and so is the rest of the Land Cruiser.
- 'Anyone Who Had a Heart' – never joined us in the first place.
- 'If Paradise is Half as Nice' – as Raqqa… – errh…
- 'Wooden Heart'
- 'Paint It Black'
- 'I'm a Believer'
- 'House of Fun' – ironic
- '(There's a Drone) – In the Air Tonight'
- 'Out of Time', and finally…
- 'Total Eclipse of the Brain'

Two now-dead zealots both did miss
The 'drone-food' fact that goes like this:
'With cheese and bread and pepper black
Two-martyrs make a pleasant snack…'

By the same author:

Brian's World Series

Brian on the Brahmaputra (with Sujan in the Sundarbans)
A Syria Situation
Sabah-taged
Cape Earth
Strip Pan Wrinkle (in Namibia and Botswana)
Crystal Balls and Moroccan Walls
Marmite, Bites and Noisy Nights (in Zambia)
The Country-cides of Namibia and Botswana
First Choose Your Congo

The Renton Tenting Trilogy

Dumpiter
Ticklers
Lollipop

Light-bites

Eggshell in Scrambled Eggs
Crats

www.davidfletcherbooks.co.uk